READING COMPREHENSION SUCCESS
IN 20 MINUTES A DAY

5th Edition

LEARNINGEXPRESS ®

NEW YORK

Library of Congress Cataloging-in-Publication Data
  Reading comprehension success in 20 minutes a day. —5th ed.
      p.   cm.
  Prev. ed. entered under: Chesla, Elizabeth L.
  ISBN-13: 978-1-57685-899-8 (alk. paper)
  ISBN-10: 1-57685-899-5 (alk. paper)
  1. Reading comprehension—Problems, exercises, etc. I. Title: Reading comprehension success in twenty min-
utes a day.
  LB1050.45.R429 2012
  428.4—dc23
                          2012010089

ISBN 13: 978-1-57685-899-8

Printed in the United States of America

9 8 7 6 5 4 3 2

Fifth Edition

For information on LearningExpress, other LearningExpress products, or bulk sales, please write to us at:
    LearningExpress
    2 Rector Street
    26th Floor
    New York, NY 10006

Or visit us at:
    www.learningexpressllc.com

Contents

CONTENTS

CONTENTS

How to Use This Book ▶

This book is designed to help you improve your reading comprehension skills by studying 20 minutes a day for 20 days. You'll start with the basics and move on to more complex reading comprehension and critical thinking strategies. Please note that although each chapter can be an effective skill builder on its own, it is important that you proceed through this book in order, from Lesson 1 through Lesson 20. Each lesson builds on skills and ideas discussed in the previous chapters. As you move through this book and your reading skills develop, the passages you read will increase both in length and in complexity.

The book begins with a pretest, which will allow you to see how well you can answer various kinds of reading comprehension questions *now,* as you begin. When you finish the book, take the posttest to see how much you've improved.

The text is divided into four sections, each focusing on a different group of related reading and thinking strategies. These strategies will be outlined at the beginning of each section and then reviewed in a special "putting it all together" final lesson.

Each lesson provides several exercises that allow you to practice the skills you learn. To ensure you're on the right track, each lesson also provides answers and explanations for all of the practice questions. Additionally, you will find practical suggestions in each chapter for how to continue practicing these skills in your daily life.

The most important thing you can do to improve your reading skills is to become an active reader. The following guidelines and suggestions will familiarize you with active reading techniques. Use these techniques as much as possible as you work your way through the lessons in this book.

Becoming an Active Reader

Critical reading and thinking skills require active reading. Being an active reader means you have to engage with the text, both mentally and physically.

The following are active reading strategies:

- Skim ahead and jump back.
- Mark up the text.
- Make specific observations about the text.

Skimming Ahead and Jumping Back

Skimming ahead enables you to see what's coming up in your reading. Page through the text you're about to read. Notice how the text is broken down, what the main topics are, and the order in which they are covered. Notice key words and ideas that are boldfaced, bulleted, boxed, or otherwise highlighted. Skimming through the text beforehand will prepare you for what you are about to read. It's a lot like checking out the hills and curves in the course before a cross-country race. If you know what's ahead, you know how to pace yourself, so you're prepared to handle what's to come.

When you finish your reading, jump back. Review the summaries, headings, and highlighted information in the text. Notice both what the author highlighted and what you highlighted. By jumping back, you help solidify in your mind the ideas and information you just read. You're reminded of how each idea fits into the whole, how ideas and information are connected. When you make connections between ideas, you're much more likely to remember them.

Marking Up the Text

Marking up the text creates a direct physical link between you and the words you're reading. It forces you to pay closer attention to the words you read and takes you to a higher level of comprehension. Use these three strategies to mark up text:

1. Highlight or underline key words and ideas.
2. Circle and define any unfamiliar words or phrases.
3. Record your reactions and questions in the margins.

Highlighting or Underlining Key Ideas

When you highlight or underline key words and ideas, you are identifying the most important parts of the text. There's an important skill at work here: You can't highlight or underline everything, so you have to distinguish between the facts and ideas that are most important (major ideas) and those facts and ideas that are helpful but not so important (minor or supporting ideas). Highlight only the major ideas, so you don't end up with a text that's completely highlighted.

An effectively highlighted text will make for an easy and fruitful review. When you jump back, you'll be quickly reminded of the ideas that are most important to remember. Highlighting or underlining major points as you read also allows you to retain more information from the text.

Circling Unfamiliar Words

One of the most important habits to develop is that of circling and looking up unfamiliar words and phrases. If possible, don't sit down to read without a dictionary by your side. It is not uncommon for the meaning of an entire sentence to hinge on the meaning of a single word or phrase, and if you don't know what that word or phrase means, you won't understand the sentence. Besides, this habit enables you to quickly and steadily expand your vocabulary, so you'll be a more confident reader and speaker.

If you don't have a dictionary readily available, try to determine the meaning of the word as best you can from its context—that is, the words and ideas around it. (There's more on this topic in Lesson 3.) Then, make sure you look up the word as soon as possible so you're sure of its meaning.

Making Notes in the Margins

Recording your questions and reactions in the margins turns you from a passive receiver of information into an active participant in a dialogue. (If you're reading a library book, write your reactions in a notebook.) You will get much more out of the ideas and information you read about if you create a "conversation" with the writer. Here are some examples of the kinds of reactions you might write down in the margin or in your notebook:

- **Questions** often come up when you read. They may be answered later in the text, but by that time, you may have forgotten the question! And if your question isn't answered, you may want to discuss it with someone: "Why does the writer describe the new welfare policy as 'unfair'?" or "Why does the character react in this way?"

- **Agreements and disagreements** with the author are bound to arise if you're actively reading. Write them down: "That's not necessarily true!" or "This policy makes a lot of sense to me."

- **Connections** may arise either between the text and something that you read earlier or between the text and your own experience. For example, "I remember feeling the same way when I . . ." or "This is similar to what happened in China."

- **Evaluations** are your way of keeping the author honest. If you think the author isn't providing sufficient support for what he or she is saying or that there's something wrong with that support, say so: "He says the dropping of the bomb was inevitable, but he doesn't explain why" or "This is a very selfish reason."

Making Observations

Good readers know that writers use many different strategies to express their ideas. Even if you know very little about those strategies, you can make useful observations about what you read to better understand and remember the author's ideas. You can notice, for example, the author's choice of words; the structure of the sentences and paragraphs; any repetition of words or ideas; important details about people, places, and things; and so on.

This step—making observations—is essential because your observations (what you notice) lead you to logical inferences about what you read. *Inferences* are conclusions based on reason, fact, or evidence. You are constantly making inferences based on your observations, even when you're not reading. For example, if you notice that the sky is full of dark, heavy clouds, you might infer that it is going to rain; if you notice that your coworker has a stack of gardening books on her desk, you might infer that she likes gardening.

If you misunderstand what you read, it is often because you haven't looked closely enough at the text. As a result, you base your inferences on your own ideas and experiences, not on what's actually written in the text. You end up forcing your own ideas on the author (rather than listening to what the author has to say) and then forming your own ideas about it. It's critical, then, that you begin to really pay attention to what writers say and how they say it.

If any of this sounds confusing now, don't worry. Each of these ideas will be thoroughly explained in the lessons that follow. In the meantime, start practicing active reading as best you can. Begin by taking the pretest.

Pretest ▶

Before you start your study of reading skills, you may want to get an idea of how much you already know and how much you need to learn. If that's the case, take the pretest that follows. The pretest consists of 50 multiple-choice questions covering all the lessons in this book. Naturally, 50 questions can't cover every single concept or strategy you will learn by working through this book. So even if you get all the questions on the pretest right, it's almost guaranteed that you will find a few ideas or reading tactics in this book that you didn't already know. On the other hand, if you get many questions wrong on this pretest, don't despair. This book will show you how to read more effectively, step by step.

You should use this pretest to get a general idea of how much you already know. If you get a high score, you may be able to spend less time with this book than you originally planned. If you get a low score, you may find that you will need more than 20 minutes a day to get through each chapter and improve your reading skills.

There's an answer sheet you can use for filling in the correct answers on page 3. Or, if you prefer, simply circle the answer numbers in this book. If the book doesn't belong to you, write the numbers 1–50 on a piece of paper and record your answers there. Take as much time as you need to do this short test. When you finish, check your answers against the answer key at the end of this lesson. Each answer references the lesson(s) in this book that teaches you about the reading strategy in that question.

1.	ⓐ	ⓑ	ⓒ	ⓓ	18.	ⓐ	ⓑ	ⓒ	ⓓ	35.	ⓐ	ⓑ	ⓒ	ⓓ
2.	ⓐ	ⓑ	ⓒ	ⓓ	19.	ⓐ	ⓑ	ⓒ	ⓓ	36.	ⓐ	ⓑ	ⓒ	ⓓ
3.	ⓐ	ⓑ	ⓒ	ⓓ	20.	ⓐ	ⓑ	ⓒ	ⓓ	37.	ⓐ	ⓑ	ⓒ	ⓓ
4.	ⓐ	ⓑ	ⓒ	ⓓ	21.	ⓐ	ⓑ	ⓒ	ⓓ	38.	ⓐ	ⓑ	ⓒ	ⓓ
5.	ⓐ	ⓑ	ⓒ	ⓓ	22.	ⓐ	ⓑ	ⓒ	ⓓ	39.	ⓐ	ⓑ	ⓒ	ⓓ
6.	ⓐ	ⓑ	ⓒ	ⓓ	23.	ⓐ	ⓑ	ⓒ	ⓓ	40.	ⓐ	ⓑ	ⓒ	ⓓ
7.	ⓐ	ⓑ	ⓒ	ⓓ	24.	ⓐ	ⓑ	ⓒ	ⓓ	41.	ⓐ	ⓑ	ⓒ	ⓓ
8.	ⓐ	ⓑ	ⓒ	ⓓ	25.	ⓐ	ⓑ	ⓒ	ⓓ	42.	ⓐ	ⓑ	ⓒ	ⓓ
9.	ⓐ	ⓑ	ⓒ	ⓓ	26.	ⓐ	ⓑ	ⓒ	ⓓ	43.	ⓐ	ⓑ	ⓒ	ⓓ
10.	ⓐ	ⓑ	ⓒ	ⓓ	27.	ⓐ	ⓑ	ⓒ	ⓓ	44.	ⓐ	ⓑ	ⓒ	ⓓ
11.	ⓐ	ⓑ	ⓒ	ⓓ	28.	ⓐ	ⓑ	ⓒ	ⓓ	45.	ⓐ	ⓑ	ⓒ	ⓓ
12.	ⓐ	ⓑ	ⓒ	ⓓ	29.	ⓐ	ⓑ	ⓒ	ⓓ	46.	ⓐ	ⓑ	ⓒ	ⓓ
13.	ⓐ	ⓑ	ⓒ	ⓓ	30.	ⓐ	ⓑ	ⓒ	ⓓ	47.	ⓐ	ⓑ	ⓒ	ⓓ
14.	ⓐ	ⓑ	ⓒ	ⓓ	31.	ⓐ	ⓑ	ⓒ	ⓓ	48.	ⓐ	ⓑ	ⓒ	ⓓ
15.	ⓐ	ⓑ	ⓒ	ⓓ	32.	ⓐ	ⓑ	ⓒ	ⓓ	49.	ⓐ	ⓑ	ⓒ	ⓓ
16.	ⓐ	ⓑ	ⓒ	ⓓ	33.	ⓐ	ⓑ	ⓒ	ⓓ	50.	ⓐ	ⓑ	ⓒ	ⓓ
17.	ⓐ	ⓑ	ⓒ	ⓓ	34.	ⓐ	ⓑ	ⓒ	ⓓ					

Pretest

The pretest consists of a series of reading passages with questions that follow to test your comprehension.

Cultural Center Adds Classes for Young Adults

The Allendale Cultural Center has expanded its arts program to include classes for young adults. Director Leah Martin announced Monday that beginning in September, three new classes will be offered to the Allendale community. The course titles will be Yoga for Teenagers; Hip-Hop Dance: Learning the Latest Moves; and Creative Journaling for Teens: Discovering the Writer Within. The latter course will not be held at the Allendale Cultural Center but instead will meet at the Allendale Public Library.

Staff member Tricia Cousins will teach the yoga and hip-hop classes. Ms. Cousins is an accomplished choreographer as well as an experienced dance educator. She has an MA in dance education from Teachers College, Columbia University, where she wrote a thesis on the pedagogical effectiveness of dance education. The journaling class will be taught by Betsy Milford. Ms. Milford is the head librarian at the Allendale Public Library as well as a columnist for the professional journal *Library Focus*.

The courses are part of the Allendale Cultural Center's Project Teen, which was initiated by Leah Martin, director of the Cultural Center. According to Martin, this project is a direct result of her efforts to make the center a more integral part of the Allendale community. Over the last several years, the number of people who have visited the cultural center for classes or events has steadily declined. Project Teen is primarily funded by a munificent grant from The McGee Arts Foundation, an organization devoted to bringing arts programs to young adults. Martin oversees the Project Teen board, which consists of five board members. Two board members are students at Allendale's Brookdale High School; the other three are adults with backgrounds in education and the arts.

The creative journaling class will be co-sponsored by Brookdale High School, and students who complete the class will be given the opportunity to publish one of their journal entries in *Pulse*, Brookdale's student literary magazine. Students who complete the hip-hop class will be eligible to participate in the Allendale Review, an annual concert sponsored by the cultural center that features local actors, musicians, and dancers.

All classes are scheduled to begin immediately following school dismissal, and transportation will be available from Brookdale High School to the Allendale Cultural Center and the Allendale Public Library. For more information about Project Teen, contact the cultural center's programming office at 988-0099 or drop by the office after June 1 to pick up a fall course catalog. The office is located on the third floor of the Allendale Town Hall.

1. The Creative Journaling for Teens class will be co-sponsored by
   a. the Allendale Public Library.
   b. the McGee Arts Foundation.
   c. Brookdale High School.
   d. Betsy Milford.

2. The writing in this article is
   a. emotionally charged.
   b. literary.
   c. opinionated.
   d. nonfiction.

3. According to Leah Martin, what was the direct cause of Project Teen?
   a. Tricia Cousins, the talented choreographer and dance educator, was available to teach courses in the fall.
   b. Community organizations were ignoring local teenagers.
   c. The McGee Arts Foundation wanted to be more involved in Allendale's arts programming.
   d. She wanted to make the cultural center a more important part of the Allendale community.

4. Which of the following factors is implied as another reason for Project Teen?
   a. The number of people who have visited the cultural center has declined over the last several years.
   b. The cultural center wanted a grant from the McGee Arts Foundation.
   c. The young people of Allendale have complained about the cultural center's offerings.
   d. Leah Martin thinks classes for teenagers are more important than classes for adults.

5. From the context of the passage, it can be determined that the word *munificent* most nearly means
   a. complicated.
   b. generous.
   c. curious.
   d. unusual.

6. The title of the course "Creative Journaling for Teens: Discovering the Writer Within" implies that
   a. all young people should write in a journal daily.
   b. teenagers do not have enough hobbies.
   c. writing in a journal can help teenagers become better and more creative writers.
   d. teenagers are in need of guidance and direction.

7. Which of the following correctly states the primary subject of this article?
   a. Leah Martin's personal ideas about young adults
   b. the McGee Foundation's grant to the Allendale Cultural Center
   c. three new classes for young adults added to the cultural center's arts program
   d. the needs of young adults in Allendale

8. This article is organized in which of the following ways?
   a. in chronological order, from the past to the future
   b. most important information first, followed by background and details.
   c. background first, followed by the most important information and details.
   d. as sensational news, with the most controversial topic first

Heading West: *The Grapes of Wrath* and *The Way West*
(excerpt from the opening of a literary essay)

John Steinbeck's *The Grapes of Wrath*, published in 1939, was followed ten years later by A.B. Guthrie's *The Way West*. Both books chronicle a migration, though that of Guthrie's pioneers is considerably less bleak in origin. What strikes one at first glance, however, are the commonalities. Both Steinbeck's and Guthrie's characters are primarily farmers. They look to their destinations with nearly religious enthusiasm, imagining their "promised" land the way the Biblical Israelites envisioned Canaan. Both sets of characters undergo great hardship to make the trek. But the two sagas differ distinctly in origin. Steinbeck's Oklahomans are forced off their land by the banks that own their mortgages, and they follow a false promise—that jobs as seasonal laborers await them in California. Guthrie's farmers willingly remove themselves, selling their land and trading their old dreams for their new hope in Oregon. The pioneers' decision to leave their farms in Missouri and the East is frivolous and ill-founded in comparison with the Oklahomans' unwilling response to displacement. Yet it is they, the pioneers, who are declared the heroes in our history books.

9. From the context of the passage, it can be determined that the word *frivolous* most nearly means
a. silly.
b. high-minded.
c. difficult.
d. calculated.

10. Suppose that the author is considering following this sentence with supportive detail: "Both sets of characters undergo great hardship to make the trek." Which of the following sentences would be in keeping with the comparison and contrast structure of the paragraph?
a. The migrants in *The Way West* cross the Missouri, then the Kaw, and make their way overland to the Platte.
b. The Oklahomans' jalopies break down repeatedly, while the pioneers' wagons need frequent repairs.
c. Today's travelers would consider it a hardship to spend several days, let alone several months, getting anywhere.
d. The Joad family in *The Grapes of Wrath* loses both grandmother and grandfather before the journey is complete.

11. Which of the following sentences illustrates an important difference between Steinbeck's and Guthrie's characters?
a. Steinbeck's and Guthrie's characters are primarily farmers.
b. Steinbeck's migration was forced, while the Guthrie farmers chose to leave their land.
c. They look to their destinations with nearly religious enthusiasm, imagining their "promised" land the way the Biblical Israelites envisioned Canaan.
d. none of these

12. The language in the paragraph implies that which of the following will happen to the Oklahomans when they arrive in California?
a. They will find a means to practice their religion freely.
b. They will be declared national heroes.
c. They will not find the jobs they were promised.
d. They will make their livings as mechanics rather than as farm laborers.

Barack Obama's Inaugural Address
(excerpt)

In reaffirming the greatness of our nation, we understand that greatness is never a given. It must be earned. Our journey has never been one of shortcuts or settling for less.

It has not been the path for the faint-hearted, for those who prefer leisure over work, or seek only the pleasures of riches and fame.

Rather, it has been the risk-takers, the doers, the makers of things—some celebrated, but more often men and women obscure in their labor—who have carried us up the long, rugged path toward prosperity and freedom.

For us, they packed up their few worldly possessions and traveled across oceans in search of a new life.

For us, they toiled in sweatshops and settled the West, endured the lash of the whip and plowed the hard earth.

For us, they fought and died, in places like *Concord and Gettysburg; Normandy and Khe Sanh.*

Time and again these men and women struggled and sacrificed and worked till their hands were raw so that we might live a better life. They saw America as bigger than the sum of our individual ambitions; greater than all the differences of birth or wealth or faction.

This is the journey we continue today. We remain the most prosperous, powerful nation on Earth. Our workers are no less productive than when this crisis began. Our minds are no less inventive, our goods and services no less needed than they were last week or last month or last year. Our capacity remains undiminished. But our time of standing pat, of protecting narrow interests and putting off unpleasant decisions—that time has surely passed.

13. What is the central topic of this part of the speech?
  a. Americans don't work hard enough.
  b. America is not great because it has faced too many hardships.
  c. America's greatness is based on its history of hard work and overcoming adversity.
  d. Americans can stop working hard, because they've already achieved prosperity and power.

14. The mentions of Concord, Gettysburg, Normandy, and Khe Sanh demonstrate what?
  a. that Americans have fought for the nation's freedom and prosperity all over the world
  b. that diplomacy is America's strongest asset
  c. that other countries are responsible for America's prosperity
  d. that wars have been fought in these places

15. President Barack Obama's inaugural address expresses which point of view?
  a. first-person perspective
  b. second-person perspective
  c. third-person perspective
  d. presidential perspective

16. If President Obama wanted to add a statement about the types of Americans who have helped build the country, which of the following sentences would be most consistent with the tone of his speech?
  a. Various others contributed as well.
  b. Our teachers, scientists, and countless others continue to work tirelessly to create an even better tomorrow for our nation.
  c. Today's young people do not value the efforts that our great-grandfathers and great-grandmothers made to ensure this nation's success.
  d. We should celebrate the famous Americans who have stood head and shoulders above others in their quests for greatness.

The Crossing
Chapter I: The Blue Wall
(excerpt from the opening of a 1904 novel by American writer Winston Churchill)

I was born under the Blue Ridge, and under that side which is blue in the evening light, in a wild land of game and forest and rushing waters. There, on the borders of a creek that runs into the Yadkin River, in a cabin that was chinked with red mud, I came into the world a subject of King George the Third, in that part of his realm known as the province of North Carolina.

The cabin reeked of corn-pone and bacon, and the odor of pelts. It had two shakedowns, on one of which I slept under a bearskin. A rough stone chimney was reared outside, and the fireplace was as long as my father was tall. There was a crane in it, and a bake kettle; and over it great buckhorns held my father's rifle when it was not in use. On other horns hung jerked bear's meat and venison hams, and gourds for drinking cups, and bags of seed, and my father's best hunting shirt; also, in a neglected corner, several articles of woman's attire from pegs. These once belonged to my mother. Among them was a gown of silk, of a fine, faded pattern, over which I was wont to speculate. The women at the Cross-Roads, twelve miles away, were dressed in coarse butternut wool and huge sunbonnets. But when I questioned my father on these matters he would give me no answers.

My father was—how shall I say what he was? To this day I can only surmise many things of him. He was a Scotchman born, and I know now that he had a slight Scotch accent. At the time of which I write, my early childhood, he was a frontiersman and hunter. I can see him now, with his hunting shirt and leggins and moccasins; his powder horn, engraved with wondrous scenes; his bullet pouch and tomahawk and hunting knife. He was a tall, lean man with a strange, sad face. And he talked little save when he drank too many "horns," as they were called in that country. These lapses of my father's were a perpetual source of wonder to me—and, I must say, of delight. They occurred only when a passing traveler who hit his fancy chanced that way, or, what was almost as rare, a neighbor. Many a winter night I have lain awake under the skins, listening to a flow of language that held me spellbound, though I understood scarce a word of it.

"Virtuous and vicious every man must be,
Few in the extreme, but all in a degree."

The chance neighbor or traveler was no less struck with wonder. And many the time have I heard the query, at the Cross-Roads and elsewhere, "Whar Alec Trimble got his larnin'?"

17. Why did the narrator enjoy it when his father drank too many "horns," or drafts of liquor?
   a. The father spoke brilliantly at those times.
   b. The boy was then allowed to do as he pleased.
   c. These were the only times when the father was kind.
   d. The boy was allowed to ask about his mother.

18. Judging by the sentences surrounding it, the word *surmise* in the third paragraph most nearly means
   a. to form a negative opinion.
   b. to praise.
   c. to desire.
   d. to guess.

19. The mention of the dress in the second paragraph is most likely meant to
    a. show the similarity between its owner and other members of the community.
    b. show how warm the climate was.
    c. show the dissimilarity between its owner and other members of the community.
    d. give us insight into the way most of the women of the region dressed.

20. It can be inferred from the passage that Alec Trimble is
    a. a traveler.
    b. a neighbor.
    c. the narrator's father.
    d. the narrator.

21. What is the meaning of the lines of verse quoted in the passage?
    a. People who pretend to be virtuous are actually vicious.
    b. Moderate amounts of virtuousness and viciousness are present in all people.
    c. Virtuous people cannot also be vicious.
    d. Whether people are virtuous or vicious depends on the difficulty of their circumstances.

22. Which of the following adjectives best describes the region in which the cabin is located?
    a. remote
    b. urban
    c. agricultural
    d. flat

23. The author most likely uses dialect when quoting the question, "Whar Alec Trimble got his larnin'?" in order to
    a. show disapproval of the father's behavior.
    b. show how people talked down to the narrator.
    c. show the speakers' lack of education.
    d. mimic the way the father talked.

(excerpt from a letter to a pet-sitter)

Dear Lee,

As I told you, I'll be gone until Wednesday morning. Thank you so much for taking on my "children" while I'm away. Like real children, they can be kind of irritating sometimes, but I'm going to enjoy myself so much more knowing they're getting some kind human attention. Remember that Regina (the "queen" in Latin, and she acts like one) is teething. If you don't watch her, she'll chew anything, including her sister, the cat. There are plenty of chew toys around the house. Whenever she starts gnawing on anything illegal, just divert her with one of those. She generally settles right down to a good hour-long chew. Then you'll see her wandering around whimpering with the remains of the toy in her mouth. She gets really frustrated because what she wants is to bury the thing. She'll try to dig a hole between the cushions of the couch. Finding that unsatisfactory, she'll wander some more, discontent, until you solve her problem for her. I usually show her the laundry basket, moving a few clothes so she can bury her toy beneath them. I do sound like a parent, don't I? You have to understand, my own son is practically grown up.

Regina's food is the Puppy Chow in the utility room, where the other pet food is stored. Give her a bowl once in the morning and once in the evening. No more than that, no matter how much she begs. Beagles are notorious overeaters, according to her breeder, and I don't want her to lose her girlish figure. She can share water with Rex (the King), but be sure it's changed daily. She needs to go out several times a day, especially last thing at night and first thing in the morning. Let her stay out for about ten minutes each time, so she can do *all* her business. She also needs a walk in the afternoon, after which it's important to romp with her for awhile in the yard. The game she loves most is fetch, but be sure to make her drop the ball. She'd rather play tug of war with it. Tell her, "Sit!" Then, when she does, say, "Drop it!" Be sure to tell her "good girl," and then throw the ball for her. I hope you'll enjoy these sessions as much as I do.

Now, for the other two, Rex and Paws… (*letter continues*)

24. Which effect is most likely to occur if the pet sitter does not supervise Regina and encourage her to play with her chew toys?
   a. Regina will get frustrated or damage her owner's personal property.
   b. Regina will overeat and gain weight.
   c. Regina will fight with her sister.
   d. Regina will find something else to do.

25. If the pet-sitter is a businesslike professional who watches people's pets for a living, she or he would likely prefer
   a. more first-person revelations about the owner.
   b. fewer first-person revelations about the owner.
   c. more praise for agreeing to watch the animals.
   d. greater detail on the animals' cute behavior.

26. The author uses the word *children* to describe his or her pets because
   a. the author believes her pets possess childlike qualities.
   b. the author has never had children and the pets are substitutes for the children she never had.
   c. she dresses them in clothing and indulges them with special foods.
   d. her beagle has a girlish figure and the author calls her a "good girl."

27. The information in the note is sufficient to determine that there are three animals. They are
   a. two cats and a dog.
   b. three dogs.
   c. a dog, a cat, and an unspecified animal.
   d. a cat, a dog, and a parrot.

28. Given that there are three animals to feed, which of the following arrangements of the feeding instructions would be most efficient and easiest to follow?
   a. all given in one list, chronologically from morning to night
   b. provided separately as they are for Regina, within separate passages on each animal
   c. given in the order of quantities needed, the most to the least
   d. placed in the middle of the letter, where they would be least likely to be overlooked

29. From the context of the note, it is most likely that the name Rex is
   a. Spanish.
   b. English.
   c. French.
   d. Latin.

30. If the sitter is to follow the owner's directions in playing fetch with Regina, at what point will he or she will tell Regina "good girl"?
   a. every time Regina goes after the ball
   b. after Regina finds the ball
   c. when Regina brings the ball back
   d. after Regina drops the ball

Don't Forget the Animals
(excerpt from a pro-animal rights essay)

Throughout history, through thick and thin, we have been accompanied by animals. Whether as companions, protectors, or fellow citizens of the world, animals have been the silent partners of our lives. They are more than just pets—they are intelligent, loving creatures who do not deserve to be slaughtered for meat or *sacrificed* for laboratory experiments. But who speaks for them? They have no vote, no voice in government, no one to speak up for them. We must be their voices.

Every year, more than 100 million animals are used in laboratories in the United States to test chemicals, drugs, food, and consumer products. In many cases, the animals are made to suffer greatly. How would you feel if that were your pet, forced to endure pain and suffering? You would want to intervene on their behalf—so why would you turn your back on these animals? Please consider writing a letter to your representative in Congress to end animal testing now.

31. The writer's argument relies most on which of the following techniques to convince the reader?
   a. impartial facts taken from research
   b. emotional appeals directly to scientists
   c. emotional appeals meant to sway readers on a controversial issue
   d. personal anecdotes

32. Which of the following sentences best summarizes the main idea of the passage?
   a. There are too many facilities that test on animals.
   b. Animals can't talk.
   c. Everyone should adopt a pet.
   d. If we care about animals, we should end scientific animal testing.

33. In context, the word *sacrificed* implies that
a. animals are victims of scientific testing.
b. animals are being used in religious rituals.
c. animals are choosing to be test subjects.
d. animal testing leads to great scientific breakthroughs.

The Unconventional Lives of Famous Writers
(excerpt from a literary essay)

Throughout the centuries, various writers have contributed greatly to the literary treasure trove of books lining the shelves of today's libraries. In addition to writing interesting material, many famous writers, such as Edgar Allan Poe, were larger-than-life characters with personal histories that are as interesting to read as the stories they wrote. Poe's rocky life included expulsion from the United States Military Academy at West Point in 1831 and an ongoing battle with alcohol. Yet, despite heavy gambling debts, poor health, and chronic unemployment, Poe managed to produce a body of popular works, including "The Raven" and "The Murders in the Rue Morgue."

Herman Melville, author of *Moby Dick,* once lived among the cannibals in the Marquesas Islands and wrote exotic tales inspired by his years of service in the U.S. Navy. Dublin-born Oscar Wilde was noted for his charismatic personality, his outrageous lifestyle, and creating witty catchphrases such as, "Nothing succeeds like excess." D. H. Lawrence wrote scandalous novels that were often censored, and Anne Rice led a double life writing bestselling vampire novels under her real name and using the nom de plume "A. N. Roquelaure" for the lowbrow erotica novels she penned on the side. Nonconformist author and naturalist Henry David Thoreau once fled to the woods and generated enough interesting material to fill his noted book *Walden*.

Thoreau wrote on the issue of passive resistance protest in his essay "Civil Disobedience" and served time in jail for withholding tax payments in protest of the United States government's policy towards slavery. American short story writer O. Henry's colorful life was marred by tragic events, such as being accused and sentenced for allegedly stealing money from an Austin, Texas bank. Despite his success selling his short stories, O. Henry struggled financially and was nearly bankrupt when he died.

As diverse as these famous authors' backgrounds were, they all led unconventional lives while writing great literary works that will endure throughout the ages. The next time you read an interesting book, consider learning more about the author by reading his or her biography so you can learn about the unique life experiences that shaped his or her writing.

34. Select the word that best defines *expulsion*.
a. admittance
b. entry
c. ejection
d. inclusion

35. Based on the passage, select the best choice regarding the statement: "Edgar Allan Poe was a commercially popular author."
a. The statement is false.
b. The statement is an opinion.
c. The statement is factual.
d. The statement is fictional.

36. What can you infer from the following sentence? "D. H. Lawrence wrote scandalous novels that were often censored, and Anne Rice led a double life writing bestselling novels under her real name and using the nom de plume 'A. N. Roquelaure' for the lowbrow erotica novels she penned on the side."

  a. D. H. Lawrence and Anne Rice had similar writing styles.

  b. Anne Rice used a pen name because her novels were more scandalous than D. H. Lawrence's novels.

  c. Anne Rice used different names when she wrote in different genres.

  d. none of the above

37. Which statement is false?

  a. Henry David Thoreau was passionately opposed to slavery.

  b. Anne Rice used a pen name to disguise her true identity.

  c. Herman Melville experimented with cannibalism during his naval service.

  d. Edgar Allan Poe was an alcoholic.

38. Select the word that best defines *marred*.

  a. improved

  b. soaked

  c. tarnished

  d. ended

39. The main idea of this story is

  a. Many famous writers lived nontraditional lives.

  b. Writers are troublemakers.

  c. All writers lead interesting lives.

  d. Writers' biographies are inspirational.

(excerpt from a college admissions essay)

Ever since I was a little girl, I have dreamed of attending Westfall University. My parents took me to football games, where I wore the green and gold, and cheered along with Westie the Terrier as he danced on the field in costume. However, I know that attending such a *prestigious* school requires more than cheering for the sports teams, so I have worked very hard in hopes of joining the Westfall community as a student next September.

In addition to my very strong grades (3.8 average out of 4.0), I belong to six different clubs and organizations at my high school. I am the secretary of the Key Club, which performs community service. I play the saxophone in Jazz Band and Symphonic Band, and participate in Making Music Together, which teaches young children how to play instruments. Since my freshman year, I have been the Treasurer and am now the Vice President of the Student Council; as a senior, I serve as a student liaison for the local School Board's Student Advisory Council. Being a member of these groups has taught me the importance of leadership and participation in my community—skills that I would bring with me to Westfall as a student and member of the campus.

40. This essay is written from which point of view?
a. first person
b. second person
c. third person
d. fourth person

41. What is the writer's main topic?
a. reminiscing about football games she attended as a child
b. the types of activities offered at her high school
c. describing her background and qualifications as an applicant
d. whether or not she wants to attend Westfall University

42. The writer relies primarily on which of the following techniques to make her main point?
a. emotional appeal
b. statement of facts
c. fictional embellishment
d. sarcasm

43. What is the tone of this essay excerpt?
a. boastful
b. indifferent
c. hopeful
d. humorous

44. The writer's list of extracurricular activities implies which of the following?
a. that the writer is too busy to apply to other schools
b. that she has many interests and is good at working with others in a variety of activities
c. that she wants to be the Westfall University mascot at football games
d. that Westfall University would be lucky to have her

45. In the context of this excerpt, the word *prestigious* most likely means which of the following?
a. dull
b. easy
c. impressive
d. local

(excerpt from an online review of a restaurant)

I am a longtime customer of Woody's Grill, but after the experience I had there last night, I am extremely disappointed. My family and I went to Woody's for good food and good service, like we've had so many times before. Instead, we found terrible food and even worse service.

It all started when we were asked to wait 15 minutes for a table. That was understandable—it was prime dinner time, and Woody's was very busy. However, 15 minutes came and went, and no one came to show us to a table, or let us know how much longer we'd be waiting. Then another 30 minutes passed. Finally, 45 minutes after we arrived, we were shown to a table. Our waiter didn't come over to take our drink orders for 15 more minutes. By the time we'd ordered, we had been in the restaurant for more than an hour, with no food and no drinks to show for it. When our food *finally* arrived, it was cold—and half the order was wrong! When we spoke to the waiter, he was quite rude, telling me that I must have been mistaken. I can assure you that, as a vegetarian, I did not *erroneously* order a cheeseburger. Even after this unfortunate exchange, we had to wait another 20 minutes for our check.

I have always enjoyed Woody's Grill, but if this is what their customer service has become, I will have to revise my opinion.

46. The tone of the review could best be described as which of the following?
   a. impressed
   b. angry
   c. excited
   d. neutral

47. The supporting details are organized in which of the following ways?
   a. with the most important detail first, followed by background details
   b. with the background first, followed by the most important details
   c. randomly, according to the writer's preference
   d. in a chronological narrative of the writer's restaurant visit

48. In the context of the excerpt, the word *erroneously* most likely means which of the following?
   a. mistakenly
   b. gleefully
   c. purposely
   d. loudly

49. According to the writer, how long was he or she made to wait before a waiter came to take drink orders?
   a. one hour
   b. 105 minutes
   c. 45 minutes
   d. one hour, 15 minutes

50. From this excerpt, it is implied that which of the following will likely be the outcome of the writer's visit to Woody's Grill?
   a. She/he will get an apology from the waiter.
   b. Woody's Grill will close.
   c. She/he will not go back to the restaurant.
   d. She/he will stop being a vegetarian.

Answers

If you miss any of the answers, you can find help for that kind of question in the lesson(s) shown to the right of the answer.

1. c. Lesson 1
2. d. Lesson 4
3. d. Lesson 9
4. a. Lesson 16
5. b. Lesson 3
6. c. Lesson 12
7. c. Lesson 2
8. b. Lessons 6 and 7
9. a. Lesson 3
10. b. Lesson 8
11. b. Lesson 8
12. c. Lesson 17
13. c. Lesson 2
14. a. Lesson 20
15. a. Lesson 11
16. b. Lesson 13
17. a. Lesson 19
18. d. Lesson 3
19. c. Lesson 8
20. c. Lesson 19
21. b. Lesson 19
22. a. Lesson 16
23. c. Lesson 13
24. a. Lesson 9
25. b. Lesson 11

26. a. Lesson 18
27. c. Lesson 1
28. a. Lessons 6 and 10
29. d. Lesson 3
30. d. Lesson 6
31. c. Lesson 18
32. d. Lesson 2
33. a. Lesson 3
34. c. Lesson 3
35. c. Lesson 14
36. a. Lesson 16
37. c. Lesson 1
38. c. Lesson 3
39. a. Lesson 2
40. a. Lesson 11
41. c. Lesson 2
42. b. Lesson 18
43. c. Lesson 2
44. b. Lesson 16
45. a. Lesson 12
46. b. Lesson 14
47. d. Lesson 18
48. b. Lesson 16
49. d. Lesson 17
50. a. Lesson 17

Answer Explanations

1. Choice **a** is incorrect. The Allendale Public Library is the location for the Creative Journaling for Teens class (per the first paragraph), but is not a co-sponsor.

   Choice **b** is incorrect. The McGee Arts Foundation is an organization that helps fund Project Teen (per the third paragraph), but is not a co-sponsor of the creative journaling class.

   Choice **c** is correct. According to the fourth paragraph, the creative journaling class is co-sponsored by Brookdale High School, which also offers publication in its literary journal for all students who complete the class.

Choice **d** is incorrect. Betsy Milford, the head librarian at the Allendale Public Library, will be teaching the creative journaling class, but the passage does not suggest she is a co-sponsor.

2. Choice **a** is incorrect. The writing in this article offers neutral information about the classes available through the Allendale Cultural Center, and there is no emotional language to suggest that the author is trying to convey a particular emotion.

Choice **b** is incorrect. The article offers plain facts (what the classes are, where they will take place, who is teaching them, etc.), without descriptive literary details.

Choice **c** is incorrect. The writer does not offer personal opinions on the classes, the Allendale Cultural Center, or the people in the program.

Choice **d** is correct. The article offers facts and details about the classes, but does not take liberties with that information, or include any speculation—therefore, it is nonfiction.

3. Choice **a** is incorrect. Tricia Cousins is not mentioned by Leah Martin in the article.

Choice **b** is incorrect. The author never suggests that local teenagers have been ignored.

Choice **c** is incorrect. In paragraph 3, the author writes that the McGee Arts Foundation is devoted to bringing arts programs to young adults, but this is not part of Leah Martin's statement.

Choice **d** is correct. At the beginning of paragraph 3, the author conveys what Leah Martin said: that Project Teen is a direct result of her efforts to make the Allendale Cultural a more integral part of the local community.

4. Choice **a** is correct. Though Cultural Center director Leah Martin does not come out and say that declining numbers of visitors are the reason for Project Teen, the author implies a connection by following Leah Martin's comments directly with the statement about decreasing visitor numbers.

Choice **b** is incorrect. The article never speculates about whether or not the cultural center wanted a grant from the McGee Arts foundation, so this is not the implication referred to in the question.

Choice **c** is incorrect. The article never mentions whether or not young people have complained about the cultural center's offerings, so there is no implication that this is the reason behind Project Teen.

Choice **d** is incorrect. Leah Martin's statement (that the project is a result of wanting to be more integrated with the community) has nothing to do with whether or not she thinks classes for teenagers are more important than classes for adults—and there is no supporting information to link the two or imply a connection.

5. Choice **a** is incorrect. None of the supporting information about The McGee Arts Foundation suggests that the grant is *complicated*.

Choice **b** is correct. The author indicates that The McGee Arts Foundation provides the primary funding for Project Teen, which suggests that the grant is a significant amount of money. *Generous* is commonly used to describe charitable grants or donations, like the one described in this article.

Choice **c** is incorrect. The author presents no information that would suggest that the grant is *curious* or out of the ordinary—especially given that the author writes that the Foundation's goals are similar to the goals of Project Teen (providing arts programs for young adults).

Choice **d** is incorrect. As with choice **c**, there is no indication that the grant is odd or *unusual*, both of which are synonyms of *curious*.

6. Choice **a** is incorrect. None of the language in the title compels students to write in a journal.

Choice **b** is incorrect. The title says nothing about the numbers or types of hobbies that teenagers have.

Choice **c** is correct. "Discovering the Writer Within" suggests that teenagers already have the ability to write creatively, and that taking the course and keeping a journal will help them develop those skills.

Choice **d** is incorrect. "Discovering the Writer Within" emphasizes that students will be finding their creative writing talents for themselves—not necessarily receiving guidance or direction from others. There is nothing to support an implication that the class will provide strict guidance or direction from others.

7. Choice **a** is incorrect. The only statement from Leah Martin discusses her motivations for creating Project Teen, not her personal opinions on teenagers.

Choice **b** is incorrect. While the article mentions that Project Teen is largely funded by a grant from the McGee Arts Foundation, it is not the overall focus of the article.

Choice **c** is correct. The first sentence tells you that the Allendale Cultural Center is offering new classes for young adults, and each paragraph after that offers information and background on those classes.

Choice **d** is incorrect. The article discusses specifically what the cultural center offers, not what the author believes that young adults in Allendale need. There is no factual information to support a discussion of what local teenagers need—only that the cultural center is offering classes for those teenagers.

8. Choice **a** is incorrect. There are no words or phrases that suggest that the article is laying out information in a chronological way (like *first*, *next*, or *then*).

Choice **b** is correct. The article tells you up front that the Allendale Cultural Center is offering classes: the most important information. This is then followed by details and background that tell the reader more about those classes.

Choice **c** is incorrect. The author does not begin to offer information about the courses until the second paragraph.

Choice **d** is incorrect. The article is not sensationalistic; the author uses very plain language, backed by clear facts and background details. The point of the article is to convey information, not to editorialize by trying to present controversial information to attract the reader's attention.

9. Choice **a** is correct. *Frivolous* means *silly,* which you can tell from the way the author describes their decision to sell their land and forfeit their livelihoods, and compares them to Steinbeck's characters, who are forced from their land.

Choice **b** is incorrect. If *frivolous* meant *high-minded,* the author would likely use supporting comments to suggest that Guthrie's characters were motivated by noble ideas. Instead, the author pairs *high-minded* with the phrase *ill-founded,* which casts the decision in a negative light.

Choice **c** is incorrect. The essay's author suggests that Guthrie's farmers (as opposed to Steinbeck's displaced farmers) easily traded stability for the unknown without giving the matter deep thought or consideration, both of which would have made the decision a more *difficult* one to make.

Choice **d** is incorrect. Again, the use of *ill-founded* suggests that the author does not believe that the characters put a lot of thought into their choices, that the decision was simple and poorly considered, without calculation or regard for consequences.

10. Choice **a** is incorrect. Describing the geographic path of the characters in *The Way West* does not support the author's claim that the characters endured hardship.

Choice **b** is correct. This sentence describes problems that occur for each set of characters, which builds on the original phrase *Both sets of characters undergo great hardship. . . .*

Choice **c** is incorrect. This sentence does not describe the hardships, or even mention the books' characters. Therefore, it is not the supportive detail we're looking for.

Choice **d** is incorrect. While losing both a grandmother and a grandfather is certainly a hardship, it applies only to the Joads. The original sentence to be supported mentions both the characters in *The Grapes of Wrath* and the characters in *The Way West*, so this choice has insufficient detail to be truly supportive.

11. Choice **a** is incorrect. This choice points out a similarity between the two sets of characters, not a difference.

Choice **b** is correct. The author explicitly contrasts the origins of each family's trek in the following sentence: *The pioneers' decision to leave their farms in Missouri and the East is frivolous and ill-founded, in comparison with the Oklahomans' unwilling response to displacement.* When looking for differences in a piece of writing, look for phrases like *in comparison, as opposed to,* or *in contrast.*

Choice **c** is incorrect. Like choice **a**, this choice describes a similarity between the characters, and the question calls for a difference.

Choice **d** is incorrect. Because choice **b** fits the question criteria (describing a difference), *none of these* should not be an option.

12. Choice **a** is incorrect. While the author does make a Biblical reference with regard to how the Oklahomans saw their destination, their specific religion (or whether they are seeking to practice it freely) is not mentioned at all.

Choice **b** is incorrect. In the last sentence, *they* refers to Guthrie's pioneers being considered national historical heroes, not Steinbeck's Oklahomans.

Choice **c** is correct. The author uses words like *bleak* and *false promise* to describe the Oklahomans' journey, suggesting that they will not find the promised jobs at the end of their trek to California.

Choice **d** is correct. The author does not describe what type of jobs the Oklahomans are seeking in California, so there is not enough supporting information to determine how the family is planning to make their living.

13. Choice **a** is incorrect. This section of President Obama's speech specifically discusses the hard work that generations of Americans have done in the interest of creating freedom and prosperity for the country.

Choice **b** is incorrect. In the closing, the speech says explicitly that America has achieved prosperity and power as a result of overcoming the hardships. President Obama contrasts this achievement against ways that existing prosperity and power could decline.

Choice **c** is correct. The speech contains supporting details that discuss the types of challenges faced by Americans throughout history, supporting the statement in the first paragraph that greatness must be earned without shortcuts or settling for less.

Choice **d** is incorrect. President Obama is saying the opposite. In the last paragraph, he says that "standing pat" is not an option for maintaining the achievements of past generations of Americans.

14. Choice **a** is correct. If you look at the information around the list of places, you can see that President Obama is putting them in the context of how Americans traveled "across oceans."

Choice **b** is incorrect. The passage very clearly suggests that America's success comes from its own citizens; there is no mention of how diplomacy with other countries fits into that.

Choice **c** is incorrect. Again, as with choice **b**, while other locations are mentioned, it is only within the context of what Americans achieved there.

Choice **d** is incorrect. While the places are a list of places where battles took place, they are not just a laundry list of historical facts. The speech uses them to establish a broad range of American hardships all over the world, so the list is contextual, not factual.

15. Choice **a** is correct. Although President Obama never uses "I" in this section of his speech, the use of "we" makes it first-person perspective.

Choice **b** is incorrect. For this speech to have a second-person perspective, the President would need to address "you" instead of "we" and "us."

Choice **c** is incorrect. The President is not a narrator, discussing events from a removed perspective. He includes himself and his listeners in his discussion of Americans as a whole.

Choice **d** is incorrect. *Presidential perspective* is not a type of perspective found in writing.

16. Choice **a** is incorrect. This is a vague and short statement, unlike the longer sentences and more detail that President Obama had used in the rest of the speech.

Choice **b** is correct. The specific mention of different types of American professionals is similar to his previous mentions of entrepreneurs, soldiers, etc., as is connecting those to the country's future prosperity. The tone and theme of the sentence are in keeping with the rest of his speech.

Choice **c** is incorrect. Nowhere else in the speech does he discuss how the youth fit in with this theme of overcoming adversity, so this sentence would not fit.

Choice **d** is incorrect. In the second paragraph, he states that it has been regular Americans ("some celebrated, but more often men and women obscure in their labor") who have achieved the most over the course of history. In this context, *obscure* is the word that eliminates choice **d** as a possibility.

17. Choice **a** is correct. The author uses words like *spellbound* and *wonder* to describe the narrator's reaction to his father's speeches, implying the brilliance of his father's words.

Choice **b** is incorrect. The author describes his reaction as being trancelike and holding him almost captive of his father's speech. This suggests the opposite of the narrator having the freedom to do whatever he wants.

Choice **c** is incorrect. In this excerpt, the narrator never says that his father is *unkind*—so the passage is unlikely to support the conclusion that this was the only time the narrator's father was kind.

Choice **d** is incorrect. Earlier in the passage, the narrator states that when he questioned his father about his mother, he received no answers. There is no supporting detail after that to suggest that there was ever a time when he received answers.

18. Choice **a** is incorrect. By the time the word *surmise* is used, there have been no details that suggest that the narrator has a negative view of his father.

Choice **b** is incorrect. Similarly, there is no information to support the idea that the narrator has a positive view of his father, either.

Choice **c** is incorrect. The first sentence, *My father was—how shall I say he was?* implies that the narrator is searching for a way to describe his father, not that he wants (or desires) his father to do something particular.

Choice **d** is incorrect. The narrator uses *surmise* in the context of his questions about his father, and the lack of information he received about his father/mother. Therefore, *to guess* is the likeliest choice when you consider that the narrator is trying to construct his own information.

19. Choice **a** is incorrect. By describing the silk dress as "fine" and the wool dresses as "coarse," the narrator is setting up a contrast between the two, not a similarity.

Choice **b** is incorrect. The narrator uses the dresses to contrast between the people who wore them. He offers no supporting information or commentary on the climate.

Choice **c** is correct. Again, by describing the silk as "fine" and suggesting its luxury compared to the "coarse" wool and sunbonnets, the narrator tries to establish that his mother was likely different from the other women in town.

Choice **d** is incorrect. Before he compares the types of dresses, the narrator mentions that he is speculating on the matter, which implies he is probably not trying to provide factual information about women's dresses.

20. Choice **a** is incorrect. The "traveler" is the person talking about Alec Trimble—he or she is not Alec Trimble.

Choice **b** is incorrect. The neighbor is the person speaking, so it is highly unlikely that he is talking about himself in the third person.

Choice **c** is correct. The narrator is discussing his father's speeches and their effects on people who pass by; therefore, when that passerby makes a comment, you can infer that he or she is talking about the narrator's father: Alec Trimble.

Choice **d** is incorrect. The people commenting on Alec Trimble are talking about his words, which we know are not the narrator's, because the narrator is listening with delight too.

21. Choice **a** is incorrect. The phrase *every man must be* suggests that being vicious or virtuous is not an either/or.

Choice **b** is correct. Again, that every man must be vicious *and* virtuous connects the two elements. And in the second line, the phrase *all in a degree* suggests the moderation.

Choice **c** is incorrect. If all people must have both, as implied in the first line, then being virtuous does not exclude being vicious.

Choice **d** is incorrect. There is no mention of virtuosity or viciousness being affected by circumstances, so the text cannot support this interpretation of the meaning.

22. Choice **a** is correct. The narrator establishes the remoteness of the cabin in the first paragraph ("a wild land of game and forest and rushing waters") and also in the second, when he mentions that the nearest town is 12 miles away.

Choice **b** is incorrect. Again, the narrator talks about how removed the cabin is from the town, so *urban*, or city-like, is not an accurate description.

Choice **c** is incorrect. The narrator emphasizes that hunting and fishing are the main attributes of his region (discussing the "game" in the first paragraph, and the "pelts" that decorate the cabin in the second paragraph), so *agricultural* is not an accurate description either. The narrator's father is clearly described as a frontiersman and a hunter, not a farmer.

Choice **d** is incorrect. The narrator opens by saying he was born in the Blue Ridge, which the reader can infer is a mountain region. Therefore, *flat* is not the correct choice in the context of this excerpt.

23. Choice **a** is incorrect. The narrator says in the third paragraph that his father's talkative moments cause "delight." It is unlikely that the narrator would also disapprove of his father's behavior.

Choice **b** is incorrect. The narrator shows that the speakers are praising his father (with "wonder"), not talking to or about him—so it is unlikely that he feels that the speakers are talking down to him.

Choice **c** is incorrect. There is no other information about whether or not the speakers are educated, so it is unlikely that this is the narrator's reason for using the dialect.

Choice **d** is correct. The narrator is enchanted by his father's dialect, and is trying to recreate the speaker's voice and the sense of "wonder" that he or she felt at hearing Alec speak.

24. Choice **a** is correct. In the first paragraph, the writer specifically says that Regina will "chew anything," which likely includes the owner's property.

Choice **b** is incorrect. Overeating causes Regina to "lose her girlish figure," according to the second paragraph, so this is a different cause/effect relationship.

Choice **c** is incorrect. The letter says that Regina will chew on the cat, which suggests that the cat is more like a chew toy than a participant in a fight.

Choice **d** is incorrect. This choice is too vague. While Regina will technically find something else to do, the specific activities outlined in choice **a** make it the correct choice.

25. Choice **a** is incorrect. A professional pet-sitter would need as much information as possible about the pets he or she is watching. First-person revelations about the owner might tell the pet-sitter very little about the person's pets.

Choice **b** is correct. Details about the writer's own son and how much the writer enjoys playing with her dog add color to the letter, but they tell the pet-sitter very little about his or her job.

Choice **c** is incorrect. The letter is written from the pet owner's perspective, so the reader has no information about what kind of praise the pet-sitter would expect.

Choice **d** is incorrect. As with choices **a** and **b**, the personal details are descriptive and entertaining, but they do not help the pet-sitter on a professional level, and have no place in a businesslike letter.

26. Choice **a** is correct. The writer describes the antics of her pets like she would describe her child, and acknowledges this at the end of the first paragraph ("I do sound like a parent, don't I?").

Choice **b** is incorrect. The author contradicts this choice with her statement, "My son is practically grown up." Since she already has a child, the pets cannot be substitutes.

Choice **c** is incorrect. There is no mention of any of the pets wearing clothes, and the writer clearly says the pet food that Regina eats is Puppy Chow. There are no instructions for special foods.

Choice **d** is incorrect. Calling Regina a "girl" is personification, but it is used in a very general way here and it is not child-specific, which is what the question is asking.

27. Choice **a** is incorrect. Throughout the excerpt, the writer refers to a dog (Regina), a cat (Paws), and Rex (unidentified). There is not enough information in this particular excerpt to confirm that Rex is a cat.

Choice **b** is incorrect. There are three animals (Regina and "the other two," as the writer states in the last sentence), and the writer refers to Regina's sister, the cat. Therefore, all three animals can't be dogs.

Choice **c** is correct. You know for sure that Regina is a dog, and can infer the female cat is likely Paws, who is mentioned in the first paragraph but not named until the last sentence. However, although you know that Rex is male, there is not have enough information to conclude what kind of animal Rex is.

Choice **d** is incorrect. Similar to choice **a**, there is simply not enough information to conclude that Rex is a parrot, either.

28. Choice **a** is correct. If the writer were to organize the list chronologically, the reader would have all of the information arranged in the way he or she is likely to organize it him- or herself, the way the pets will actually be fed.

Choice **b** is incorrect. It is less efficient to organize the feedings by animal, because the pet-sitter will still need to figure out when each pet needs to be fed.

Choice **c** is incorrect. The quantities are important information, but organizing it this way still leaves the reader to figure out the correct feeding schedule.

Choice **d** is incorrect. This is the least efficient option. If the feeding instructions are buried in the middle, the reader needs to locate the information, then organize it to determine what the actual schedule, quantities, etc. are for each animal.

29. Choice **a** is incorrect. The writer goes out of her way to write that Regina's name means "the queen" in Latin, so it is unlikely that "the King" is in Spanish.

Choice **b** is incorrect. The letter is written in English, so if "Rex" was meant to be English, he would likely be named King instead.

Choice **c** is incorrect. As with choice **a**, there is no information to support that the writer switched languages when giving her pets names that "match" like a king and queen.

Choice **d** is correct. Because the writer specifically mentions Latin when translating Regina's name in the first paragraph, and simply describes Rex's translation without suggesting that his name means "king" in a different language, you can infer that the two names come from the same language. In this case, that language is Latin.

30. Choice **a** is incorrect. The reader is throws the ball after he or she says "good girl" as praise for dropping it.

Choice **b** is incorrect. The writer states that the reader needs to make sure that Regina drops the ball before throwing it. Regina receives praise for dropping the ball, not finding it.

Choice **c** is incorrect. The writer states that the reader needs to make sure Regina drops the ball after she brings it back. Regina receives praise for dropping the ball, not bringing it back.

Choice **d** is correct. The letter clearly states that the reader is to say "good girl" after saying "Drop it!" After Regina drops the ball, the reader is to praise her.

31. Choice **a** is incorrect. Although the writer does offer the number of animals used in laboratory testing each year, the excerpt does not rely on factual information to convey the writer's point.

Choice **b** is incorrect. While the writer is using an emotional appeal (including asking the reader to think of his or her own pets), there is no evidence to suggest that he or she is writing with scientists in mind.

Choice **c** is correct. By trying to connect the reader and the animals ("we must be their voices") and asking the reader to consider his or her own pets when thinking about animal testing, it is clear that the writer is attempting to use the reader's emotions to agree with the main topic.

Choice **d** is incorrect. Although this essay is written from the first-person plural perspective at times ("we"), the author gives no insight into his or her own personal experiences.

32. Choice **a** is incorrect. In this excerpt, the writer never mentions the actual facilities where the testing is done.

Choice **b** is incorrect. While the writer does say that humans need to be the voices of animals, this is not the primary point of the passage.

Choice **c** is incorrect. In this excerpt, the writer discusses mostly the plight of animals who are subject to testing, not animals who need homes.

Choice **d** is correct. The writer links concern for animals to a condemnation of scientific animal testing. In the last sentence, the writer directly asks the reader to reach out to Congress in order to help end animal testing.

33. Choice **a** is correct. *Sacrificed* implies that humans are using animals for their own gain (in this case, scientific study).

Choice **b** is incorrect. In this excerpt, the writer focuses on scientific testing. There is no information to support the idea that the author is taking a stand on religious rituals.

Choice **c** is incorrect. In the first paragraph, the writer specifically tells you that animals do not have voices or choices. Therefore, it is unlikely that the word *sacrificed* means that animals are willingly subjecting themselves to scientific testing.

Choice **d** is incorrect. The writer never discusses what the types of research are, or the potential outcomes of that research. Also, he or she sees animal testing as a negative activity that should be ended, so it is unlikely that he or she sees the animals as being sacrificed to a greater good.

34. Choice **a** is incorrect. The writer uses "rocky" to describe Poe's life, which suggests that he or she is not going to talk about the more successful aspects. *Expulsion* is the opposite of *admittance*.

Choice **b** is incorrect. For the same reasons that *admittance* is incorrect, its synonym *entry* is incorrect as well.

Choice **c** is correct. The writer talks about instability, so the reader can infer that Poe's experience with the United States Military Academy at West Point was not a stable or productive one. Out of the choices, only *ejection* fits that line of thought.

Choice **d** is incorrect. The information that comes next (that Poe was an unemployed gambler in poor health) does not support the idea that the author was included in a stable institution like the Academy.

35. Choice **a** is incorrect. The writer specifically mentions that Poe produced "popular" books in spite of his personal problems.

Choice **b** is incorrect. Poe is a well-known author and historical figure, so stating his popularity is not an opinion in this case.

Choice **c** is correct. As with choice **b**, that Poe is widely known for his books makes this a factual statement.

Choice **d** is incorrect. This essay is a nonfiction literary essay, meaning the author is using facts and opinions to express the main ideas. Because this statement is considered truthful (and can be verified by book sales and history), the statement about Poe's popularity is not fictional. If the author made it up or made a statement that was unverifiable, then it could be considered fictional.

36. Choice **a** is correct. Because the only point of similarity mentioned by the author is Lawrence's "scandalous" novels and Rice's "lowbrow erotica novels," you can infer that the author is comparing the two authors' writing styles.

Choice **b** is incorrect. There is no supporting information that tells you exactly how scandalous each author's novels were, so you cannot make a conclusion about whose books were more scandalous.

Choice **c** is incorrect. This is a fact, stated directly in the writer's sentence. There's no need to infer that Anne Rice used different pen names.

37. Choice **a** is incorrect. The third paragraph states that Thoreau stopped paying taxes as a way of protesting slavery, suggesting that he supported that cause very strongly.

Choice **b** is incorrect. The second paragraph states that Anne Rice used multiple pen names for her books, so this is verifiably true.

Choice **c** is correct. The excerpt states that Melville lived *among* cannibals, but says nothing about whether he experimented with cannibalism himself.

Choice **d** is incorrect. The first paragraph declares that Poe had "an ongoing battle with alcohol," so this is also verifiably true (at least in terms of this essay).

38. Choice **a** is incorrect. O. Henry's life was *marred* by "tragic events," so you can infer that his life was not *improved* by tragedy.

Choice **b** is incorrect. If you replace *soaked* with a similar word/phrase like *drenched*, the sentence does not make sense. *O. Henry's life was drenched by tragic events.* . . .

Choice **c** is correct. As with choice **a**, you can make the inference that tragic events had a negative impact on O. Henry's life. Of the choices available, only *tarnished* really fits that criteria.

Choice **d** is incorrect. The end of O. Henry's life could have been tragic, but the writer chooses a different kind of example of the kind of event that marred his life: a robbery conviction. This event is not a life-ending one, so you can safely assume that *ended* is not the correct meaning for *marred*.

39. Choice **a** is correct. This information is found right in the title: "The Unconventional Lives of Writers." The writer also uses words and phrases like *larger-than-life* and *colorful* to emphasize that the writers experienced interesting things.

Choice **b** is incorrect. The writer writes mostly about exotic or negative things that happened in the lives of authors, but he or she does not seem to be suggesting that all of the writers were troublemakers. The writer maintains a neutral voice, not a judgmental one.

Choice **c** is incorrect. The writer highlights a handful of famous authors who had nontraditional experiences, but never suggests that all writers have similar experiences.

Choice **d** is incorrect. In the last paragraph, the writer suggests that the reader seek out author biographies for "interesting" reading, but never implies that the reader should find these anecdotes (like Poe's alcoholism or O. Henry's incarceration) inspirational.

40. Choice **a** is correct. The writer is writing about herself and her experiences, and uses "I," which signals to the reader that the perspective is first-person.

Choice **b** is incorrect. If the writer used mostly "you" as the primary perspective, then the essay could be considered second-person.

Choice **c** is incorrect. If the writer wanted to use third-person perspective, phrases like *I serve* would become *she serves*. A third-person narrator is removed from the action, but this is an essay where the writer is writing from her own perspective.

Choice **d** is incorrect. There is no such perspective as fourth-person.

41. Choice **a** is incorrect. The writer mentions attending football games as a way of adding personal detail from her essay, but the subject never comes up again in the course of the essay.

Choice **b** is incorrect. The writer lists the activities in which *she* participated, but from this essay the reader has no way of knowing how that compares to the total number of activities offered by her school.

Choice **c** is correct. This is a college applications essay, which means the writer is trying to convey her background and why she would be a good candidate for Westfall University.

Choice **d** is incorrect. The writer tells us in the very first paragraph that she wants to attend Westfall University, so there is no ongoing discussion about the matter in the rest of the essay.

42. Choice **a** is incorrect. Although the writer offers personal details, she uses very calm logic to explain why she thinks she's qualified to be a Westfall student.

Choice **b** is correct. The writer uses facts (like her GPA and her activities) to support her main idea.

Choice **c** is incorrect. Because the writer gives supporting evidence that can be verified (her grades and her extracurricular activities), it's pretty clear that she's not embellishing or inventing details.

Choice **d** is incorrect. The writer's style is very straightforward, and she doesn't seem to be making light of the school, or mocking herself.

43. Choice **a** is incorrect. While the writer is talking confidently about herself, she is presenting her experiences in a very matter-of-fact way, not trying to make them seem bigger or more significant than they are.

Choice **b** is incorrect. The writer is clearly very set on attending Westfall University, so *indifferent* (or not caring) is the opposite of what she's trying to convey in her essay.

Choice **c** is correct. Her goal is to get into Westfall University, and the information she provides supports that goal. She is *hopeful*, or optimistic, that she is a good candidate for the school.

Choice **d** is incorrect. The writer is very straightforward about the goals of her essay, and uses plain, direct language—even when she uses a lighter tone (like in the mascot example in the first paragraph), it's not *humorous*.

44. Choice **a** is incorrect. She lists her activities, not her schedule. The reader has no way of knowing how busy she really is—just that she has participated in these activities at some point in her high school career.

Choice **b** is correct. In addition to listing her academic accomplishments and her activities, the writer adds a summary sentence about how those experiences make her a better candidate for the university.

Choice **c** is incorrect. In the first paragraph, she remembers cheering along with the mascot, but never mentions wanting to *be* Westie the Terrier.

Choice **d** is incorrect. By using statements like, "I know that attending such a prestigious school requires more than cheering for the sports teams, so I have worked very hard…" the writer suggests that she knows that she is auditioning to get into the school—not the other way around.

45. Choice **a** is incorrect. Assuming the writer really does want to attend Westfall University, it's unlikely that she would describe the school as *dull*.

Choice **b** is incorrect. In the first paragraph, the writer acknowledges that getting into the school requires hard work, so it is also unlikely that she sees the application process as *easy*.

Choice **c** is correct. The writer clearly has respect for the school, so *impressive* is the closest fit out of all the choices.

Choice **d** is incorrect. There is no indication of whether Westfall University is close or far, so the reader has no way of knowing whether the school is *local* to the writer or not.

46. Choice **a** is incorrect. The writer is displeased with the experience at the restaurant, so he or she is probably not *impressed*.

Choice **b** is correct. The writer is upset about the food and the service at Woody's Grill, and words like "terrible" suggest that the tone is *angry*.

Choice **c** is incorrect. Given the negative tone, the writer is obviously not very *excited* about his or her experience, and even less excited about going back for more.

Choice **d** is incorrect. The dinner at Woody's Grill was a negative experience, and strong enough that the person wanted to review the incident to warn others.

47. Choice **a** is incorrect. While the writer states the main topic up front (the lousy experience at the restaurant), the structure is mostly chronological.

Choice **b** is incorrect. The important information is stated and then supported consistently throughout the review.

Choice **c** is incorrect. The writer uses an orderly structure: statement of topic, supporting details, and then a restatement of the main topic. No details appear to be random or out of place.

Choice **d** is correct. The second paragraph, containing most of the supporting details, is structured chronologically, outlining the family's restaurant visit event by event.

48. Choice **a** is correct. The writer is a vegetarian and knows his or her own personal preferences, so ordering meat would have been a *mistake*.

Choice **b** is incorrect. Again, if the writer is vegetarian, it is unlikely that he or she would order a burger *gleefully*, or happily.

Choice **c** is incorrect. Similar to the logic for choice **a**, the writer would probably not order meat *on purpose*.

Choice **d** is incorrect. Because the story is told from the reviewer's perspective, there is no way to tell how *loud* he or she was when ordering.

49. Choice **a** is correct. The writer says that he or she was there for 15 minutes waiting for a table, plus another 30 minutes before they were seated, then waited for 15 more minutes until the waiter came to take drink orders. 15 + 30 + 15 = 60 minutes, or one hour.

Choice **b** is incorrect. You reach 105 minutes if you add all of the numbers mentioned by the author, without reading to see if there's any context or repetition in the text. Always read the text carefully.

Choice **c** is incorrect. The writer adds the minutes halfway, saying that his or her family was in the restaurant for 45 minutes (the previously mentioned 15 minute- and 30-minute waits), before adding the final 15 minutes spent waiting for the waiter to take their order.

Choice **d** is incorrect. The writer mentions the same 15-minute waiting period twice, so always read carefully to determine a true timeline when reading text that is arranged chronologically.

50. Choice **a** is incorrect. We don't know where this review is posted, or whether or not the waiter will see it, so we have no idea whether the customer will get a response from the waiter.

Choice **b** is incorrect. There is nothing to suggest that Woody's Grill will close as a result of this bad review (or for any reason).

Choice **c** is correct. The last sentence suggests that the customer will not forget this terrible experience, making him or her unlikely to go back for another potentially bad meal.

Choice **d** is incorrect. Even though the waiter brought the writer a burger, there is nothing to suggest that it was eaten, or that the writer will stop being a vegetarian in the future.

BUILDING A STRONG FOUNDATION

You may not have thought of it this way before, but critical readers are a lot like crime scene investigators. In their search for the truth, they do not let opinions sway them; they want to know what actually happened. They collect tangible evidence and facts and use this information to draw an informed conclusion. Separating fact from opinion is essential during a crime scene investigation. It is also a crucial skill for effective reading.

When you read, look for clues to understand the author's meaning. What is this passage about? What is this writer saying? What is his or her message? At times, it may seem like authors are trying to hide their meanings from you. But no matter how complex a piece of writing may be, the author always leaves plenty of clues for the careful reader to find. It is your job to find those clues. Be a good detective when you read. Open your eyes and ask the right questions. In other words, read carefully and actively.

The five lessons that follow cover the basics of reading comprehension. By the end of this section, you should be able to

- find the basic facts in a passage.
- determine the main idea of a passage.
- determine the meaning of unfamiliar words from context.
- distinguish between fact and opinion.

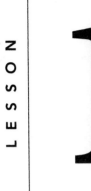

GETTING THE ESSENTIAL INFORMATION

Caress the detail, the divine detail.

—VLADIMIR NABOKOV, Russian-American novelist (1899–1977)

LESSON SUMMARY

The first step in increasing your reading comprehension is to learn how to get the basic information. Like a good detective, start with the basic facts. To get the facts, be an active reader and look for clues as you read.

magine, for a moment, that you are a detective. You have just been called to the scene of a crime; a house has been robbed. What's the first thing you should do when you arrive?

A. See what's on the TV.
B. Check what's in the fridge.
C. Get the basic facts of the case.

The answer, of course, is **C**, get the basic facts of the case: the who, what, when, where, and how. What happened? To whom? When? Where? How did it happen?

As a reader faced with a text, you go through a similar process. The first thing you should do is establish the facts. What does this piece of writing tell you? What happens? To whom? When, where, and how? If you can answer these basic questions, you're on your way to really comprehending what you read. (You'll work on answering the more difficult question—"*Why* did it happen?"—in Lesson 2.)

What Are the Facts?

Let's start with a definition. A **fact** is

- something that we know for certain to have happened.
- something that we know for certain to be true.
- something that we know for certain to exist.

Much of what you read, especially today in this "Information Age," is designed to provide you with facts. You may read, for example, about a new office procedure that you must follow; about how the new computer system works; or about what happened at the staff meeting. If you're taking a standardized test, you'll probably have to answer reading comprehension questions that ask about the facts in a reading passage. These facts are not always easy to determine, especially if the writing is dense or complicated. To make it simpler, ask yourself these questions as you read: What facts am I expected to know? What am I to learn or be aware of? What happened? What is true? What exists?

Practice Passage 1

Jump right into the task of finding facts. The following brief passage is similar to something you might see in a newspaper. Read the passage carefully, and then answer the questions that follow. Remember, careful reading is active reading (see the Introduction), so mark up the text as you go. Underline key words and ideas; circle and define any unfamiliar words or phrases; and record your reactions and questions in the margins.

On Friday, October 21, at approximately 8:30 A.M., Judith Reynolds, owner of The Cupcake Factory, arrived at her establishment to find that it had been robbed and vandalized overnight. The front window of the shop at 128 Broad Street was broken, and chairs and tables were overturned throughout the café area. Additionally, the cash register had been pried open and emptied of money. The thieves attempted to open the safe as well, but were unsuccessful. Ms. Reynolds used her cell phone to report the crime to the police. She also phoned the proprietor of Primo Pizza, located at 130 Broad Street, as she noticed that the door of that restaurant showed signs of forced entry. The police department is asking anyone with information to call 555-2323.

1. What happened to The Cupcake Factory?

2. When was the crime discovered?

3. Where did it happen?

4. What was stolen? Who called the police?

5. What other businesses were affected?

Remember, good reading is active reading. Did you mark up the passage? If so, it may have looked something like this:

when   who

what happened— robbery and vandalization

On Friday, October 21, at approximately 8:30 A.M., Judith Reynolds, owner of The Cupcake Factory, arrived at her establishment to find that it had been robbed and vandalized overnight. The front window of the shop at 128 Broad Street was broken, and chairs and tables were overturned throughout the café area. Additionally, the cash register had been pried open and emptied of money.

where

interesting detail

The thieves attempted to open the safe as well, but were unsuccessful. Ms. Reynolds used her cell phone to report the crime to the police. She also phoned the proprietor of Primo Pizza, located at 130 Broad Street, as she noticed that the door of that restaurant showed signs of forced entry. The police department is asking anyone with information to call 555-2323.

money was stolen

another business was affected

unclear from this report if anything was taken from Primo Pizza

You'll notice that the answers to the questions have all been underlined, because these are the key words and ideas in this passage. But here are the answers in a more conventional form.

1. What happened to The Cupcake Factory? *It was robbed and vandalized.*

2. When was the crime discovered? *At 8:30 A.M. on Friday, October 21.*

3. Where did it happen? *128 Broad Street.*

4. What was stolen? *Money from the cash register.*

5. Who called the police? *Judith Reynolds, owner of The Cupcake Factory.*

6. What other businesses were affected? *Possibly Primo Pizza.*

Notice that these questions went beyond the basic who, what, when, and where to include some of the details, like why the proprietor of the restaurant next door was called. This is because details in reading comprehension, as well as in detective work, can be very important clues that may help answer the remaining questions: Who did it, how, and why?

Practice Passage 2

This passage provides instructions for renewing a driver's license. Read it carefully and answer the questions that follow.

Instructions for License Renewal

A driver's license must be renewed every four years. A renewal application is sent approximately five to seven weeks before the expiration date listed on the license. Individuals who fail to renew within three years of the license expiration date are not eligible for a renewal and must repeat the initial licensing process. To renew a license, you must visit a Department of Motor Vehicles office. You must present a completed renewal application; your current driver's license; acceptable proof of age, identification, and address; and proof of Social Security in the form of a Social Security card, a state or federal income tax return, a current pay stub, or a W-2 form. You must also pay the required fee. If all the documents and payment are in order, your photo will be taken and a new license will be issued.

7. What documents does one need to renew a driver's license?

8. What documents represent proof of Social Security?

9. How often must one renew a driver's license?

10. How does one obtain the renewal form?

11. True or False: You can renew your driver's license by mail.

Before you look at the answers, look at the next page to see how you might have marked up the passage to highlight the important information.

Instructions for License Renewal

how often I need to renew

A driver's license must be renewed every four years. A renewal application is sent approximately five to seven weeks before the expiration date listed on the license.

application will be mailed

Individuals who fail to renew within three years of the license expiration date are not eligible for a renewal and must repeat the initial licensing process. To

must go in person, find out nearest location

renew a license, you must visit a Department of Motor Vehicles office. You must present a completed renewal application; your current driver's license; acceptable proof of age, identification, and address; and proof of Social Security in the form of a Social Security card, a state or federal income tax return, a current pay stub,

documents needed for renewal

bring checkbook!

or a W-2 form. You must also pay the required fee. If all the documents and payment are in order, your photo will be taken and a new license will be issued. With a marked-up text like this, it's very easy to find the answers.

7. What documents does one need to renew a driver's license?
Completed renewal application
Current driver's license
Acceptable proof of age, identification, and address
Proof of Social Security
Money to pay required fee

8. What documents represent proof of Social Security?
Social security card
State or federal income tax return
Current pay stub
W-2 form

9. *How often must one renew a driver's license?*
Every four years.

10. How does one obtain the renewal form? *It is sent five to seven weeks before current license expires.*

11. True or False: You can renew your driver's license by mail. *False: You can renew only by visiting a Department of Motor Vehicles office.*

TIP

Set out to read with an explorer's eye and sense of curiosity by probing into details behind key actions and events. If you are unfamiliar with a specific factual detail in a passage, consider asking a friend or family member for help, or check a reference source such as a dictionary, atlas, encyclopedia, or Internet database. There are print and Internet archive collections and specialized libraries covering almost every imaginable subject—from space missions and history to the performing arts.

- Example: Louis B. Mayer Library— Library of the American Film Institute
- Example: Margaret Herrick Library— Academy of Motion Picture Arts and Sciences

Practice Passage 3

Now look at one more short passage. Again, read carefully and answer the questions that follow.

Today's postal service is more efficient and reliable than ever before. Mail that used to take months to move by horse and foot now moves around the country in days or hours by truck, train, and plane. First-class mail usually moves from New York City to Los Angeles in three days or fewer. If your letter or package is urgent, the U.S. Postal Service offers Priority Mail and Express Mail services. Priority Mail is guaranteed to go anywhere in the United States in two to three days or less. Express Mail will get your package there overnight.

12. Who or what is this passage about?

13. How was mail transported in the past?

14. How is mail transported now?

15. How long does first-class mail take?

16. How long does Priority Mail take?

17. How long does Express Mail take?

Once again, here's how you might have marked up this passage:

then → Today's postal service is more efficient and reliable than ever before. Mail that used to take <u>months</u> to move by <u>horse</u> and <u>foot</u> now moves around the country — *now*
What a long time! in days or hours by <u>truck, train, and plane</u>. <u>First-class mail</u> usually moves from New York City to Los Angeles in three days or fewer. If your letter or package is urgent, the U.S. Postal Service offers <u>Priority Mail</u> and <u>Express Mail</u> services.
Are there other services? Priority Mail is guaranteed to go anywhere in the United States in two to three days or less. Express Mail will get your package there overnight.

3 services listed:
First class–3 days
Priority–2–3 days
Express–Overnight
Fastest

You can see how marking up a text helps make it easier to understand the information a passage conveys.

12. Who or what is this passage about? *The U.S. Postal Service.*

13. How was mail transported in the past? *By horse and foot.*

14. How is mail transported now? *By truck, train, and plane.*

15. How long does first-class mail take? *Usually three days or fewer.*

16. How long does Priority Mail take? *Two to three days or fewer.*

17. How long does Express Mail take? *Overnight.*

Summary

Active reading is the first essential step to comprehension. Why? Because active reading forces you to really *see* what you're reading, to look closely at what's there. Like a detective who arrives at the scene of a crime, if you look carefully and ask the right questions (who, what, when, where, how, and why), you're on your way to really comprehending what you read.

L E S S O N

2 ▶ FINDING THE MAIN IDEA

There is an art of reading, as well as an art of thinking.
—Isaac Disraeli, British writer (1804–1881)

LESSON SUMMARY
A detective finds the facts to determine "whodunit" and what the motive was. A reader determines the facts not only for their own sake but also to find out why the author is writing: What's the main idea? This lesson shows you how to determine the main idea of what you read.

When Lesson 1 talked about establishing the facts—the who, what, when, where, and how—it omitted one very important question: Why? Now you're ready to tackle that all-important question. Just as there's a motive behind every crime, there's also a motive behind every piece of writing.

All writing is communication. A writer writes to convey his or her thoughts to an audience, the reader: you. Just as you have something to say (a motive) when you pick up the phone to call someone, writers have something to say (a motive) when they pick up a pen or pencil to write. Where a detective might ask, "Why did the butler do it?" the reader might ask, "Why did the author write this? What idea is he or she trying to convey?" What you're really asking is, "What is the writer's main idea?"

Finding the main idea is much like finding the motive of the crime. It's the motive of the crime (the *why*) that usually determines the other factors (the *who, what, when, where,* and *how*). Similarly, in writing, the main idea also determines the *who, what, when,* and *where* the writer will write about, as well as *how* he or she will write.

Subject vs. Main Idea

There's a difference between the *subject* of a piece of writing and its *main idea*. To see the difference, look again at the passage about the postal system. Don't skip over it! You read it in Lesson 1, but please read it again, and read it carefully.

Today's postal service is more efficient and reliable than ever before. Mail that used to take months to move by horse and foot now moves around the country in days or hours by truck, train, and plane. First-class mail usually moves from New York City to Los Angeles in three days or fewer. If your letter or package is urgent, the U.S. Postal Service offers Priority Mail and Express Mail services. Priority Mail is guaranteed to go anywhere in the United States in two to three days or less. Express Mail will get your package there overnight.

You might be asked on a standardized test, "What is the main idea of this passage?"

For this passage, you might be tempted to answer, "the post office."

But you'd be wrong.

This passage is *about* the post office, yes—but "the post office" is not the main idea of the passage. "The post office" is merely the *subject* of the passage (*who* or *what* the passage is about). The main idea must say something *about* this subject. The main idea of a text is usually an *assertion* about the subject. An assertion is a statement that requires evidence ("proof") to be accepted as true.

The main idea of a passage is an assertion about its subject, but it is something more: It is the idea that also holds together or controls the passage. The other sentences and ideas in the passage will all relate to that main idea and serve as "evidence" that the assertion

is true. You might think of the main idea as a net that is cast over the other sentences. The main idea must be general enough to hold all of these ideas together.

Thus, the main idea of a passage is

- an assertion about the subject.
- the general idea that controls or holds together the paragraph or passage.

Look at the postal service paragraph once more. You know what the subject is: "the post office." Now, see if you can determine the main idea. Read the passage again and look for the idea that makes an assertion about the postal service *and* holds together or controls the whole paragraph. Then answer the following question:

Which of the following sentences best summarizes the main idea of the passage?

A. Express Mail is a good way to send urgent mail.
B. Mail service today is more effective and dependable than it was in the past.
C. First-class mail usually takes three days or fewer.

Because choice **a** is specific—it tells us *only* about Express Mail—it cannot be the main idea. It does not encompass the rest of the sentences in the paragraph—it doesn't cover Priority Mail or first-class mail. Choice **c** is also very specific. It tells us only about first class mail, so it, too, cannot be the main idea.

But choice **b**—"Mail service today is more effective and dependable than it was in the past"—*is* general enough to encompass the whole passage. And the rest of the sentences *support* the idea that this sentence asserts: Each sentence offers "proof" that the postal service today is indeed more efficient and reliable. Thus, the writer aims to tell us about the efficiency and reliability of today's postal service.

Topic Sentences

You'll notice that in the paragraph about the postal service, the main idea is expressed clearly in the first sentence: "Today's postal service is more efficient and reliable than ever before." A sentence, such as this one, that clearly expresses the main idea of a paragraph or passage is often called a *topic sentence.*

In many cases, as in the postal service paragraph, the topic sentence is at the beginning of the paragraph. You will also frequently find it at the end. Less often, but on occasion, the topic sentence may be in the middle of the passage. Whatever the case, the topic sentence—like "Today's postal service is more efficient and reliable than ever before"—is an assertion, and it needs "proof." The proof is found in the facts and ideas that make up the rest of the passage. (Not all passages provide such a clear topic sentence that states the main idea. Less obvious passages will come up in later lessons.)

Practice in Identifying Topic Sentences

Remember that a topic sentence is a clear statement of the main idea of a passage; it must be general enough to encompass all the ideas in that passage, and it usually makes an assertion about the subject of that passage. Knowing all that, you can answer the following question even without reading a passage.

Practice 1

Which of the following sentences is general enough to be a topic sentence?
- **a.** The new health club has a great kickboxing class.
- **b.** Many different classes are offered by the health club.
- **c.** Pilates is a popular class at the health club.
- **d.** The yoga class is offered on Saturday mornings.

The answer is choice **b**, "Many different classes are offered by the health club." Choices **a**, **c**, and **d** are all specific examples of what is said in choice **b**, so they are not general enough to be topic sentences.

Practice 2

Now look at the following paragraph. Underline the sentence that expresses the main idea, and notice how the other sentences work to support that main idea.

Erik always played cops and robbers when he was a boy; now, he's a police officer. Suzanne always played school as a little girl; today, she is a high-school math teacher. Kara always played store; today, she owns a chain of retail clothing shops. Long before they are faced with the question, "What do you want to be when you grow up?" some lucky people know exactly what they want to do with their lives.

Which sentence did you underline? You should have underlined the *last* sentence: "Long before they are faced with the question 'What do you want to be when you grow up?' some lucky people know exactly what they want to do with their lives." This sentence is a good topic sentence; it expresses the idea that holds together the whole paragraph. The first three sentences—about Erik, Suzanne, and Kara—are *specific examples* of these lucky people. Notice that the topic sentence is found at the *end* of the paragraph.

Practice 3

Among the following eight sentences are two topic sentences. The other sentences are supporting sentences. Circle the two topic sentences. Then write the numbers of the supporting sentences that go with each topic sentence.

1. In addition, two new pet stores have opened in the past year, and last March a new dog park opened on Delancey Street.
2. Furthermore, I'd sit in on various committee meetings to watch members debate and come to a consensus (if we were lucky!).
3. In recent years, the number of dog owners in the neighborhood has dramatically increased, and so have the amenities for dog owners.
4. The dog park is open and available to neighborhood residents from 6 A.M. to 10 P.M., seven days a week.
5. For instance, every morning I'd start my day by reading the news and answering letters and emails from Senator Lane's constituents.
6. For example, when you are out and about on a Saturday, you will likely see dozens of people walking their furry friends, en route to the park or just out for a stroll.
7. As a summer intern for Senator Ellen Lane, I learned a lot about the daily life of a congressional staffer.
8. I learned so much about the Senator's duties and her district, and how it takes a busy staff of dozens to keep everything running smoothly.

Sentences 3 and 7 are the two topic sentences because both make assertions about a general subject. The supporting sentences for topic sentence 3, "In recent years, the number of dog owners in the neighborhood has dramatically increased, and so have the amenities for dog owners," are sentences 1, 4, and 6. The supporting sentences for topic sentence 7, "As a summer intern for Senator Ellen Lane, I learned a lot about the daily life of a congressional staffer," are the remaining sentences 2, 5, and 8.

Here's how they look as paragraphs:

In recent years, the number of dog owners in the neighborhood has dramatically increased, and so have the amenities for dog owners. For example, when you are out and about on a Saturday, you will likely see dozens of people walking their furry friends, en route to the park or just out for a stroll. In addition, two new pet stores have opened in the past year, and last March a new dog park opened on Delancey Street. The dog park is open and available to neighborhood residents from 6 A.M. to 10 P.M., seven days a week.

As a summer intern for Senator Ellen Lane, I learned a lot about the daily life of a congressional staffer. For instance, every morning I'd start my day by reading the news and answering letters and emails from Senator Lane's constituents. Furthermore, I'd sit in on various committee meetings to watch members debate and come to a consensus (if we were lucky!). I learned so much about the Senator's duties and her district, and how it takes a busy staff of dozens to keep everything running smoothly.

You might have noticed that the supporting sentences in the first paragraph about the increased dog population began with the following words: *for example* and *in addition*. These words are often used to introduce support or specific instances. The second paragraph uses different words, but they have the same function: *for instance* and *furthermore*.

Summary

Now you can answer the last question—the *why*. What is the writer's motive? What's the main idea he or she wants to convey? By finding the sentence that makes an assertion about the subject of the paragraph and that encompasses the other sentences in the paragraph, you can uncover the author's motive.

3 ▶ DEFINING VOCABULARY IN CONTEXT

Language is the dress of thought.

—SAMUEL JOHNSON, English author (1709–1784)

LESSON SUMMARY

An active reader looks up unfamiliar words. But what if you don't have a dictionary? In a testing situation (or, for that matter, if you're reading on the bus), you almost certainly won't be able to look up words you don't know. Instead, you can use the context to help you determine the meaning.

Sometimes in your reading, you come across words or phrases that are unfamiliar to you. You might be lucky and have a dictionary handy to look up that word or phrase, but what if you don't? How can you understand what you're reading if you don't know what all of the words mean? The answer is that you can use the rest of the passage, the *context,* to help you understand the new words.

Finding Meaning from Context

The following paragraph is about one of our nation's favorite pastimes, reality TV. Read it carefully, marking it up as you go—but do not look up any unfamiliar words or phrases in a dictionary.

> Most reality TV shows center on two common motivators: fame and money. The shows transform waitresses, hairdressers, investment bankers, counselors, and teachers, to name a few, from obscure figures to household names. A lucky few successfully parlay their 15 minutes of fame into celebrity. Even if you are not interested in fame, you can probably understand the desire for lots of money. Watching people eat large insects, reveal their innermost thoughts to millions of viewers, and allow themselves to be filmed 24 hours a day for a huge financial reward makes for interesting entertainment. Whatever their attraction, these shows are among the most popular on television, and every season, they proliferate like weeds in an untended garden. The networks are quickly replacing more traditional dramas and comedies with reality TV programs, which earn millions in advertising revenue. Whether you love it or hate it, one thing is for sure—reality TV is here to stay!

As you read, you may have circled some words that are unfamiliar. Did you circle *obscure* and *proliferate*? If so, don't look them up in a dictionary yet. If you do a little detective work, you can determine their definitions by looking carefully at how they are used in the paragraph.

What Does Obscure Mean?

Start with *obscure*. How is this word used?

> The shows transform waitresses, hairdressers, investment bankers, counselors, and teachers, to name a few, from *obscure* figures to household names.

Even if you have no idea what *obscure* means, you can still learn about the word by how it is used, by examining the words and ideas surrounding it. This is called determining word meaning through *context*. Like detectives looking for clues at a crime scene, we must look at the passage for clues that will help us define this word.

So, given the sentence we have here, what can we tell about *obscure*? Well, since the shows transform waitresses, hairdressers, investment bankers, counselors, and teachers from one position(*obscure* figures), to another position (household names), that immediately tells us that an *obscure* figure and a household name are two different things.

Furthermore, we know from the sentence that the people in question are involved in typical, everyday jobs (waitresses, hairdressers, bankers, etc.) and that from this position, they are transformed into household names, which means they achieve some level of fame and notoriety. Now you can take a pretty good guess at the meaning of *obscure*.

1. Before they become household names, the waitresses, hairdressers, investment bankers, counselors, and teachers are
   a. famous and notorious.
   b. unknown and undistinguished.
   c. unique and distinctive.

The correct answer, of course, is choice **b**. It certainly can't be choice **a**, because we know that these people are not yet famous. The reality shows will make them famous, but until that happens, they remain *obscure*. Choice **c** doesn't really make sense because we know from the passage that these people are waitresses, hairdressers, investment bankers, counselors, and teachers. Now, these are all very respectable jobs, but they are fairly common, so they wouldn't be described as unique or distinctive. Furthermore, we can tell that choice **b** is the correct answer because we can substitute the word *obscure* with the words *unknown* or *undistinguished* in the sentence and both would make sense.

Review: Finding Facts

Here's a quick review of what you learned in question 1. Reality TV has the ability to take ordinary people and make them famous.

2. Another reason people participate in reality TV shows is
   a. for money.
   b. because they feel lucky.
   c. because they are bored.

A quick check of the facts in the paragraph will tell you the answer is choice **a**, for money.

What Does Proliferate Mean?

Look again at the sentence in the passage in which *proliferate* is used:

Whatever their attraction, these shows are among the most popular on television, and every season, they *proliferate* like weeds in an untended garden.

Again, even if you have no idea what *proliferate* means, you can still tell what kind of word it is by the way it is used. You know, for example, that these shows proliferate like weeds in an untended garden. Therefore, you can answer this question:

3. *Proliferate* is a word associated with
   a. growth.
   b. reduction.
   c. disappearance.

The answer, of course, is choice **a**, growth. How can you tell? Well, we all know that weeds have a tendency to grow wherever they can.

Now that you've established that *proliferate* relates to growth, you can determine a more specific meaning by looking for more clues in the sentence. The sentence doesn't only tell us that these shows proliferate like weeds. It also tells us that they proliferate like weeds in an untended garden. Just imagine a neglected garden, one that has been left to its own devices. Weeds will begin to grow in every nook and cranny of that garden. In fact, they'll quickly take over, to the detriment of the plants. The phrase "weeds in an untended garden" is quite descriptive, and as such, it serves as a wonderful clue. Based on the words and phrases surrounding it, an active reader should have no problem determining the meaning of the word *proliferate*.

4. *Proliferate* in this passage means
   a. decrease, shrink.
   b. underestimate, play down.
   c. increase, spread at a rapid rate.
   d. fail, fall short.

The correct answer is choice **c**, "increase, spread at a rapid rate." It can't be choices **a** or **d** because these are things associated with reduction, not growth. And everyone knows that weeds in an untended garden will grow fast and aggressively. Choice **b** is not an appropriate answer because if you replace *proliferate* with *underestimate* or *play down*, it doesn't really make sense. In addition, you can tell that choice **c** is the right answer because the rest of the passage provides other clues. It tells you that reality TV shows are replacing other network programs, that they are popular, and that they are earning millions of dollars in advertising revenue. All these clues would indicate that reality TV shows are spreading and growing in number, not shrinking or declining. Hence, the meaning of *proliferate* must be **c**, "increase, spread at a rapid rate."

How Much Context Do You Need?

In the previous example, you would still be able to understand the main message of the passage even if you didn't know—or couldn't figure out—the meaning of *obscure* and *proliferate*. In some cases, however, your understanding of a passage depends on your understanding of a particular word or phrase. Can you understand the following sentence, for example, without knowing what *adversely* means?

Reality TV shows will *adversely* affect traditional dramas and comedies.

What does *adversely* mean in this sentence? Is it something good or bad? As good a detective as you may be, there simply aren't enough clues in this sentence to tell you what this word means. But a passage with more information will give you what you need to determine meaning from context.

Reality TV shows will *adversely* affect traditional dramas and comedies. As reality TV increases in popularity, network executives will begin canceling more traditional dramas and comedies and replacing them with the latest in reality TV.

5. In the passage, *adversely* most nearly means
   a. mildly, slightly.
   b. kindly, gently.
   c. negatively, unfavorably.
   d. immediately, swiftly.

The correct answer is choice **c**, "negatively, unfavorably." The passage provides clues that allow you to determine the meaning of *adversely*. It tells you that as reality TV becomes more popular, network executives will cancel more traditional dramas and comedies and replace them with reality TV programming. So the meaning of *adversely* is neither choice **a**, "mild or slight," nor choice **b**, "kindly or gently." And based on the passage, you can't really tell if these changes will be immediate or swift (choice **d**) because the sentence doesn't say anything about the exact time frame in which these changes will occur. Remember, good detectives don't make assumptions they can't support with facts—and there are no facts in this sentence to support the assumption that changes will occur immediately. Thus, choice **c** is the best answer.

You may also have noticed that ***adversely*** is very similar to ***adversary***. If you know that an *adversary* is a hostile opponent or enemy, then you know that *adversely* cannot be something positive. Or, if you know the word ***adversity***—hardship or misfortune—then you know that *adversely* must mean something negative or difficult. All these words share the same root—*advers*. Only the endings change.

TIP

If you are unfamiliar with a particular word, use context clues to try to figure out its meaning. Draw upon the important clues in the sentences that appear directly before and after the unfamiliar word or passage. Punctuation can help you decipher unfamiliar words:

- Parentheses are often used to highlight or explain words or phrases and elaborate on the words that precede them.
- An exclamation point appears in a sentence in which some kind of surprise, shock, or excitement is taking place.
- Commas often set off non-restrictive elements that provide additional information and elaboration on a word. Example: *I wanted to buy a digital camera with a zoom lens, which is very costly.* (The phrase "which is very costly" provides added information that can be used to figure out the meaning of the words that come before the phrase.)

Practice

Read the following passages and determine the meaning of the words from their context. The answers appear immediately after the questions.

Although social work is not a particularly *lucrative* career, I wouldn't do anything else. Knowing I'm helping others is far more important to me than money.

6. *Lucrative* means
   a. highly profitable.
   b. highly rewarding.
   c. highly exciting.

When you are in an interview, try not to show any *overt* signs that you are nervous. Don't shift in your chair, shake, or stutter.

7. *Overt* means
   a. embarrassing, awkward.
   b. subtle, suggestive.
   c. obvious, not hidden.

By the time our staff meeting ended at 8:00, I was *ravenous.* I had skipped lunch and hadn't eaten since breakfast.

8. *Ravenous* means
   a. like a raven, birdlike.
   b. extremely hungry, greedy for food.
   c. exhausted, ready for bed.

Answers

   6. a. The writer says money is not important to him. If money is not an issue, it is okay that social work is not *highly profitable,* that it doesn't earn a lot of money.
   7. c. Shifting, shaking, and stuttering are all *obvious, not hidden* signs of nervousness. They are not subtle or suggestive (choice **b**); and though they may make the interviewee feel embarrassed or awkward (choice **a**), the signs themselves are not embarrassing or awkward.
   8. b. Because the writer hadn't eaten since breakfast, she is *extremely hungry, greedy for food.* She may also be exhausted (choice **c**), but the context tells us that this word has something to do with eating.

Summary

The ability to determine the meaning of unfamiliar words from their context is an essential skill for reading comprehension. Sometimes, there will be unfamiliar words whose meaning you can't determine without a dictionary. But more often than not, a careful look at the context will give you enough clues to meaning.

TIP

The general tone or theme of the text can help you figure out the meaning of an unfamiliar word. Titles can also provide clues about the tone of a story and the type of vocabulary words that are likely to be found in the text. What overall tone does each of the following titles convey?

- "Babylon Revisited" by F. Scott Fitzgerald
- *Paradise Lost* by John Milton
- "The Fall of the House of Usher" by Edgar Allan Poe
- *The Devil Wears Prada* by Lauren Weisberger

LESSON 4 ▶ THE DIFFERENCE BETWEEN FACT AND OPINION

Force yourself to reflect on what you read, paragraph by paragraph.

—Samuel Taylor Coleridge, English poet (1772–1834)

LESSON SUMMARY
To make sense of what you read, you must be able to tell whether you're reading fact or opinion. This lesson tells you how to distinguish what someone knows for certain from what someone believes.

What's the difference between fact and opinion, and what does it matter, anyway? It matters a great deal, especially when it comes to reading comprehension. During your life, you'll be exposed to a wide variety of literature, ranging from analytical articles based on cold hard facts to fictional novels that arise wholly from the author's imagination. However, much of what you read will be a mixture of facts and the author's opinions. Part of becoming a critical reader means realizing that opinions are not evidence; for opinions to be valid, they must be supported by cold, hard facts.

Facts are

- things *known* for certain to have happened.
- things *known* for certain to be true.
- things *known* for certain to exist.

Opinions, on the other hand, are

- things *believed* to have happened.
- things *believed* to be true.
- things *believed* to exist.

As you can see, the key difference between fact and opinion lies in the difference between *believing* and *knowing*. Opinions may be based on facts, but they are still what we *think*, not what we *know*. Opinions are debatable; facts are not.

Using Facts to Support Opinions

Reasonable opinions are those *based on fact*; and indeed, that is what much of writing is: the writer's opinion (an assertion about his or her subject) supported by facts or other evidence.

Think about the topic sentences you formed after you finished Lesson 2. Perhaps you made an assertion like this:

James is a terrific boss.

This sentence is a good topic sentence; it's an assertion about the subject, James. And it is also an opinion. It is, after all, debatable; someone could just as easily take the opposite position and say:

James is a terrible boss.

This is another good topic sentence, and it's another opinion. Now, a good writer will show his or her readers that this opinion is *valid* by supporting it with facts. For example:

James is a terrific boss. He always asks us how we're doing. He lets us leave early or come in late when we have to take care of our children. He always gives holiday bonuses. And he offers tuition reimbursement for any course, even if it has nothing to do with our positions.

Notice how the topic sentence states an opinion, whereas the rest of the sentences support that opinion with facts about how James treats his employees. That paragraph is much more effective than something like this:

James is a terrible boss. I really don't like him. He just can't get along with people. And he has stupid ideas about politics.

Why is the first paragraph so much better? Because it's not just opinion. It's opinion supported by evidence. The second paragraph is all opinion. Every sentence is debatable; every sentence tells us what the author *believes* is true, but not what is *known* to be true. The author of the second paragraph doesn't provide any evidence to support why he or she thinks that James is such a lousy boss. As a result, we're not likely to take his or her opinion very seriously.

In the first paragraph, on the other hand, the writer offers concrete evidence for why he or she *believes* James is a great boss. After the initial opinion, the writer provides facts—specific things James does (which can be verified by other observers) that make him a good boss. You may still not agree that James is a great boss, but at least you can see exactly why this writer thinks so.

Distinguishing Fact from Opinion

When you read academic materials, very often you will have to distinguish between fact and opinion—between what the writer thinks and how the writer supports what he or she thinks, between what is proven to be true and what needs to be proved.

A good test for whether something is a fact or opinion might be to ask yourself, "Can this statement be debated? Is this known for certain to be true?" If you answer *yes* to the first question, you have an opinion; if you answer *yes* to the second, you have a fact.

TIP

Sometimes "facts" are incorrect or skewed because they were obtained from invalid or biased sources. When you are reading a nonfiction text, it's important to note the author's credentials and his or her sources. Use that information to validate the legitimacy of the "facts" being presented.

Practice 1

Try these questions on the following statements. Read them carefully, and then write F in the blank if the statement is a fact and O if it is an opinion. The answers appear right after the questions.

_____ **1.** The Academy Awards honor the film industry.

_____ **2.** The Academy Awards are always fun to watch.

_____ **3.** More independent films should win Academy Awards.

_____ **4.** The Academy Awards are an annual event.

_____ **5.** Best Director is the most interesting Academy Award category.

Answers

1. Fact
2. Opinion
3. Opinion
4. Fact
5. Opinion

Practice 2

Now try the same exercise with a complete paragraph. Underline the facts and use a highlighter or colored pen to highlight the opinions. Be careful—you may find fact and opinion together in the same sentence. When you've finished, you can check your answers against the marked passage that follows.

There are many different ways to invest your money to provide for a financially secure future. Many people invest in stocks and bonds, but I think good old-fashioned savings accounts and CDs (certificates of deposit) are the best way to invest your hard-earned money. Stocks and bonds are often risky, and it doesn't make sense to risk losing the money you've worked so hard for. True, regular savings accounts and CDs can't make you a millionaire overnight or provide the high returns some stock investments do. But by the same token, savings accounts and CDs are fully insured and provide steady, secure interest on your money. That makes a whole lot of cents.

Answers

How did you do? Was it easy to distinguish between the facts and the opinions? Here's what your marked-up passage should look like. The facts are underlined and the opinions are in boldface type.

There are many different ways to invest your money to provide for a financially secure future. Many people invest in stocks and bonds, **but I think good old-fashioned savings accounts and CDs (certificates of deposit) are the best way to invest your hard-earned money.** Stocks and bonds are often risky, **and it doesn't make sense to risk losing the money you've worked so hard for.** True, regular savings accounts and CDs can't make you a millionaire overnight or provide the high returns some stock investments do. But by the same token, savings accounts and CDs are fully insured and provide steady, secure interest on your money. **That makes a whole lot of cents.**

Practice 3

To strengthen your ability to distinguish between fact and opinion, try this. Take a fact, such as:

FACT: *Wednesday is the fourth day of the week.*

Now, turn it into an opinion. Make it something debatable, like this:

OPINION: *Wednesday feels like the longest day of the week.*

Here's another example.

FACT: *You must be 18 years old to vote in the United States.*

OPINION: *The voting age should be lowered to 16 years of age.*

Try these next. Suggested answers come after the questions.

6. FACT: *Healthcare costs have risen over the last several years.*

OPINION:

7. FACT: *The 22nd Amendment of the United States Constitution establishes a two-term limit for the presidency.*

OPINION:

8. FACT: *More than 58,000 Americans lost their lives in the Vietnam War.*

OPINION:

THE DIFFERENCE BETWEEN FACT AND OPINION

9. FACT: *The Motion Picture Association of America's R (Restricted) rating requires anyone under 17 to be accompanied by a parent or adult guardian.*

OPINION:

10. FACT: *Use of performance-enhancing drugs is strictly prohibited in both amateur and professional sports.*

OPINION:

Answers

There are, of course, many opinions you could form from these subjects. Here are some possible answers.

6. Our government should make healthcare a higher priority.
Companies should give employees several healthcare programs from which to choose.
People should stop complaining about healthcare costs.

7. Presidents should be allowed to serve for three terms.
Limiting service to two terms makes U.S. presidents more effective.
Term limits are a very bad idea.

8. American soldiers should not have been sent to Vietnam.
Our government did all the right things concerning the Vietnam War.

9. The Motion Picture Association of America should not be able to rate films.
The Motion Picture Association of America ratings should be taken seriously by all parents.
Movie ratings are useless.

10. Performance-enhancing drugs should be legal.
Competitive sports would be more interesting to watch if performance-enhancing drugs were legal.
Performance-enhancing drugs are the worst thing that ever happened to competitive sports.

Summary

The ability to differentiate between fact and opinion is a very important skill. Like a detective, you need to know the difference between what people *think* and what people *know*, between what people *believe* to be true and what has been *proven* to be true. Then you will be able to see whether writers support their opinions, and if they do, how they do it. This will allow you to judge for yourself the validity of those opinions.

TIP

When you are reading a nonfiction text, seek out contradictory statements. They serve as red flags, signaling that what is being presented as "fact" might actually be a half-truth or opinion.

PUTTING IT ALL TOGETHER

There is creative reading as well as creative writing.
—RALPH WALDO EMERSON, American poet (1803–1882)

LESSON SUMMARY
This lesson reviews what you learned in Lessons 1–4: getting the facts, finding the main idea, determining what words mean in context, and distinguishing between fact and opinion. In this lesson, you'll get vital practice in using all four skills at once.

In order to solve a crime, a detective cannot *just* get the facts of the case, *just* discover the motive, *just* decipher difficult clues, or *just* distinguish between fact and opinion. To be successful, a detective must do all these things at the same time. Similarly, reading really can't be broken down into these separate tasks. Reading comprehension comes from employing all of these strategies simultaneously. This lesson gives you the opportunity to combine these strategies and take your reading comprehension skills to the next level.

Review: What You've Learned So Far

These are the strategies you studied in the previous four lessons:

- **Lesson 1: Find the facts in what you read.** You practiced looking for the basic information that was being conveyed in the paragraphs: the who, what, when, where, and how.
- **Lesson 2: Find the main idea.** You learned about topic sentences and how they express an assertion about the subject of the paragraph. You saw how the main idea must be general enough to encompass all other sentences in the paragraph; it is the thought that controls the paragraph, and the other sentences work to support that main idea.
- **Lesson 3: Determine the meaning of words from context.** You practiced looking for clues to determine meaning in the words and sentences surrounding the unfamiliar word or phrase.
- **Lesson 4: Distinguish between fact and opinion.** You learned that a fact is something *known* to be

true, whereas an opinion is something *believed* to be true. You practiced distinguishing between the two and saw how good paragraphs use facts to support opinions.

> If any of these terms or strategies sound unfamiliar to you, STOP. Take a few minutes to review whatever lesson is unclear.

Practice

In this lesson, you will sharpen your reading comprehension skills by using all of these strategies at once. This will become more natural to you as your reading skills develop.

Practice Passage 1

Begin by looking at the following paragraph. Remember to read actively; mark up the text as you go. Then answer the questions. An example of how to mark up the passage, as well as the answers to the questions, follow.

It is clear that the United States is a nation that needs to eat healthier and slim down. One of the most important steps in the right direction would be for school cafeterias to provide healthy, low-fat options for students. In every town and city, an abundance of fast-food restaurants lure teenage customers with fast, inexpensive, and tasty food, but these foods are typically unhealthy. Unfortunately, school cafeterias—in an effort to provide food that is appetizing to young people—mimic fast food menus, often serving items such as burgers and fries, pizza, hot dogs, and fried chicken. While these foods do provide some nutritional value, they are relatively high in fat. Many of the lunch selections school cafeterias currently offer could be made healthier with a few simple and inexpensive substitutions. Veggie burgers, for example, offered alongside beef burgers, would be a positive addition. A salad bar would also serve the purpose of providing a healthy and satisfying meal. And tasty grilled chicken sandwiches would be a far better option than fried chicken. Additionally, the beverage case should be stocked with containers of low-fat milk.

1. What is the subject of this passage?

2. According to the passage, which of the following options would make healthy, low-fat additions to a school cafeteria's offerings? (Circle all correct answers.)
   a. tofu
   b. veggie burgers
   c. low-fat milk
   d. salad bar

3. The meaning of *mimic* is
   a. reject.
   b. copy.
   c. ignore.
   d. disregard.

4. The fast-food restaurants described in the article are noted for serving
   a. veggie burgers and salads.
   b. tasty, inexpensive food.
   c. seafood specialties.
   d. home-cooked meals at an inexpensive price.

5. True or False: "One of the most important steps in the right direction would be for school cafeterias to provide healthy, low-fat options for students" is a topic sentence.

6. True or False: "One of the most important steps in the right direction would be for school cafeterias to provide healthy, low-fat options for students" is an opinion.

Marking Practice Passage 1

Before you check the answers, look again at the paragraph. Did you mark it up? If so, it may look something like this:

It is clear that the United States is a nation that needs to eat healthier and slim down. <u>One of the most important steps in the right direction would be for school cafeterias to provide healthy, low-fat options for students</u>. In every town and city, an abundance of fast-food restaurants lure teenage customers with fast, inexpensive, and tasty food, but these foods are typically unhealthy. Unfortunately, school cafeterias—in an effort to provide food that is appetizing to young people—(mimic) fast food menus, often serving items such as <u>burgers and fries, pizza, hot dogs, and fried chicken</u>. While these foods do provide some nutritional value, they are relatively high in fat. Many of the lunch selections school cafeterias currently offer could be made healthier with a few simple and inexpensive substitutions. <u>Veggie burgers</u>, for example, offered alongside beef burgers, would be a positive addition. <u>A salad bar</u> would also serve the purpose of providing a healthy and satisfying meal. And <u>tasty grilled chicken sandwiches</u> would be a far better option than fried chicken. Additionally, the beverage case should be stocked with containers of <u>low-fat milk</u>.

main idea

to copy

high-fat lunch offerings

possible healthy low-fat lunch options

Answers

1. The subject of the passage is *healthier, low-fat lunch options in school cafeterias*. Remember, the subject of a passage is who or what the passage is about.

2. **b.** These results are mentioned in the passage. Tofu (**a**) is a healthy, low-fat lunch option, but it is not mentioned *in the passage*.

   Remember, you're looking for the facts that the *author* has provided. It is extremely important, especially in test situations, not to choose an answer that isn't present in the text. Logic may tell you that tofu is a healthy, low-fat lunch option, but the paragraph doesn't tell you this. You need to stick to the facts. Any assumption that you make about a passage must be grounded in evidence found in that passage itself.

3. **b.** *Mimic* means to copy. The most obvious clue is the way the word is used in the sentence: "Unfortunately, school cafeterias—in an effort to provide food that is appetizing to young people— mimic fast food menus, often serving items such as burgers and fries, pizza, hot dogs, and fried chicken." Burgers and fries, pizza, hot dogs, and fried chicken are all foods served by fast-food restaurants, and if school cafeterias are also serving those foods, they are clearly *copying* fast-food menus, not *rejecting*, *ignoring*, or *disregarding* them.

4. **b.** This is the correct answer because the text describes the food served by fast-food restaurants as "fast, inexpensive, and tasty." Although the article mentions veggie burgers (cited in choice **c**), and while it is true that salads are served in some fast food restaurants, *tasty* and *inexpensive* are the qualities that are mentioned in connection to fast-food restaurant menus in this article. Seafood and home-cooked meals are never mentioned.

5. **True.** This sentence expresses the main idea.

6. **True.** This sentence is an opinion. It is debatable. Someone else might think that altering the menu in school cafeterias isn't one of the most important steps to be taken in order to make the United States a healthier, slimmer nation. They might think that launching a public service ad campaign about the dangers of fast food or implementing more rigorous classroom education about eating healthy is more important than changing the menus of school cafeterias.

How did you do? If you got all six answers correct, congratulations! If you missed one or more questions, check the following table to see which lessons to review.

IF YOU MISSED:	THEN STUDY:
Question 1	Lesson 2
Question 2	Lesson 1
Question 3	Lesson 3
Question 4	Lesson 2
Question 5	Lesson 2
Question 6	Lesson 4

Practice Passage 2

Try one more paragraph to conclude this first section. Once again, mark up the paragraph carefully and then answer the questions that follow.

Robert Johnson is the best blues guitarist of all time. There is little information available about this legendary blues guitarist, and the information is as much rumor as fact. What is indisputable, however, is Johnson's tremendous impact on the world of rock and roll. Some consider Johnson the father of modern rock: His influence extends to artists from Muddy Waters to Led Zeppelin, from the Rolling Stones to the Allman Brothers Band. Eric Clapton has called Johnson the most important blues musician who ever lived. Considering his reputation, it is hard to believe that Johnson recorded only 29 songs before his death in 1938, purportedly at the hands of a jealous husband. He was only 27 years old, yet he left an indelible mark on the music world. Again and again, contemporary rock artists return to Johnson, whose songs capture the very essence of the blues, transforming our pain and suffering with the healing magic of his guitar. Rock music wouldn't be what it is today without Robert Johnson.

7. According to the passage, from what musical tradition did Robert Johnson emerge?
a. rock and roll
b. jazz
c. blues

8. Johnson died in
a. 1927.
b. 1938.
c. 1929.

9. True or False: Johnson influenced many rock artists, including Led Zeppelin and the Rolling Stones.

10. Contemporary rock artists turn to Robert Johnson for
a. musical influence.
b. life lessons.
c. recovery from painful injuries.

11. The most appropriate title for this article would be
a. "A Fleeting Life"
b. "The World's Greatest Musician"
c. "Blues Guitar Legend Robert Johnson"

12. The main idea of this paragraph is best expressed in which sentence in the paragraph?

13. Indicate whether the following sentences are *fact* or *opinion*:
a. "Robert Johnson is the best blues guitarist of all time."
b. "Eric Clapton has called Johnson the most important blues musician who ever lived."
c. "Rock music wouldn't be what it is today without Robert Johnson."

Answers

7. **c.** See the first and second sentences. The next-to-last sentence also provides this information.

8. **b.** See the sixth sentence.

9. **True.** See the fourth sentence.

10. **a.** In sentence five, the author mentions that contemporary rock bands such as Muddy Waters and Led Zeppelin were influenced by Johnson's music. In the last sentence, Johnson's legendary musical influence is communicated when the author writes, "Again and again, contemporary rock artists return to Johnson." Based on the text, the logical conclusion is that the contemporary artists are turning to Johnson for musical inspiration.

11. **c.** Although "A Fleeting Life" might be an appropriate description for Johnson's brief life span, it describes only one aspect of his life. On the other hand, specifying that Robert Johnson is a blues guitar legend is more specific and descriptive. Although some of his fans might consider Johnson to be "The World's Greatest Musician," there are many who would disagree. The term "musician" covers music in general, and while Johnson might have been great in his particular genre, he would not likely be recognized as "the greatest musician" in all other music genres, such as classical or country music.

12. **The third sentence.** The point of the whole passage, which is Johnson's impact on rock and roll, is very clearly stated in the third sentence, "What is indisputable, however, is Johnson's tremendous impact on the world of rock and roll."

13. Choice **a** is **opinion**. It is debatable whether Johnson is the best blues guitarist of all time.
Choice **b** is **fact**. This is verifiable information.
Choice **c** is **opinion** because this is a debatable proposition.

How did you do this time? Better? If you missed any questions, this time, *you* figure out which questions correspond with which lessons. This will help you see with what categories you most need help.

TIP

The more often you read, the more likely it is that you will learn new words. Because it is sometimes difficult to know how to pronounce a word solely by reading it, consider using an electronic dictionary with a pronunciation feature. That way, you can learn the correct pronunciation of an unfamiliar word at the same time that you learn its definition.

▶ STRUCTURE

Now that you've covered the basics, you can begin to focus on one specific reading comprehension strategy: structure. How do writers organize their ideas?
You might want to think of a writer as an architect. Every building has a number of rooms. But how these rooms are arranged is up to the architect. The same goes for a piece of writing—how the sentences and ideas are arranged is entirely up to the writer. However, most architects—and most writers—generally follow certain patterns, not because they can't think on their own, but because these patterns work. In this section, you'll study four organizational patterns that work for writers:

1. Chronological order
2. Order of importance
3. Compare and contrast
4. Cause and effect

You'll learn to recognize these patterns and some of the reasons why writers use them.

LESSON

6 ▶ START FROM THE BEGINNING: CHRONOLOGICAL ORDER

Nothing is so difficult as a beginning / In poesy, unless perhaps the end.

—LORD BYRON, British poet (1788–1824)

LESSON SUMMARY
This lesson focuses on one of the simplest structures writers use: chronological order, or arrangement of events by the order in which they occured.

There are many ways to tell a story. Some stories start in the middle and flash backward to the beginning; a few start at the end and tell the story in reverse. In media res is a technique in which the author begins a story in the thick of a conflict or the middle of the story and then flashes back to the key events leading up to the present situation or conflict. The difference between a flashback and simply remembering a past event is that in a flashback a character is actually viewed reliving the past event as if it were occurring in the present. Most of the time, however, stories start at the beginning. Writers often begin with what happened first and then tell what happened next, and next, and so on, until the end. When writers tell a story in this order, from beginning to end in the order in which things happened, they are telling it in *chronological* order. *Chronology* is the arrangement of events in the order in which they occurred.

Chronology and Transitions

Much of what you read is arranged in chronological order. Newspaper and magazine articles, minutes of meetings, and explanations of procedures are usually arranged this way. For example, look at the following paragraph that might be found in a company newsletter:

This year's employee award ceremony was a tremendous success. The first award was given to Carlos Fe for Perfect Attendance. The second award, for Most Dedicated Employee, went to Jennifer Steele. Then our president, Martin Lucas, interrupted the awards ceremony to announce that he and his wife were having a baby. When he finished, everyone stood up for a congratulatory toast. Afterward, the third award was given to Karen Hunt for Most Inspiring Employee. Finally, President Lucas ended the ceremony by giving everyone a bonus check for $100.

You'll notice that this paragraph tells what happened at the ceremony from start to finish. You'll also notice that you can tell the order in which things happened in two ways. First, you can tell by the order of the sentences themselves—first things first, last things last. Second, you can tell by the use of *transitional words and phrases*, which signal a shift from one idea to the next. Here is the same paragraph with the transitional words underlined:

This year's employee award ceremony was a tremendous success. The <u>first</u> award was given to Carlos Fe for Perfect Attendance. The <u>second</u> award, for Most Dedicated Employee, went to Jennifer Steele. <u>Then</u> our president, Martin Lucas, interrupted the awards ceremony to announce that he and his wife were having a baby. <u>When</u> he finished, everyone stood up for a congratulatory toast. <u>Afterward</u>, the <u>third</u> award was given to Karen Hunt for Most Inspiring Employee. <u>Finally</u>, President Lucas ended the ceremony by giving everyone a bonus check for $100.

The underlined words—*first, second, then, when, afterward, third,* and *finally*—are transitional words that keep these events linked together in chronological order. Look at how the paragraph sounds without these words:

This year's employee award ceremony was a tremendous success. The award was given to Carlos Fe for Perfect Attendance. The award for Most Dedicated Employee went to Jennifer Steele. Our president, Martin Lucas, interrupted the awards ceremony to announce that he and his wife were having a baby. He finished; everyone stood up for a congratulatory toast. The award was given to Karen Hunt for Most Inspiring Employee. President Lucas ended the ceremony by giving everyone a bonus check for $100.

It doesn't sound quite as good, does it?

Practice with Transitional Words and Phrases

Practice Passage 1

Here's a more extreme example of a paragraph with the transitional words and phrases omitted:

I went to work early to get some extra filing done. I got there; the phone started ringing. My boss walked in. He asked me to type a letter for him. He asked me to make arrangements for a client to stay in town overnight. I looked at my watch; it was already 11:00.

Now, take the paragraph and add the following transitional words and phrases:

immediately   yesterday
as soon as   a moment later
when   then

_____ I went to work early to get some extra filing done. _____ I got there, the phone started ringing. _____ my boss walked in. _____ he asked me to type a letter for him. _____ he asked me to make arrangements for a client to stay in town overnight. _____ I looked at my watch, it was already 11:00.

Answers

You might have come up with a slightly different version, but here's one good way to fill in the blanks:

Yesterday, I went to work early to get some extra filing done. As soon as I got there, the phone started ringing. A moment later, my boss walked in. Immediately, he asked me to type up a letter for him. Then he asked me to make arrangements for a client to stay in town overnight. When I looked at my watch, it was already 11:00.

See how much better the paragraph sounds with transitional words and phrases to guide you?

Practice Passage 2

Here is a series of events listed in random order. Use the transitional words and phrases in each sentence to help you put them in proper chronological order. Number the sentences from 1–6 in the blanks provided.

_____ If the penalty structure is to your liking, make sure that the money market account is FDIC insured.

_____ After you've found the best terms, be sure to find out what the minimum account balance is and ask what the penalties are if your account drops below the limit.

_____ In order to open a money market account, you should follow several steps.

_____ Then you should shop around for the best terms and yields available.

_____ Finally, once the account is opened and you are earning interest, you should consider using that interest to pay off outstanding credit card debt.

_____ First, you should decide what features are important to you.

Answers

You should have numbered the blanks in this order: 5, 4, 1, 3, 6, 2. Here's how the sentences look together in a paragraph.

In order to open a money market account, you should follow several steps. First, you should decide what features are important to you. Then you should shop around for the best terms and yields available. After you've found the best terms, be sure to find out what the minimum account balance is and ask what the penalties are if your account drops below the limit. If the penalty structure is to your liking, make sure that the money market account is FDIC insured. Finally, once the account is opened and you are earning interest, you should consider using that interest to pay off outstanding credit card debt.

Practice Passage 3

Read the following paragraph, which describes a local community event.

The International Dinner raised $15,000 to renovate the Berkshire Park Community Center. Three hundred and fifty people attended the dinner, which was held in the ballroom of a local hotel. Tickets were sold in advance for $50 each. The attendees left the event feeling very good about their community. The Berkshire Park Community Center was damaged in a fire six months ago. An energetic committee of eight community members came up with the idea of the International Dinner to raise funds to repair the damages. The plan was to celebrate the diversity of the Berkshire Park Neighborhood Association by serving ethnic food that represents the various cultures in the neighborhood. The committee also organized a silent auction with prizes donated by local businesses to take place during the dinner. The committee chairperson talked to a local newspaper reporter at the dinner and stated that the goal was to raise $10,000. A follow-up letter to community members thanked everyone for the huge success of the fundraiser and outlined a schedule for the renovation.

Notice that this paragraph is not arranged in chronological order. Take the ten different events that make up the story and rearrange them so that they are in chronological order.

Here's the order of events as they are presented in the story.

- The International Dinner raised $15,000 to renovate the Berkshire Park Community Center.
- Three hundred and fifty people attended the dinner.
- Tickets were sold for $50 each.
- The attendees left the event feeling very good about their community.
- The Community Center was damaged in a fire six months ago.
- A committee of eight community members came up with the idea of the International Dinner to raise funds for repairs.
- The plan was to serve foods that represent the various cultures in the neighborhood.
- The committee organized a silent auction to take place during the dinner.
- The chairperson talked to a local newspaper reporter, stating that the goal was to raise $10,000.
- A letter to community members thanked everyone and outlined the schedule for renovation.

Next, put the events in chronological order.

1.

2.

3.

4.

5.

6.

7.

8.

9.

10.

Now, take these chronologically ordered events and make them into a cohesive paragraph. To do this, you need to add transitional words and phrases. Here is a list of transitional words and phrases often used in chronologically organized passages:

first	soon
second	after
third	before
next	during
now	while
then	meanwhile
when	in the meantime
as soon as	at last
immediately	eventually
suddenly	finally

Write your paragraph, putting the events in chronological order with transitional phrases, below or on a separate piece of paper.

Answers

There are, of course, many possible ways of using transitional words and phrases to put this story in chronological order. One paragraph might look like this:

Veteran news anchor and reporter Benny Armstrong has announced his retirement <u>after</u> nearly 30 years with News Network. Armstrong, who joined the fledgling cable news channel shortly <u>after</u> he graduated from Columbia University in 1982, began as a business reporter, covering Wall Street and various economic topics. He then went on to cover international business as News Network's primary economics correspondent, winning a Piedmont Prize for his coverage of insider trading scandals in 1987. <u>By 1992</u>, Armstrong was the host of the popular *Dollars and Sense* show on News Network, showcasing international economic developments and featuring in-depth discussion with experts. <u>After the show ended</u> in 1999, Armstrong was named the co-anchor of News Network's flagship *Evening News*, in addition to providing special reports from around the world. <u>Before</u> Tuesday night's broadcast, rumors swirled that Armstrong would be leaving the network. <u>At the end</u> of the hour-long show, he announced that he would be stepping down at the end of April. News Network has not yet announced who will be replacing Armstrong on *Evening News*.

Practice Passage 4

Chronological order is very important, especially when it comes to procedures. If you perform the steps out of chronological order, you won't get the results you desire. Just imagine, for example, that you are trying to bake a cake. What happens when you do things out of order? You go without dessert.

Of course, the consequences of not following proper chronological order at work can be much more serious, so it's important that you strengthen this skill. Read the following paragraph, marking it up to help you keep track of the steps that an employee must follow to get tuition reimbursement.

Our company will be happy to reimburse you for college courses that enhance your job performance. Before you register for the course, you must get approval first from your immediate supervisor and then from Human Resources. If you are taking the course for credit, you must receive a C+ or better in the course. If you are not taking it for credit, you must pass the course. After you have completed the course, you must write a report explaining the content of the course and its relevance to your position. Then, you must fill out a reimbursement request. Attach a tuition payment receipt, your report, and a copy of your grades to this request and promptly submit this request to your supervisor. Once your supervisor has approved the request, you can then submit all these forms to Human Resources, and you should receive your check within two weeks.

There are eight separate steps an employee must take to be reimbursed for college course work. What are they? List them below in the order in which the employee must do them.

1.

2.

3.

4.

5.

6.

7.

8.

If you marked up your paragraph, you should easily see the different steps. Here's how you might have marked it up. The transitional words and phrases are highlighted in bold.

1   Our company will be happy to reimburse you for college courses that enhance your job performance. **Before** you register for the course, you must get approval
2   **first** from your immediate supervisor and **then** from Human Resources. If you
3   are taking the course for credit, you must receive a C+ or better in the course. If you are not taking it for credit, you must pass the course. **After** you have com-
4   pleted the course, you must write a report explaining the content of the course
5   and its relevance to your position. **Then**, you must fill out a reimbursement
6   request. Attach a tuition payment receipt, your report, and a copy of your grades
7   to this request and **promptly** submit this request to your supervisor. Once your
8   supervisor has approved the request, you can **then** submit all these forms to Human Resources, and you should receive your check within two weeks.

need approval before registering!

1ˢᵗ –get supervisor approval
2ⁿᵈ –get HR approval
3ʳᵈ –take course–get C+ or better!
4ᵗʰ –write report
5ᵗʰ –fill out reimb. request
6ᵗʰ –attach tuition, report + grades to request
7ᵗʰ –submit to supervisor
8ᵗʰ –submit to HR

If you miss a step in this process, you won't be reimbursed. Thus, it's critical that you be able to identify each step and the order in which the steps must be taken.

Summary

Chronological structure is, of course, a very useful organizational pattern. Events happen in a certain order, so writers often present them in that order. Keep an eye out for the transitional words and phrases that signal this type of organization.

TIP

Both newspaper reporters and detectives possess a keen eye for determining and reporting on a sequence of events. As you are reading a newspaper article, detective story, or novel, note the methods and language that journalists and detectives use to describe the timing, setting, and sequence of key events. Transitional words and phrases that pinpoint the timing of an event include:

- Then
- When
- After
- Before
- Yesterday

LESSON

7 ▶ ORDER OF IMPORTANCE

In my beginning is my end.

—T. S. ELIOT, poet and literary critic (1888–1965)

LESSON SUMMARY

Continuing your study of the structure of reading material, this lesson shows you how writers use order of importance—from least to most important or from most to least important. Understanding this commonly used structure improves your reading comprehension by helping you see what's most important in a piece of writing.

I t's a scientifically proven fact: People remember most what they learn *first* and *last* in a given session. Writers have known this instinctively for a long time. That's why many pieces of writing are organized not in chronological order but *by order of importance.*

Imagine again that the writer is like an architect. How would this type of writer arrange the rooms? By hierarchy. A *hierarchy* is a group of things arranged by rank or order of importance. In this type of organizational pattern, *hierarchy*, not chronology, determines order. Thus, this architect would lay the rooms out like so: When you walk in the front door, the first room you encounter would be the president's office, then the vice president's, then the assistant vice president's, and so on down to the lowest ranking worker. Or, vice versa, the architect may choose for you to meet the least important employee first, the one with the least power in the company. Then the next, and the next, until at last, you reach the president.

Likewise, in writing, ideas may be arranged in order of importance. In this pattern, which idea comes first? Not the one that *happened* first, but the one that is *most*, or *least*, important.

Most Important to Least Important

In the following paragraph, the writer starts with what is most important, hoping that by putting this item first, the reader will be sure to remember it. After you read the passage, answer the questions that follow. Each question is followed by its answer to guide you through your reading of the passage.

> Choosing a doctor is an important decision. Here are some things you can do to make the best choice. The single most important thing is to interview the doctors you are considering. Ask questions about the practice, office hours, and how quickly he or she responds to phone calls. Pay attention to the doctor's communication skills and how comfortable you are with him or her. The second thing you should do is check the doctor's credentials. One way to do this is to ask your health insurance company how they checked the doctor's credentials before accepting him or her into their network. Another thing you can do is to look at the environment of the doctor's office. Be sure patients aren't waiting too long and that the office is clean and professional. Finally, spend some time talking with the receptionist. Keep in mind that this is the person you'll come into contact with every time you call or come into the office. If he or she is pleasant and efficient, it will certainly make your overall experience better.

1. According to the passage, what's the most important thing you can do to be sure you choose the right doctor?

The answer should be clear: The writer tells you clearly that the "single most important thing is to interview the doctors you are considering."

2. What is the second most important thing you can to choose the right doctor?

When a writer starts out by saying "the most important thing," you know that the writer will be starting with the most important idea and ending with the least important. The second most important thing, therefore, is the second piece of advice offered in the paragraph: "Check the doctor's credentials."

3. What's the third most important thing?

The writer is going from most to least important, so according the passage, the third most important thing is to "look at the environment of the doctor's office."

4. Finally, what is the *least* important tip the writer offers?

The answer is the last piece of advice the writer offers: "Spend some time talking with the receptionist."

Least Important to Most Important

Some writers prefer the opposite approach, depending on the subject and the effect they want their writing to have. Rather than *starting* with the most important idea, they prefer to *end* with what is most important. Not only do they leave you with a strong concluding impression, but they also take advantage of the "snowball effect." The snowball effect is the "buildup" or force that a writer gets from starting with what's least important and moving toward what's most important. Like a snowball, the writer's idea builds and builds, getting bigger and bigger, more and more important. By starting with the least important point, writers can also create suspense—the reader is waiting for that final idea. And each idea or item builds upon the ones that come before it.

Here's an example of a passage that builds from least important to most important. Read the passage, marking it up as you go along. Answer the questions that follow.

There are a number of reasons why the current voting age of 18 should be lowered to 16. First, a lower voting age in the United States would encourage other countries to follow this example. Many countries are discussing and debating the pros and cons of lowering the voting age, and if the United States gives 16-year-olds the right to vote, it will serve as an important example for the rest of the world.

More importantly, if 16-year-olds are old enough to engage in other adult activities, then they are old enough to vote. In many states, 16-year-olds can work, get a driver's license, and engage in many other adult activities that make them mature enough to vote. If, at 16, young people are old enough to manage the responsibilities of work and school, then it is clear that they are responsible enough to make informed decisions about politics and politicians.

But the most important reason why the voting age should be lowered to 16 is that it will decrease apathy and cynicism while stimulating a lifelong interest in political participation. Many young people feel as though their opinion doesn't matter. By the time they reach voting age, they are often disenchanted with politics and cynical about the entire political process. If the voting age were lowered to 16, young people would know that their opinion does count. They would be inspired to exercise their right to vote not just as young adults but throughout their lives. The long-term results—a much higher percentage of interested voters and better voter turnout—will benefit our entire nation.

In the following spaces, list the reasons the author provides for why the voting age should be lowered *in the order in which they are listed in the passage*. In the next set of blanks, list those same reasons *in their order of importance*.

Order of Presentation
1.

2.

3.

Order of Importance
1.

2.

3.

You can see that the orders are reversed: The author starts with what is least important and ends with what is most important. Why? Why not the other way around?

This author uses a least-to-most-important organizational strategy because he is making an argument. He's trying to convince you that the United States should lower the voting age to 16. In order to be convincing, he must have a strong argument. If he starts with what he feels is his most important (and most convincing) point, he has already shown his hand, so to speak. Especially when the issue is controversial, writers often use the least-to-most-important structure. That way, if their less important points make sense to the reader, then their more important points will come off even stronger. Also, if they were to organize their ideas in the reverse order, most to least important, readers might feel let down.

Thus, you can often expect to see this type of structure—least to most important—in an argument. As the saying goes, "save the best for last." In an argument, that's usually where "the best" has the most impact.

In the first example, about choosing a doctor, the writer was not trying to convince. She was simply giving some advice. There's no need, then, for a buildup. Indeed, in that kind of paragraph, readers might stop reading after the first tip if they don't find it helpful. That's why the most important ideas come first—to make sure they'll be read.

In other words, the writer's purpose—his or her motive for writing—influences the choice of organizational patterns. In turn, the structure influences how you take in and understand what you read.

Practice

Look at the following list of reasons to read more often. If you were to put these reasons together in a paragraph to convince readers that they should read more, how would you organize them? Rank these reasons first in order of importance and then in the order in which you would present them.

Five Reasons to Read More Often
- It will improve your vocabulary.
- It will improve your reading comprehension.
- It will increase your reading speed.
- It will broaden your understanding of yourself and others.
- It will introduce you to new information and ideas.

Order of Importance to You

1.

2.

3.

4.

5.

Order of Presentation

1.

2.

3.

4.

5.

In which order did you choose to present your ideas? Most important to least important? Or least to most? Either structure will work beautifully with these ideas. You may want to hit your readers with what's most important from the start so that you make sure you catch their attention. Or you may want to save your best idea for last so that your readers get through all the other ideas first and build up to the most important.

You might present the ideas differently, but here are two versions of the resulting paragraph as examples.

Example: Most to Least Important

There are many benefits to reading more often. First and foremost, reading more will broaden your understanding of yourself and of other people. It will also introduce you to new information and ideas. Furthermore, it will improve your overall reading comprehension so you'll begin to understand more of what you read. In addition, reading more will improve your vocabulary and increase your reading speed.

Example: Least to Most Important

There are many benefits to reading more often. First, it will increase your reading speed, so that you can read more in less time. Second, it will improve your vocabulary. Third, it will improve your overall reading comprehension, and you'll understand more of what you read. In addition, reading more will introduce you to new information and ideas. Most importantly, it will broaden your understanding of yourself and of other people.

Review
Transitions

Notice how the transitional words and phrases are used in these paragraphs. Go back to each paragraph and underline the transitional words and phrases.

Here are the words you should have underlined in the first paragraph: *first and foremost, also, furthermore,* and *in addition.* The second paragraph uses different transitional words and phrases: *first, second, third, in addition,* and *most importantly.*

Main Idea

By the way, what is the main idea of these two paragraphs? Do you see a topic sentence? Write the main idea of the paragraphs in this space.

You can probably recognize by now that the first sentence in each paragraph, "There are many benefits to reading more often," is the topic sentence that governs each paragraph. This sentence is general enough to encompass each of the different reasons given, and it makes an assertion about reading—that you should do it more often.

TIP

Three main ways that authors organize their ideas are

- Time order—the chronological sequence of events
- Space order—describing the placement of a particular person, thing, or setting using words and phrases such as: *below, next to, behind, in the middle, beyond,* before, and *in front of*
- Order of importance—grabbing attention and creating a strong first impression by organizing ideas from most important to least important, or building suspense and tension by organizing ideas from least important to most important

Summary

Organizing ideas by order of importance is a structure you will see often. Whether a passage is organized from most to least important or least to most, this technique should now be easy for you to recognize.

TIP

Serial plotting is a plotting technique that builds anticipation by creating suspenseful chapter endings that leave the reader wondering what will happen next.

8 ▶ SIMILARITIES AND DIFFERENCES: COMPARE AND CONTRAST

It is well to read everything of something, and something of everything.

—LORD HENRY P. BROUGHAM, British statesman (1778–1868)

LESSON SUMMARY

This lesson explores another organizational pattern writers often use to structure their writing: comparison and contrast.

W e spend a good deal of our lives comparing and contrasting things. Whenever we want to explain something, for example, we often use **comparison** (showing how two or more things are *similar*). We might say, for example, that mint chocolate chip ice cream tastes just like a peppermint candy; or that the new manager looks just like Clint Eastwood. When we want to show how things are *different* or not alike, we **contrast** them. We might say that peppermint candies are mintier than any mint chocolate chip ice cream; or that the new manager may look like Eastwood, but he doesn't have Eastwood's dimple.

How Comparison and Contrast Work

When writers compare and contrast, they provide a way of classifying or judging the items they are discussing. They show how two (or more) things are similar or different when placed side by side. Consider, for example, the following paragraph. Read it carefully, and then answer the questions that follow.

Planting a garden is a lot like having a family. Both require a great deal of work, especially as they grow and as the seasons change. As summer days lengthen, your plants become dependent on you for sustenance, much like your children depend on you for food and drink. Like a thirsty child asking for a drink of water, your plants do the same. Their bent, wilted "body" language, translated, issues a demand much the way your child requests milk or juice. When their collective thirsts are quenched, you see the way they both thrive in your care. The fussy child becomes satisfied, and the plant reaches toward the sun in a showy display. You might also find that you have to clean the space around your plants much like you would pick up toys and clothes that have been thrown helter-skelter in your toddler's room. Similarly, plants shed spent petals, roses need to be pruned, and weeds need to be pulled. To keep children healthy, parents protect their children against disease with medicine, and gardeners do the same with insect repellent. To nourish them, parents give children vitamins, and gardeners use fertilizer, as both promote healthy growth. As children grow and become adults, they need less and less care. However, here's where the similarity ends. While plants die and become dormant during winter, children still maintain a vital role in the family unit.

Finding the Facts

1. What two things are being compared and contrasted here?

2. In what ways are these two things similar? (There are four similarities; list them here.)
   a.
   b.
   c.
   d.

3. In what ways are these two things different? (There is one aspect that is different; write it here.)

Answers

1. The two things being compared and contrasted are a parent and a gardener.
2. Gardeners are like parents in that: a) plants are dependent on gardeners as children are on parents; b) plants require care from gardeners as children do from their parents; c) gardeners tidy up after their plants, as parents do after children; and d) gardeners protect their plants, as parents protect their children.
3. Gardeners are unlike parents in that their responsibility for their plants ends when the plant dies or goes into winter dormancy.

Finding the Main Idea

Now that you've answered those questions, consider one more. Read the passage again, and then answer this question:

4. What is the main idea of this passage?

Did you notice that the opening sentence, "Planting a garden is a lot like having a family," is the topic sentence that expresses the main idea of this paragraph? The paragraph does mention a *difference* between these two roles, but notice that the topic sentence does not claim that gardeners and parents are *exactly* alike. Instead, it asserts that they are "a lot" alike.

Transitional Devices

As you read the paragraph about gardeners and parents, did you notice the transitional words and phrases that show you when the writer is comparing (showing similarity) and when the writer is contrasting (showing difference)? Here's the passage once more. As you read it this time, underline the transitional words and phrases you find.

Planting a garden is a lot like having a family. Both require a great deal of work, especially as they grow and as the seasons change. As summer days lengthen, your plants become dependent on you for sustenance, much like your children depend on you for food and drink. Like a thirsty child asking for a drink of water, your plants do the same. Their bent, wilted "body" language, translated, issues a demand much the way your child requests milk or juice. When their collective thirsts are quenched, you see the way they both thrive in your care. The fussy child becomes satisfied, and the plant reaches toward the sun in a showy display. You might also find that you have to clean the space around your plants much like you would pick up toys and clothes that have been thrown helter-skelter in your toddler's room. Similarly, plants shed spent petals, roses need to be pruned, and weeds need to be pulled. To keep children healthy, parents protect their children against disease with medicine, and gardeners do the same with insect repellent. To nourish them, parents give children vitamins, and gardeners use fertilizer, as both promote healthy growth. As children grow and become adults, they need less and less care. However, here's where the similarity ends. While plants die and become dormant during winter, children still maintain a vital role in the family unit.

Writers use several transitional words and phrases to show comparison and contrast. In this paragraph, you should have underlined the following words: *much like, in the same way, similarly,* and *however.*

These words and phrases show similarity:

similarly	in the same way
likewise	in a like manner
like	and
just as	also

These words and phrases show difference:

but	yet
on the other hand	on the contrary
however	nevertheless
conversely	

Structure

Now look more closely at the sample paragraph to examine its structure. Exactly how is this paragraph organized?

First, you've noticed that the paragraph begins with a topic sentence that makes the initial comparison: "Gardeners are like parents." Then, the paragraph identifies four ways in which gardeners are like parents:

1. Plants become dependent upon gardeners as children do on parents.

2. Plants require care from their gardeners as children do from parents.

3. Gardeners clean up after their plants as parents do after children.

4. Gardeners protect plants from "dangers" as parents protect children.

Finally, after pointing out these similarities, the paragraph concludes by pointing out an important difference between parents and gardeners:

1. A gardener's responsibility for his or her plants ends with time, while a parent's doesn't.

Perhaps you noticed something else in the way this paragraph is organized. Did you notice that every time the paragraph mentions something about a parent's role, it also mentions something about a gardener? Each aspect of the gardener's role is followed by a comparable aspect of the parent's role. Thus, for every aspect of "A" (the gardener), the paragraph provides a comparable aspect of "B" (the parent) to compare or contrast. The paragraph is therefore organized like this: ABABABABAB.

This is called the *point-by-point* method of comparison and contrast. Each aspect of A discussed is immediately paired with that aspect of B (being dependent, requiring care, cleaning up, and protecting).

On the other hand, some writers prefer to deal first with all aspects of A and then with all aspects of B. This is called the *block* method of comparison and contrast; it goes AAAAABBBBB. Here is the same paragraph arranged using the block method:

Planting a garden is a lot like having a family. A plant becomes dependent on the gardener and begs for water on a hot summer day. Gardeners also have to clean up the space around their plants as they shed spent petals, as they require pruning, and as they become choked with weeds. Gardeners also provide for the health of their plants through insecticide and fertilizer applications. A gardener's responsibility for his or her plants lessens as they die at the end of the season or they go into winter dormancy.

Like gardeners, parents find their children dependent upon them for food and nourishment. Like gardeners, parents are constantly picking up after their children, as toys and clothes are scattered throughout the house. Like gardeners, parents provide for the nourishment and well-being of their children with vitamin supplements, food, and medicines. However, unlike gardeners, parents will find that their responsibility lessens as the child grows, but it does not come to an end.

Here, the passage treats each of the things being compared and contrasted separately—first, all aspects of the gardener, then all aspects of the parent—rather than one aspect of the gardener, one of the parent; another of the gardener, another of the parent. So the organization is quite different.

But you should notice one thing that is similar in both passages: They compare and contrast aspects of A and B that are comparable or parallel. If an aspect of A is discussed, that same aspect of B (whether similar to or different from A) must be discussed at some point in the passage. This correspondence of parts is essential for the compare and contrast technique. Look what happens, for example, when the writer does not discuss corresponding parts:

Being a parent is a lot like being a gardener. Parents must bathe, clothe, and feed their children. Parents must also create and maintain guidelines for acceptable behavior for children. Also, parents must see to it that their children get a proper education.

Gardeners nurture the plants in their gardens. They pull weeds and prune them to encourage them to grow. They feed them and apply insecticides. They watch them flower and then witness their demise.

You'll notice that this passage seems to focus on differences between gardeners and parents rather than the similarities. But is this really a fair contrast? Look at the aspects of A (the gardener) that are described here. Do they have any relationship to the aspects of B (the parent) that are described? No. And a compare and contrast passage can't be successful unless the aspects of A and B are discussed comparably. These two paragraphs don't really seem to have a point—there's no basis for comparison between gardeners and parents.

Practice

Suppose you were going to write a paragraph that compares and contrasts readers and detectives. The following lists describe five aspects of being a reader and five aspects of being a detective. Only *three* items in each list are comparable. Find those three items in each list and pair each one with its matching item. Remember, these items may be either similarities or differences. What's important is that they are comparable aspects.

A reader:

1. looks for clues to meaning.
2. has many different types of books to read.
3. can choose what book to read.
4. builds vocabulary by reading.
5. becomes a better reader with each book.

A detective:

1. has a dangerous job.
2. gets better at solving crimes with each case.
3. requires lots of training.
4. doesn't get to choose which cases to work on.
5. looks for clues to solve the crime.

Did you find the aspects that are comparable? Did you match reader 1 with detective 5 (similarity)? Reader 3 with detective 4 (difference)? And reader 5 with detective 2 (similarity)? If so, you did terrific work.

Here's how this information might work together in a paragraph:

In many ways, readers are a lot like detectives. Like detectives looking for clues at the scene of the crime, readers look for clues to meaning in the books that they read. And, like detectives who get better and better at solving crimes with each case, readers get better and better at understanding what they read with each book. Unfortunately for detectives, however, they cannot choose which cases they get to work on, whereas readers have the pleasure of choosing which books they'd like to read.

Why Compare and Contrast?

In addition to following the ABABAB or AAABBB structure, compare and contrast passages must, like all other passages, have a point. There's a reason that these two items are being compared and contrasted; there's something the writer is trying to point out by putting these two things side by side for analysis. This reason or point is the main idea, which is often stated in a topic sentence.

The main idea of the first paragraph you looked at in this lesson was, "Planting a garden is a lot like having a family." In this paragraph, you learned that the writer sees a significant similarity between these two roles. Likewise, in the previous paragraph, you see a significant similarity between readers and detectives.

In both cases, you may never have thought of making such comparisons. That's part of the beauty of the compare and contrast organization: It often allows you to see things in a new and interesting way. In addition, it serves the more practical function of showing you how two things measure up against each other so that you can make informed decisions, like about which car to buy (a compare and contrast essay might tell you which car is better) or which savings bond to invest in (a compare and contrast essay will show you which bond is best for you).

TIP

When you are reading a comparison/contrast essay or article, focus on the words or phrases that point out key similarities or differences.

The following are some topics that lend themselves well to comparison and contrast:

- Fashion trends of the 1960s and the 1980s
- baseball and football games
- high school years and college years
- teenagers and senior citizens
- art students and computer science majors
- fast food and health food
- living on a farm and living in an urban area

Can you think of any other significant comparison/contrast topics?

9 ▶ WHY DO THINGS HAPPEN? A LOOK AT CAUSE AND EFFECT

Be sure that you go to the author to get at his meaning, not to find yours.

—JOHN RUSKIN, poet and critic (1819–1900)

LESSON SUMMARY

"One thing leads to another"—that's the principle behind cause and effect. Understanding cause and effect, and the relationship between them, will make you a better reader.

For every action," famous scientist Sir Isaac Newton said, "there is an equal and opposite reaction." Every action results in another action (a *reaction*); or, for every action, there is an *effect* caused by that action. Likewise, each action is *caused* by a previous action. In other words, each action has a *cause*—something that made it happen—and each action has an *effect*—something it makes happen.

- **Cause:** a person or thing that makes something happen or produces an effect
- **Effect:** a change produced by an action or cause

Much of what you read is an attempt to explain either the cause of some action or its effect. For example, an author might try to explain the causes of World War I or the effect of underwater nuclear testing; the reason behind a change in policy at work; or the effect a new computer system will have on office procedure. Let's take a look at how writers explaining cause or effect might organize their ideas.

Distinguishing Cause from Effect

A passage that examines cause generally answers the question *why* something took place: Why was the company restructured? Who or what made this take place? A passage that examines effect generally answers the question *what happened* after something took place: What happened as a result of the restructuring? How did it affect the company?

Practice

To help you distinguish between cause and effect, carefully read following the sentences. You'll see that cause and effect work together; you can't have one without the other. That's why it's very important to be able to distinguish between the two. See if you can determine both the cause and the effect in each of the following sentences:

Example: Robin got demoted when she talked back to the boss.
Cause: Robin talked back to the boss.
Effect: Robin got demoted.

1. Inflation has caused us to raise our prices.
   Cause:

   Effect:

2. Since we hired Joan, the office has been running smoothly.
   Cause:

   Effect:

3. He realized that his car had stopped not because it needed repair but because it ran out of gas.
   Cause:

   Effect:

4. The company's budget crisis was created by overspending.
   Cause:

   Effect:

5. As a result of our new marketing program, sales have doubled.
   Cause:

   Effect:

Answers

1. **Cause:** *Inflation*
   Effect: *We had to raise our prices.*
2. **Cause:** *We hired Joan.*
   Effect: *Our office has been running smoothly.*
3. **Cause:** *The car ran out of gas.*
   Effect: *The car stopped.*
4. **Cause:** *Overspending*
   Effect: *Budget crisis*
5. **Cause:** *The new marketing program*
   Effect: *Sales have doubled.*

If you are having trouble connecting causes and effects, look for significant events or actions and reword the situations in the form of a question. The phrase "because of" is helpful in generating potential causes, and the phrase "resulted in" can be used to formulate questions leading to effects.

- Why did Jane lose her job?
- Jane lost her job "because of" [cause]
- What happened when Jane was constantly late?
- Jane's constant lateness "resulted in" [effect]

Here is a partial list of words and phrases that indicate when a cause or effect is being examined.

Words Indicating Cause

because (of)	created (by)
since	caused (by)

Words Indicating Effect

since	therefore
hence	consequently
so	as a result

When Cause and Effect Are Interrelated

Notice how the signal words listed on the previous page are used in the following paragraph. Underline the signal words as you come across them.

Ed became a mechanic largely because of his father. His father was always in the garage working on one car or another, so young Ed would spend hours watching his father work. As a result, he became fascinated by cars at an early age. His father encouraged him to learn about cars on his own, so Ed began tinkering with cars himself at age eight. Consequently, by the time he was 13, Ed could tear an engine apart and put it back together by himself. Since he was already so skilled, when he was 15, he got a job as the chief mechanic at a local repair shop. He has been there ever since.

You should have underlined the following signal words and phrases in this paragraph: *because of, so* (twice), *as a result, consequently,* and *since.*

Notice that this paragraph's purpose—to explain *why* Ed became a mechanic—is expressed in the topic sentence, "Ed became a mechanic largely because of his father." This paragraph's purpose, then, is to explain cause, and the primary cause is Ed's father.

You'll notice, however, that some of the sentences in this paragraph also deal with effect. This may seem like a contradiction at first. After all, why would a paragraph about cause deal with effect? But it's not a contradiction. That's because there isn't just *one* thing that led to Ed's becoming a mechanic. Although Ed's dad may have been the initial cause, there was still a *series* of actions and reactions that occurred—a series of causes and effects. Once A causes B, B then becomes the cause for C.

In fact, six different sets of cause and effect are listed in this paragraph. What are they? The first cause is provided to get you started.

Cause 1: Ed's father was always in the garage.

Effect 1:

Cause 2:

Effect 2:

Cause 3:

Effect 3:

Cause 4:

Effect 4:

Cause 5:

Effect 5:

Cause 6:

Effect 6:

Answers

Cause 1: Ed's father was always in the garage.
Effect 1: Ed would spend hours watching.

Cause 2: Ed would spend hours watching.
Effect 2: Ed became fascinated by cars.

Cause 3: Ed became fascinated by cars.
Effect 3: Ed began tinkering with cars.

Cause 4: Ed began tinkering with cars.
Effect 4: Ed's father encouraged him.

Cause 5: Ed's father encouraged him.
Effect 5: Ed could tear an engine apart by himself.

Cause 6: Ed could tear an engine apart by himself.
Effect 6: He got a job as the chief mechanic.

Variations

When One Cause Has Several Effects

Sometimes, one cause may have several effects: Several things may happen as a result of one action. In the following passage, the writer explains several effects of the new marketing campaign:

> Our new marketing campaign has been a tremendous success. Since we've been advertising on the radio, sales have increased by 35%. Our client references have doubled, and we've had greater client retention rates. Furthermore, we've been able to hire five new sales representatives and expand our territory to include the southwestern United States.

According to the paragraph, what were the effects of the new marketing campaign?

1.

2.

3.

4.

5.

Answers

1. Sales have increased 35%.
2. Client references have doubled.
3. Client retention rates have increased.
4. Five new sales representatives have been hired.
5. Territory has been expanded to include the southwestern United States.

When One Effect Has Several Causes

Just as one action can have many results, one action can have many causes as well. The following announcement is an example.

TO: All Commuters
FROM: The Station Management

Unfortunately, we will no longer provide an afternoon snack concession at the train station. Although poor sales are one of the reasons that this service will no longer be provided, there are actually several reasons why the concession is no longer a viable option. In addition to poor sales, the south wall of the train station (where the concession is located) will be undergoing a six-month renovation that will force the closure of the snack concession. In fact, the ticket windows on that wall will be closed as well. Furthermore, from this point forward, the station will close its doors at 6 P.M. due to new town regulations, which will cut the rush-hour commuter traffic coming through the station in half. Finally, Mike Alberti, the proprietor of the concession, has decided to say farewell to his concession business, and after 35 years on the job, Mike will be retiring next month. While none of these factors on their own would have caused the long-term closure of the concession, combined, they make it impossible to continue running an afternoon snack concession for the foreseeable future.

Why is the afternoon snack concession at the train station being discontinued?

1.

2.

3.

4.

Answers

You should have noticed four causes in the announcement:

1. Poor sales.
2. A renovation on the side of the train station where the concession is located.
3. Town regulations will now close the station at 6 P.M., which will decrease commuter traffic significantly.
4. The proprietor of the concession has decided to retire.

Contributing vs. Sufficient Cause

You'll notice that the previous announcement informs commuters that "none of these factors on their own would have caused the long-term closure of the concession." This means that each of these causes is a *contributing* cause. A contributing cause *helps* make something happen but can't make that thing happen by itself. It is only one factor that *contributes* to the cause.

On the opposite end of the cause spectrum is the **sufficient** cause. A sufficient cause is strong enough to make something happen by itself. Sufficient cause is demonstrated in the following paragraph.

Dear Mr. Miller:

It has come to our attention that you have breached your lease. When you signed your lease, you agreed that you would leave Apartment 3A at 123 Elm Street in the same state that you found it when you moved in. You also agreed that if the apartment showed signs of damage upon your departure, then we (Livingston Properties) would not return the security deposit that you gave us at the time you moved into the building. Upon inspection, we have found a great deal of damage to the appliances in the apartment as well as the wood floors. Consequently, we will not be returning your security deposit.

Here, you can see that there is one clear reason why Livingston Properties will not return Mr. Miller's security deposit. He breached his lease by damaging the apartment he rented from them. (If you don't know what *breach* means, you should be able to determine the meaning from the context.)

Evaluating Opinions about Cause and Effect

Sometimes, in a cause and effect passage, an author will offer his or her *opinion* about the cause or effect of something, rather than *facts* about the cause or effect. In that case, readers must judge the validity of the author's analysis. Are the author's ideas logical? Does he or she support the conclusions he or she comes to? Consider, for example, two authors' opinions about instituting mandatory school uniforms.

Paragraph A

Mandatory school uniforms are a bad decision for our district. If students are required to wear a uniform, it will greatly inhibit their ability to express themselves. This is a problem because dress is one of the major ways that young people express themselves. A school uniform policy also directly violates the freedom of expression that all Americans are supposed to enjoy. Consequently, young people will doubt that their basic rights are protected, and this will affect their larger outlook on civil liberties. Furthermore, school uniforms will interfere with the wearing of certain articles of religious clothing, which will create tensions among certain religious groups that can lead to feelings of discrimination. In addition, school uniforms will place an undue financial burden on many low-income families who may not have the money to spend on new uniforms every year, especially if they have several children. Finally, school uniforms will negate one of the most important concepts we can teach our children—individuality. When push comes to shove, we'd all be better off choosing individuality over uniformity. Mandatory school uniforms are a step in the wrong direction.

Paragraph B

Mandatory school uniforms will have a tremendously positive impact on our district. If students are required to wear a uniform, it will greatly inhibit gang behavior since they will no longer be able to wear gang colors. As a result, schools will experience an overall decrease in school violence and theft. Since violence is one of the major concerns that parents, teachers, and students raise about our district, this change will be welcomed with open arms. In addition, school uniforms will instill a much-needed sense of discipline in our student body, and discipline is something that is, unfortunately, in short supply in our school district. Also, students dressed in uniforms will feel a strong sense of community with their peers, which will lead to a more harmonious school environment. Finally, if students were wearing school uniforms, administrators and teachers would no longer have to be clothing police, freeing them to focus on more important issues than whether someone is wearing a dress that is too short or a T-shirt with an inappropriate message. You can make our schools a better place by supporting mandatory school uniforms.

What effects does the author of paragraph A think mandatory uniforms would have?

1.

2.

3.

4.

5.

What effects does the author of paragraph B think mandatory uniforms would have?

1.

2.

3.

4.

5.

You'll notice that both authors take one cause—mandatory school uniforms—and offer several possible effects. Often, authors will use the cause and effect structure to make arguments like the ones we've just seen: one for and one against mandatory school uniforms. It is up to the reader to determine whose argument seems most valid.

Summary

Understanding cause and effect is an important skill not only for reading comprehension, but also for your daily life. To analyze the events happening around you, you must be able to understand *why* those events happened—what caused them. Similarly, to make decisions or evaluate the decisions of others, you must be able to consider the effects of a possible decision. "Reading" not only texts, but also events and situations, requires you to understand cause and effect.

TIP

Whenever you read the newspaper, be sure to read with a skeptical eye—sometimes causes and effects aren't entirely black and white. For example, parents, teachers, superintendents, and students might provide different opinions on why a particular school is failing based on their own personal biases or hidden agendas.

- Don't be swayed by the use of emotional rhetoric and finger-pointing tactics.
- Focus on judging the cause (why something happened) and the effect (what exactly happened) by determining which party is presenting the most logical and valid conclusion based on documented factual information, examples, and specific, detailed explanations of a cause or sequence of causes that resulted in a particular effect.

LESSON

10 ▶ BEING STRUCTURALLY SOUND: PUTTING IT ALL TOGETHER

Reading is to the mind what exercise is to the body.

—RICHARD STEELE, Irish writer (1672–1729)

LESSON SUMMARY

Today's lesson pulls together what you've learned in Lessons 6–9 and gives you more practice in discerning the structure of a reading passage.

Like an architect designing a building, a writer must have a blueprint—a plan for how he or she will organize the passage. So far in this section, we've looked at several ways that authors may organize their information and ideas:

- **Lesson 6: Chronological order.** Ideas are arranged in the order in which they occurred (or in the order in which they should occur).
- **Lesson 7: Order of importance.** Ideas are arranged in order of *increasing* importance (least important idea to most important idea) or in order of *decreasing* importance (most important idea to least important idea).
- **Lesson 8: Compare and contrast.** Ideas are arranged so that parallel aspects of item A and item B are compared and contrasted either in block style (AAAABBBB) or point-by-point style (ABABABAB).
- **Lesson 9: Cause and effect.** Ideas are arranged so that readers can see what event or series of events *caused* something to take place or what *effect* an event or series of events had.

Practice

Although writers often rely on one particular structure to organize their ideas, in many cases, writers use a combination of these structures. For example, a writer may want to compare and contrast the causes of World War I and those of World War II; or a writer may want to describe, in chronological order, the events that led to (caused) the failure of a computer system. Thus, today we will look at how writers may combine these strategies. In addition, we'll continue to strengthen your reading comprehension skills by including strategies from the first week:

- Finding the facts
- Determining the main idea
- Defining vocabulary words in context
- Distinguishing between fact and opinion

Practice Passage 1

Begin with the following paragraph. Read it carefully, marking it up as you go. Then answer the questions that follow.

There were several reasons behind our decision to move to Flemington. The first occurred about 18 months ago when Mark and I decided to start a family. We were living in a one-bedroom apartment and we knew that we wanted to move into larger quarters before we had a baby. We began to look at houses. Then, much sooner than expected, I got pregnant. Soon after that, Mark's company announced that they were relocating to Flemington, which was in a less expensive part of the state, about 90 miles south of us. Mark's company had been good to him, and they were one of the few around with excellent benefits, family-friendly policies, and a child-care center on site. With a baby on the way, these things were imperative for us. Since I ran my graphic arts business from home, I wasn't bound to any particular place, so we began looking at real estate in Flemington and also did some research on their school system as well as the overall community. We were very excited about what we found—reasonable housing costs, great schools, and a lively town. Mark then accepted the relocation offer and we found a beautiful old Tudor house. We'll be moving about a month before the baby is due. Let's hope she doesn't decide to come early.

1. Which two organizational strategies does this writer use?
  a. chronological order
  b. order of importance
  c. compare and contrast
  d. cause and effect

2. *Imperative* means
  a. trivial, unimportant.
  b. luxurious, lavish.
  c. pressing, crucial.

3. What prompted the initial decision to move?

4. What happened after the initial cause set things in motion?

   a.

   b.

   c.

   d.

   e.

   f.

Answers

1. a, d. The writer tells you the causes, in the order in which they occurred, that resulted in her move to Flemington.

2. c. The sentence before the one that uses the word *imperative* is describing the attractive family-friendly benefits that Mark's company offers. Since we know that the writer is pregnant, it would make sense that these benefits would be pressing or crucial for her, as opposed to the other two options.

3. The decision to begin a family sparked the initial desire to move.

4. After the writer and her husband decided to start a family, the following events occurred in this order:

   a. They began to look at houses.

   b. The writer got pregnant.

   c. Mark's company announced plan to relocate.

   d. The couple began researching real estate, schools, and community life in Flemington.

   e. Mark accepted the relocation offer.

   f. They found a house.

How did you do? Were you able to see how each cause led to an effect, and how that effect caused something else to happen (another effect)? If you missed any of the questions, here's what you should do:

IF YOU MISSED:	THEN STUDY:
Question 1	Lessons 6 and 9
Question 2	Lesson 3
Question 3	Lesson 9
Question 4	Lesson 9

Practice Passage 2

Now try the following passage. Again, read it carefully, marking it up as you go, and then answer the questions that follow.

There are several changes in the procedure for employees who wish to apply for vacant positions within the company. These changes make it much easier for in-house employees to fill vacancies that occur.

First, the most important difference is that employees will now be notified of all available positions *before* the positions are advertised for the general public. Accordingly, all in-house candidates will be interviewed before we see any outside candidates, and we will offer the job to outside candidates only if no current employees are able to fill the position.

Second, under the new procedure, in-house employees can be hired even if they don't meet all job requirements. Under our old policy, in-house employees had to meet all job qualifications in order to obtain the vacant position. Now, however, employees who have proven themselves dedicated to the company will be hired for a vacant position even if they are lacking some minor qualifications; training will be provided.

A third change involves recommendations. From now on, employees do not need to be recommended for an in-house position before they apply. Instead, employees may apply as soon as they are aware of the vacancy. The remaining procedures and policies (those regarding increase in pay, interview procedure, and hiring approval) remain the same.

5. Which two organizational strategies does this writer use?
  a. chronological order
  b. order of importance
  c. compare and contrast

6. The author organizes her ideas in order of
  a. decreasing importance (most important to least important).
  b. increasing importance (least important to most important).
  c. which points she likes best.

7. Underline the sentence in this passage that expresses the main idea.

8. The sentence you underlined is a(n)
  a. fact.
  b. opinion.
  c. neither.

Answers

5. b, c. The author uses order of importance in comparing the old procedure to the new one.

6. a. The author organizes her ideas in order of decreasing importance. She starts with the most important change ("First, the most important difference is . . .") and moves downward to the second and third most important changes.

7. The sentence that expresses the main idea of all four paragraphs is the second sentence in the first paragraph: "These changes make it much easier for in-house employees to fill vacancies." Although the first sentence tells us what all the paragraphs will be about (the changes in the procedure), it is the second sentence that expresses an opinion—how the author feels about this subject—and therefore, it is the main idea.

8. b. This sentence expresses an opinion, not a fact. There have indeed been changes—that is a fact—but whether those changes make things easier for most employees is debatable. There may be some things about the old procedure that we don't know. Perhaps, for example, they opened the job to both in-house employees and the general public at the same time, but they interviewed all in-house employees first anyway. Because of our limited information about the old procedure, we cannot accept the idea that the change is better as fact.

If you missed some of these questions, now it's up to you to figure out which lessons to review.

Practice Passage 3

Now it's your turn. In this exercise, you'll take a paragraph that is organized one way—by cause and effect—and add another structure: order of importance.

Here's what you should do: Reread the following two paragraphs about mandatory school uniforms. Decide which author you agree with most. Then, look carefully at the effects the author predicts. Which effect do you think is most important? Which is least important? Rank these effects in order of importance. Then, decide whether you want to start with the most important idea and end with the least important, or vice versa, start with the least important idea and end with the most important. Finally, put it all together in a paragraph in the space provided.

Paragraph A

Mandatory school uniforms are a bad decision for our district. If students are required to wear a uniform, it will greatly inhibit their ability to express themselves. This is a problem because dress is one of the major ways that young people express themselves. A school uniform policy also directly violates the freedom of expression that all Americans are supposed to enjoy. Consequently, young people will doubt that their basic rights are protected, which will affect their larger outlook on civil liberties. Furthermore, school uniforms will interfere with the wearing of certain articles of religious clothing, and this will create tensions among certain religious groups that can lead to feelings of discrimination. In addition, school uniforms will place an undue financial burden on many low-income families who may not have the money to spend on new uniforms every year, especially if they have several children. Finally, school uniforms will negate one of the most important concepts we can teach our children—individuality. When push comes to shove, we'd all be better off choosing individuality over uniformity. Mandatory school uniforms are a step in the wrong direction.

Paragraph B

Mandatory school uniforms will have a tremendously positive impact on our district. If students are required to wear a uniform, it will greatly inhibit gang behavior since they will no longer be able to wear gang colors. As a result, schools will experience an overall decrease in school violence and theft. Since violence is one of the major concerns that parents, teachers, and students raise about our district, this change will be welcomed with open arms. In addition, school uniforms will instill a much-needed sense of discipline in our student body, and discipline is something that is, unfortunately, in short supply in our school district. Also, students dressed in uniforms will feel a strong sense of community with their peers, which will lead to a more harmonious school environment. Finally, if students were wearing school uniforms, administrators and teachers would no longer have to be clothing police, freeing them to focus on more important issues than whether someone is wearing a dress that is too short or a T-shirt with an inappropriate message. You can make our schools a better place by supporting mandatory school uniforms.

1. Rank the ideas of the paragraph you have chosen in order of their importance to you.

2. Now write a paragraph, choosing whether to put the ideas in the order of increasing importance or decreasing importance.

Creating a brief outline is the best way to ensure that your ideas are organized according to your chosen method of ordering.

Some students prefer to discuss all of the similarities of a topic or issue first and then move on to discuss the contrasting elements in the separate blocks of paragraphs that follow. Still others prefer to alternate their focus by shifting from comparison to contrast on a point-by-point basis throughout the entire essay. Either style is fine, as long as the key points are restated in your concluding paragraph.

LANGUAGE AND STYLE

In most of the passages you have read so far, the author's ideas and intentions have been very clear. But what happens when they're not? What if the writer doesn't provide a topic sentence that clearly expresses the main idea? Or what if the writer gives you a poem instead of a clear-cut memorandum? How do you figure out what the author is trying to say?

The good news is that no matter how cryptic a piece of writing may seem, the author always leaves clues to help you figure out what he or she means. These clues can be found in the writer's *language* and *style*—the words used and the type of sentences in which he or she uses them. The next four lessons, therefore, focus on four different aspects of language and style:

- point of view
- diction
- style
- tone

You'll learn how authors use these elements to create meaning for their readers. Then you'll put it all together in Lesson 15 to see how language, style, structure, and meaning work together.

11 ▶ A MATTER OF PERSPECTIVE: POINT OF VIEW

Reading is a means of thinking with another person's mind; it forces you to stretch your own.

—CHARLES SCRIBNER JR., American publisher (1921–1995)

LESSON SUMMARY

This lesson introduces you to the concept of *point of view*, one strategy writers use to convey their meaning to readers. Aspects such as whether writers use the more subjective *I* or the more objective *one*, whether they address readers as *you* or merely refer to an anonymous *they*, influence how readers understand what the writer has written.

Picture this: You are walking along a tree-lined street late in the afternoon. Just ahead of you, a woman is sitting on a bench; a dog lies in the shade at her feet. You watch them and nod hello as you walk by.

Now, picture this: You are that dog. You're sitting in the shade under a bench next to your owner's feet. Suddenly, someone walks down the street in front of you. If you look up, you can see that person nod as he or she walks by.

Although you've just pictured the same thing—a person walking by a woman with a dog—you've really pictured two very different scenes, haven't you? The scenario looks quite different from the dog's point of view than from the walker's.

This shift in perspective happens in writing by changing the point of view. *Point of view* is one of the first choices writers make when they begin to write, because it is the point of view that determines who is speaking to the reader.

Point of view is the person or perspective through which the writer channels his or her information and ideas. Just as we may look at a physical object from a number of different perspectives (from above it, below it, behind it, beside it, and so on), we can look at information and ideas from different perspectives as well (mine, yours, his or hers, the professor's, the country's, and so on).

Three Kinds of Point of View

When it comes to expressing point of view, writers can use three distinct approaches:

- **First-person point of view** is a highly individualized, personal point of view in which the writer or narrator speaks about his or her own feelings and experiences directly to the reader using these pronouns: *I, me, mine; we, our, us.*
- **Second-person point of view** is another personal point of view in which the writer speaks directly to the reader, addressing the reader as *you.*
- **Third-person point of view** is an impersonal, objective point of view in which the perspective is that of an outsider (a "third person") who is not directly involved in the action. There is no direct reference to either the reader (second person) or the writer (first person). The writer chooses from these pronouns: *he, him, his; she, her, hers; it, its;* and *they, them, theirs.*

All these points of view are available to writers, but not all of them may be appropriate for what they're writing, and only one will create the exact effect a writer desires. That's because each approach establishes a particular relationship between the reader and the writer.

When Writers Use First Person

Imagine you get one of the following messages from your company's head office:

A. The company congratulates you on the birth of your child.
B. We congratulate you on the birth of your child.

Which message would you rather receive?

Most of us would probably prefer to receive message B over message A. Why? What is the difference between these two messages? Both messages use the second-person pronoun, right? They both address the reader as *you.* But you probably noticed that the writers chose different points of view to refer to themselves. Message A uses the third-person point of view (*the company*) whereas message B uses the first person pronoun *we.* As a result, message B seems more sincere because it comes *from* a person *to* a person rather than from *the company* (a thing) to a person (*you*).

But those messages do more than just express congratulations to the reader. They also seem to indicate something about how the people in the head office want to be perceived. In fact, their choice of point of view shows whether they want to be seen as people (*we*) or as an entity (*the company*). Read the messages again and then decide how you think each writer wants to be perceived.

Which message seems to tell the reader, "We can speak directly to you because we are real people behind this company"?

Message _____

Which message seems to tell the reader, "We have a very formal relationship; let's not get too personal"?

Message _____

The company that sends message A suggests to the reader, "We have a very formal relationship; let's not get too close or too personal." Message B, on the other hand, tells the reader something more like this: "*We* can speak directly to *you* because we are real people behind this company." Thus, the point of view reflects the way the senders of the message wish to be perceived—as a distant entity (message A) or as friendly colleagues (message B).

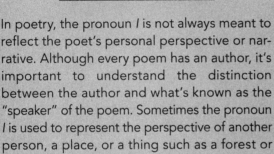

TIP

In poetry, the pronoun *I* is not always meant to reflect the poet's personal perspective or narrative. Although every poem has an author, it's important to understand the distinction between the author and what's known as the "speaker" of the poem. Sometimes the pronoun *I* is used to represent the perspective of another person, a place, or a thing such as a forest or the sun. For example, an inanimate object such as a pen could be the speaker in a haiku poem called "Always Writing."

Distance vs. Intimacy

Whether writers intend it or not (though they almost always do), the third-person point of view establishes a certain distance between the writer and the reader. There's no direct person-to-person contact that way (*me* to *you*). Rather, with the third-person point of view, someone (or something) else is speaking to the reader.

The first-person point of view, on the other hand, establishes a certain intimacy between the writer and the reader. The writer uses *I, my, mine, we, our,* or *us* as if expressing his or her own personal feelings and ideas directly to the reader. "*We* congratulate you" makes message B much more personal than message A, where *the company* congratulates you.

- First-person point of view establishes intimacy. The writer wants to be close to the reader.
- Third-person point of view establishes distance. The writer wants to distance him- or herself from the reader.

When Writers Use Third Person

In a business environment, it's not always practical to be personal. Though the first-person point of view may make the reader feel close to the writer, the first-person point of view also implies a certain *subjectivity*. That is, the writer is expressing a very personal view from a very personal perspective.

Subjectivity vs. Objectivity

There's nothing wrong with expressing personal views, but in the business world, writers may not always be at an advantage using the first-person point of view. They're more likely to be taken seriously when they're *objective*, presenting things from an outsider's point of view, than when they're *subjective*, presenting things from their own possibly selfish or biased point of view.

- **Subjective:** based on the thoughts, feelings, and experiences of the speaker or writer (first-person point of view)
- **Objective:** unaffected by the thoughts, feelings, and experiences of the speaker or writer (third-person point of view)

Thus, if you wanted to complain about a new office policy, which of the following points of view do you think would be more effective?

A. I think our new office policy is a failure.
B. The new office policy appears to be a failure.

Most people would agree that sentence B is more effective. The question is, *why?*

1. The point of view of sentence B is more effective than that of sentence A because
   a. sentence A is too subjective.
   b. sentence B is too subjective.
   c. sentence A is too objective.
   d. all of the above.

The answer is choice **a**. Sentence A uses the first-person point of view, and because *I* is so subjective and personal, it doesn't carry as much weight as the objective sentence B. In sentence B, there is no personal perspective; someone from the outside (a third person, not the reader or the writer) is looking at the policy and evaluating it. The third-person point of view is almost always considered to be more objective because the third person is not directly involved in the action. *I*, however, *is* directly involved in the action (the policy) and therefore cannot have an objective opinion about the policy's success or failure. *I*'s opinion may be prejudiced by the writer's personal experience.

Of course, even when a writer uses third person, he or she can still express his or her own opinion. When that opinion is expressed in the third person, however, it *appears* much more objective.

When Writers Use Second Person

When is *you* an appropriate pronoun? What effect does it create for you, the reader? *You* generally is used to address the reader directly, particularly when the writer is giving directions. Imagine, for example, that you have registered for a financial planning class at the local community college. Prior to the first class, you receive the following note:

Note A
As a student in our financial planning class, you will need several items. First, you must purchase the book *Financial Planning: The Basics* by Robin Wexel. Second, you must outline your current financial situation by making a list of your income sources as well as your bank accounts, investments, and retirement plans. Finally, you should prepare a financial wish list that documents where you would like to see yourself financially ten years from now.

You should be as specific as possible when putting this list together.

Now, imagine you receive this note instead:

Note B
Students in our financial planning class will need several items. First, they must purchase the book *Financial Planning: The Basics* by Robin Wexel. Second, they must outline their current financial situation by making a list of income sources as well as bank accounts, investments, and retirement plans. Finally, they should prepare a financial wish list that documents where they would like to see themselves financially ten years from now. They should be as specific as possible when putting this list together.

Which note would you rather receive? _____

Most likely you'd rather receive note A. Now, here's the tougher question:

2. The point of view of note A is more effective than the point of view of note B because
 a. note A feels less formal.
 b. note A speaks personally to the reader.
 c. note A addresses the reader as an individual.
 d. all of the above.

Many people would prefer note A for all of these reasons, so the answer is **d**. First of all, in note A, the writer speaks directly to the reader (*you*). In note B, the writer speaks in the third person ("students"); the note never acknowledges that *you* are a student. As a result, note B sounds more formal or official. The second-person point of view, however, addresses you personally. It singles you out as an individual, not as a category (student). It is almost like note A was written just for you.

Second Person and Audience

In fact, because note A uses the second-person point of view, you can make certain assumptions about the audience for this note. Reread note A and then answer this question:

3. Note A was most likely written for
  a. students considering the financial planning class for next year.
  b. instructors at the school.
  c. students enrolled in the financial planning class only.
  d. all students at the community college.

Because note A uses the second-person pronoun *you*, you can assume that it is written for **c**, *only* students enrolled in the financial planning class. It must be; it can't work for any other audience because of its pronoun.

Note B, on the other hand, could be used for a much larger audience. In fact, the note could be a description in a course catalogue designed for all students at the college as well as the general public. So, the third-person point of view may have been used in note B not to create a distance between the reader and the writer, but to allow for a wider audience.

Writers may also use *you* to make readers feel as if they are taking part in the action or ideas being expressed in the text. For example, let's imagine that a writer wants to convince readers in a particular town that a community garden is a good idea. The writer could use the third-person point of view, as in the following paragraph:

Paragraph A

Imagine how wonderful it would be if local residents had access to a community garden. Rather than gardening in isolation, residents would come together in an appealing designated spot to plant a bountiful garden. They would be given a plot of land within the large garden to plant as they see fit. They could plant flowers, vegetables, herbs, or any other greenery they desire. The requirement would be that they spend at least one hour in the garden every week and that they bring a few gardening implements to share, such as watering cans, gardening gloves, fertilizer, and shovels. The benefits of a community garden would be numerous. Residents would have access to land to garden they might not otherwise have. They would be part of a worthwhile and rewarding community activity that would allow them to meet other residents who love gardening and who might have excellent gardening skills and hints to share. Additionally, a community garden would be a wonderful oasis in the middle of our busy town where residents can come to walk, sit, or just enjoy the company of neighbors in a lush and friendly setting.

Or, the writer could use the second-person point of view to express the same ideas:

Paragraph B

Imagine how wonderful it would be if you had access to a community garden. Rather than gardening in isolation, you would come together in an appealing designated spot to plant a bountiful garden. You would be given a plot of land within the large garden to plant as you see fit. You could plant flowers, vegetables, herbs, or any other greenery you desire. The requirement would be that you spend at least one hour in the garden every week and that you bring a few gardening implements to share, such as watering cans, gardening gloves, fertilizer, and shovels. The benefits of a community garden would be numerous. You would have access to land to garden you might not otherwise have. You would be part of a worthwhile and rewarding community activity that would allow you to meet other residents who love gardening and who might have excellent gardening skills and hints to share. Additionally, a community garden would be a wonderful oasis in the middle of our busy town where you can come to walk, sit, or just enjoy the company of neighbors in a lush and friendly setting.

Did you notice the differences between the paragraphs? What pronouns does each paragraph use?

4. Paragraph A uses
 a. first-person pronouns (*I, we*).
 b. second-person pronouns (*you*).
 c. third-person pronouns (*he, she, they*).

5. Paragraph B uses
 a. first-person pronouns (*I, we*).
 b. second-person pronouns (*you*).
 c. third-person pronouns (*he, she, they*).

Paragraph A uses the third person (**c**), while paragraph B uses the second person (**b**). Now, which paragraph do you find more convincing? Most people would be more convinced by paragraph B. Why?

6. Paragraph B seems more convincing because
 a. *you* puts the readers into the action of the paragraph.
 b. *you* makes readers pay more attention.
 c. *you* makes readers imagine themselves in that situation.
 d. all of the above.

The second-person point of view does all of these things (**d**), and that's why it is often more convincing than the other points of view. The second-person point of view puts you, the reader, directly into the situation. As soon as you read the word *you*, you start to pay extra attention because the writer is addressing you directly. And you can't help but imagine yourself enjoying the benefits of a community garden because the writer puts you in each scenario. The writer of this paragraph knows that if you imagine yourself in these situations, you are much more likely to see the benefits of a community garden.

Summary

You can see by now how important point of view is in writing, for each point of view creates a certain effect. Sometimes, it brings the reader and the writer closer together; sometimes, it pushes them apart. Sometimes, it makes an argument more convincing through third-person objectivity; sometimes, an argument is more convincing through second-person involvement; and sometimes, it's more convincing through first-person intimacy. Writers choose their points of view carefully in order to create a certain relationship both with their ideas and with the reader.

TIP

Omniscient point of view occurs when an outside narrator discusses the thoughts of the characters in the story. **Limited point of view** is when one character tells the story, thereby limiting the retelling and interpretation of events to his or her perspective and personal bias.

One way to experiment with point of view is to select a newspaper article in which a crime occurred and then retell the article from different perspectives: the police officer's perspective, the crime victim's perspective, the witnesses' perspectives, and the perspectives of other participants, such as the jury members.

12 ▶ DICTION: WHAT'S IN A WORD?

Words are, of course, the most powerful drug used by mankind.
—RUDYARD KIPLING, English author and poet (1865–1936)

LESSON SUMMARY

Today's lesson focuses on *diction*, the words writers choose to convey their meaning. The smallest change in choice of words can significantly change the tone and meaning of a passage. Today's lesson shows you how to pick up on the clues to meaning writers give through their choice of words.

What made Sherlock Holmes such a good detective? Was he just much smarter than everyone else? Did he have some sort of magical powers? Could he somehow see into the future or into the past? No, Sherlock Holmes was no medium or magician. So what was his secret?

His powers of observation.

You may recall that the introduction to this book talked about *active reading.* As an active reader, you should have been marking up the passages you've read in this book: identifying unfamiliar vocabulary, underlining key words and ideas, and recording your reactions and questions in the margin. But there's another part of active reading we haven't talked about: making observations.

Making Observations

Making observations means looking carefully at the text and noticing specific things about *how it is written.* You might notice, for example, the point of view the author has chosen. You could also notice

- particular words and phrases the writer uses.
- the way those words and phrases are arranged in sentences and paragraphs.
- repeated word or sentence patterns.
- important details about people, places, and things.

When you make observations, you can then make valid *inferences.* As a matter of fact, you did this in Lesson 11, when you made assumptions about how the writer wanted to be perceived based on the point of view he or she used.

Observations and Inferences

Inferences, as you may recall, are conclusions based on reason, fact, or evidence. Good inferences come from good observations. The observations are the evidence for the inferences. Good inferences—ones based on careful observation—can help you determine meaning, as they helped Sherlock Holmes solve crimes.

To be better readers, then, we need to be more like Sherlock Holmes: We need to be better observers. In the story "The Adventure of the Blanched Soldier," Sherlock Holmes tells a client: "I see no more than you, but I have trained myself to notice what I see." You don't have to be Einstein to be a good reader; you just have to train yourself to notice what you see.

Observing Diction

Test your observation skills on these two sentences:

A. The town's new parking policy, which goes into effect on Monday, should significantly reduce traffic congestion on Main Street.

B. The town's draconian new parking policy, which goes into effect on Monday, should significantly reduce traffic congestion on Main Street.

You don't need Sherlock Holmes's magnifying glass to see the difference between sentence A and sentence B: B uses the words *draconian* and *new* to describe the parking policy, while A uses only *new.* (Review Lesson 3 if you've forgotten what *draconian* means.) Now that you have noticed this, why is it important?

1. What does sentence B tell you that sentence A doesn't?
   a. what type of policy is being discussed
   b. how the writer feels about the policy
   c. when the policy begins

The answer is **b.** Both sentences tell you that the policy is a new parking policy, and both say that the policy goes into effect on Monday. But sentence B, because it adds the word *draconian*, tells you how the writer *feels* about the new policy: He doesn't like it. His opinion is implied through his choice of the word *draconian.* Rather than directly saying, "I think the policy is very severe," the writer *suggests* or *implies* that this is the way he feels.

Denotation and Connotation

Now, suppose sentence A also had another adjective to describe the new policy:

A. The town's firm new parking policy, which goes into effect on Monday, should significantly reduce traffic congestion on Main Street.

B. The town's draconian new parking policy, which goes into effect on Monday, should significantly reduce traffic congestion on Main Street.

Do the two sentences now mean the same thing? Yes and no. Both *firm* and *draconian* suggest that the policy is strict, but each word has a specific implication or suggested meaning about *how* strict that policy is. A *firm* policy is not as strict as a *draconian* policy. Furthermore, *draconian* suggests that the policy is not only strict but unfairly or unreasonably so.

So, the words writers choose, even though they may mean the same thing when you look them up in the dictionary, actually have another level of meaning. This is called their connotation. *Connotation* is the implied meaning, the meaning that evolves when the dictionary definition (*denotation*) develops an emotional or social register or a suggestion of degree. The specific words writers choose—their *diction* or word choice—can therefore reveal a great deal about how authors feel about their subjects.

TIP

Homographs are words that are spelled alike but have greatly different meanings. When you look up a homograph in the dictionary you will find separate entries for each meaning of the word. For example: The talk show is filmed live in New York City," versus "I really want to live my life fully before I die."

For practice, look up the following homographs and use them in practice sentences:

- ellipses
- converse
- commune

How Diction Influences Meaning

Put your powers of observation to work on the following sentences. Read them carefully and then write down what you notice about each writer's specific choice of words. See if you can use the writers' diction to determine what they are inferring about the seriousness of the situation they are describing:

A. The political parties are meeting with the hope of clearing up their differences.

B. The political parties have entered into negotiations in an attempt to resolve their conflict.

Both sentences convey the same information: Two parties are meeting because they have a disagreement of some sort to address. But the differences in the diction of each sentence tell us that these two situations aren't exactly the same—or at least that the two writers have different perceptions about the situations. What differences did you notice between these two sentences? List them below (an example has been provided to get you started):

Your Observations:

> **Example:** *I noticed that sentence A says the political parties are "meeting," whereas sentence B says they "have entered into negotiations."*

Now that you've listed your observations, answer this question: In which sentence do you think the situation is more serious, and *why* do you think so? (The *why* is especially important.)

The difference in word choice should tell you that sentence B describes the more serious situation. Here are some of the observations you might have made about the writers' diction that would have told you so:

- The political parties in sentence B are not just "meeting," they've "entered into negotiations." This phrase is often used to describe disagreements between warring parties. And "negotiations" are much more formal than "meetings," suggesting that there is a serious difference to be resolved in sentence B.

- Whereas in sentence A they are ironing things out, the parties in sentence B only "attempt to" resolve the problems. This important difference suggests that the problem between the parties in sentence A is not that serious—the problem is likely to be resolved. In sentence B, on the other hand, "in an attempt" suggests that the problem is quite serious and that it will be difficult to resolve; the outlook is doubtful rather than hopeful.

- In sentence A, the parties are seeking to "clear up their differences," whereas in sentence B, the parties want to "resolve their conflict." The phrase "clear up" suggests that there is merely some sort of confusion between the two. However, "resolve" suggests that there is a matter that must be solved or settled, and "conflict" indicates a more serious problem than "differences."

TIP

Another style of language that influences meaning is **vernacular**. Vernacular is the style of language or native speech used in a particular geographical region. A person's vernacular can sometimes (but not always) indicate where he or she was raised or has lived most recently.

Vernacular is similar to diction in that a particular way of speaking might change the meaning of what is being said. For example, a person living in New York City and a person living in Texas could attempt to convey the same message, each using his or her regional language to write or verbalize their thoughts. If their vernaculars differ, the reader (or listener) would be provided with two messages that essentially mean the same thing, but that have been expressed in very different ways due to the speakers' geographical distance from one another.

Reading between the Lines

Looking at diction can be especially helpful when the writer's main idea isn't quite clear. For example, in the following paragraph—an excerpt from a letter of recommendation—the author doesn't provide a topic sentence that expresses the main idea. Instead, you must use your powers of observation to answer the question about how the author feels about the described employee.

Your Observations and Inferences:

Example: *I noticed that the writer says Nicole Bryan "usually" completes her work on time* (observation), *which suggests that Nicole Bryan is good but not perfect; she doesn't always get her work done on schedule* (inference).

Paragraph A

Nicole Bryan usually completes her work on time and checks it carefully. She is a competent lab technician and is familiar with several ways to evaluate test results. She has some knowledge of the latest medical research, which has been helpful.

2. What message does the writer of paragraph A convey about Nicole Bryan?
   a. Nicole Bryan is an exceptional employee. Hire her immediately!
   b. Nicole Bryan is an average employee. She doesn't do outstanding work, but she won't give you any trouble.
   c. Nicole Bryan is a lousy worker. Don't even think about hiring her.

To answer this question, you made an inference. Now, support your inference with specific observations about the language in this paragraph. Why do you think your answer is correct? (An example has been provided to get you started.)

The diction of the paragraph best supports choice **b**: The writer feels that "Nicole Bryan is an average employee. She doesn't do outstanding work, but she won't give you any trouble." You might have supported this inference with observations like these:

- The writer uses the word *usually* in the first sentence, which means that Nicole Bryan is good, but not great; she doesn't always meet deadlines.
- The writer describes Nicole Bryan as a "competent" lab technician. This tells us that Nicole Bryan does her work well enough for the position, but she is not exceptional. She could be better.
- The writer tells us that Nicole Bryan is "familiar with" several ways to evaluate test results. This means that she can do her work using those evaluation techniques, but she is no expert and does not know all there is to know about evaluating test results.
- The writer tells us that Nicole Bryan has "some knowledge of the latest medical research," which tells us that Nicole Bryan knows a little, but not a lot; again, she's better than someone who knows nothing, but she's no expert.

Now, take a look at a revised letter of recommendation. The diction (the word choice) has been changed so that the paragraph sends a different message. Read the paragraph carefully and determine how the writer feels about Nicole Bryan:

Paragraph B

Nicole Bryan always submits her work promptly and checks it judiciously. She is an excellent lab technician and has mastered several ways to evaluate test results. She has an extensive knowledge of the latest medical research, which has been invaluable.

3. What message does the writer of paragraph B convey about Nicole Bryan?
- **a.** Nicole Bryan is an exceptional employee. Hire her immediately!
- **b.** Nicole Bryan is an average employee. She doesn't do outstanding work, but she won't give you any trouble.
- **c.** Nicole Bryan is a lousy worker. Don't even think about hiring her.

This time, you should have selected choice **a**. The change in diction tells you that this writer thinks Nicole Bryan is a fantastic employee. To ensure the difference in word choice is clear, write the words used in paragraph B to replace the words in paragraph A. The first replacement has been filled in to get you started.

PARAGRAPH A	PARAGRAPH B
usually	always
on time	
carefully	
competent	
is familiar with	
some knowledge	
helpful	

Summary

Just as Sherlock Holmes learned to notice what he saw when he arrived at the scene of a crime, you can also learn to notice what you see when you look carefully at a piece of writing. By noticing the specific words a writer has chosen to use, you can help ensure that you fully comprehend the writer's message.

TIP

- Think about how you choose the words you use when you speak to people. Do you use different types of words for different people? Do you think carefully about what you say and which words you will use? How much are you aware of your own diction?
- Notice how much the meaning of a sentence can change when a single word is altered. Form a simple sentence, like: "Experts say the economy is unhealthy." Now, replace *unhealthy* with synonyms that have slightly different connotations, like: *sick, feeble, ill, dying, under the weather, feverish, infected*. Each word will express a slightly different attitude about your subject to the reader. Insert each of these words into your sentence and see how much the meaning is altered. (This exercise will work well if you choose words like *rich, tired, happy*, or *sad* that have many synonyms with a wide range of connotations.)

13 ▶ STYLE: IT'S NOT WHAT THEY SAY BUT HOW THEY SAY IT

Proper words in proper places mark the true definition of style.
—JONATHAN SWIFT, Irish satirist (1667–1745)

LESSON SUMMARY

How a writer puts words together to express meaning is as important as *what* the writer says. This lesson shows you how to analyze the style of a piece of writing in order to get a better understanding of what the writer means.

Style?" you ask. "What does style have to do with reading comprehension?"

Actually, style has a good deal to do with reading comprehension. Just as writers use different structures to organize their ideas and information, they also use different styles to express their ideas and information. Thus, the more aware you are of the elements of style, the more successfully you can determine a writer's purpose and understand his or her ideas.

Style is also important because it is often what attracts us to, or repels us from, certain writers or types of writing. Though an awareness of style might not make us change our taste, it can at least help us appreciate different writers and different styles.

What Is Style?

Style, in writing, generally consists of three elements:

1. Sentence structure
2. Degree of detail and description
3. Degree of formality

Diction is also an aspect of style, but because diction is so essential to meaning, it had its own lesson in this book (p. 95).

Sentence Structure

Looking at sentence structure means looking at the type of sentences the writer has used. Are they short, simple sentences? Are they long and complex, with a lot of clauses and phrases? Or does the writer use a mix? Does every sentence sound the same, or is there variety in the word order and structure? Is the complexity or simplicity of the sentences at the right level for the intended readers?

Read the following sentences and then answer the questions that describe their sentence structure.

A. The meeting began. Mr. Thomas described the policy. Then, Mr. Underwood spoke in favor of it. Afterward, Ms. Villegas spoke against it.
B. After the meeting, when everyone had already left the room, Ms. Villegas stayed behind to speak with Mr. Thomas. She carefully explained her position on the new policy, hoping she'd get him to change his mind.

1. Which version uses simple sentences?
   a. version A
   b. version B

2. Which version uses the same sentence structure throughout?
   a. version A
   b. version B

3. Which version uses complex sentences?
   a. version A
   b. version B

4. Which version varies the sentence structures, using different kinds of sentences?
   a. version A
   b. version B

You probably noticed that version A is the one that uses simple sentences with essentially the same sentence structure throughout. (You might also have noticed that these sentences sound rather dull because they are so simple and unvaried.) In version B, the sentences are far more complex with more variation in their structure.

Degree of Detail and Description

When you look at degree of detail and description, ask two things:

1. How specific is the author? Does she write "dog" (general) or "Labrador retriever" (specific detail)? Does she write "some" (general) or "three and a half pounds" (specific detail)?
2. How much description does the author provide? Does he write "Mr. B is my manager" (nondescriptive) or "Mr. B, my manager, is a tall man with piercing eyes and a mustache" (descriptive)? Or, does he go even further: "Mr. B, my manager, is six foot ten with eyes that pierce like knives and a mustache like a caterpillar" (very descriptive)?

Try your hand at deciding whether words are specific and descriptive, or general and nondescriptive.

5. Which of the following word(s) or phrases are more specific and descriptive? Underline them. Which words or phrases are more general and nondescriptive? Circle them.

    a. car

    b. red 1968 Ford

    c. on the corner of 58th and Broadway

    d. on the corner

Choices **b** and **c** are the more specific and descriptive ones, while choices **a** and **d** are more general and nondescriptive.

Degree of Formality

The *degree of formality* of a piece of writing has to do with how formal or casual the writer's language is. For example, does the writer use slang as if speaking to a friend, or jargon (specific, technical language) as if speaking to colleagues? Does the writer address the reader by his or her first name (casual), or by his or her title (formal)?

6. Which sentences are more informal? Underline them. Which are more formal? Circle them.

    a. Let's get together after work on Thursday.

    b. We kindly request that you join us for a social gathering at the close of business on Thursday.

    c. These figures indicate the sales have increased significantly.

    d. Sales are up!

Sentences **a** and **d** are more informal, and sentences **b** and **c** are more formal.

How the Three Elements of Style Work Together

Look at how these three elements of style work together in the two following letters. Both convey essentially the same information, but they are written in radically different styles. Read the letters carefully and then list your observations. What do you notice that's different between these two letters?

Letter A

Lucy:

Listen, a while ago, I ordered some invitations from your website. I haven't gotten them yet. What happened? Where are they? Find out! I need them!

—Isabel

Letter B

Dear Ms. Mirabella:

Three weeks ago, on April 14, I rush ordered two boxes of personalized party invitations from your website (Order #123456). To date, I have not received my order. Please look into this matter immediately, as I am in dire need of this product.

Sincerely,

Ms. Lindsey

What did you notice about these two letters? How are they different? Consider sentence structure, degree of description and detail, and degree of formality. List your observations in the space below (an example has been provided to get you started):

Your Observations:

Example: *I notice that letter A addresses the reader as "Lucy," whereas letter B addresses her as "Ms. Mirabella."*

Now, answer the following questions:

7. Which letter is more formal?
  a. letter A
  b. letter B

8. Which letter seems to have been written by someone who knows the recipient well?
  a. letter A
  b. letter B

9. In which letter is the sentence structure more complex?
  a. letter A
  b. letter B

10. Which letter is more descriptive and detailed?
  a. letter A
  b. letter B

You probably noticed immediately the difference in degree of formality between these two letters. Letter A is written in a very casual style, as if the writer knows the reader very well and therefore does not need to use a professional approach. Our first clue to this casual relationship is the way the letter is addressed. Letter A addresses the reader as "Lucy," while letter B begins with a formal "Dear Ms. Mirabella." The same difference can be seen in the closing of the letters: "Isabel" vs. "Sincerely, Ms. Lindsey."

The (in)formality of each relationship is also reflected in the sentence structure and degree of description and detail. You probably noticed, for example, that letter A uses short, choppy sentences, and exclamation points, which make the letter sound less formal, more urgent, and more demanding. The writer also uses casual words like "listen" so that the writing sounds conversational. On the other hand, letter B uses longer, more complex sentences to make the letter sound more formal and sophisticated.

At the same time, you may have noticed that letter A does not provide the kind of specific information that letter B does. Letter A tells us the writer placed an order for "some invitations" "a while ago," but letter B tells us the order was placed "three weeks ago, on April 14" and that the order was for "two boxes of personalized party invitations." The fact that letter A does not provide specific details is further evidence that the reader knows the writer very well, for the writer doesn't have to provide specific details. Furthermore, in letter A, the writer uses a command—"Find out!"—whereas in letter B, the writer *asks,* rather than demands, that the matter be looked into. This politeness reflects a professional distance between writer and reader.

In business, as in most writing, the audience usually determines the writer's style. The writer of letter A is probably capable of writing in the style of letter B, but because she has a casual relationship with her reader, she doesn't need to use a formal style.

TIP

An **idiom** is a regional or cultural expression that is used to add style and color to a story. Since the language is often figurative rather than literal it can sometimes be hard to figure out the meaning. It's best to use a dictionary or reference book if you're stumped by what appears to be an illogical or confusing phrase or expression.

- ***Don't air your dirty laundry in public*** means that you should not discuss embarrassing personal matters publicly, just as you would not want to air your dirty clothing on a clothesline for the entire world to see!
- "Mr. Simmons is giving a final exam tomorrow, so his students will be ***burning the midnight oil*** tonight" means that his students will be staying up late studying for the exam. This expression dates back to an earlier time when would need to burn oil in a lamp if you stayed up late reading or working.

The Effect of Description and Detail

In business, what some people call "flowery" style—lots of description and detail—is almost never appropriate. Why? Because in business, as they say, "time is money," so readers don't want to spend time reading lengthy descriptions or extensive detail. They just want the facts: when the meeting will be held and where; what the new product is designed to do and how much it costs; how the new training manual is coming along. In most cases, the more straightforward, the better.

Other times, however, when they want readers to imagine a situation or to experience something through language, writers need a "flowery" style. That is, they need a high degree of description and detail. The following two passages show the difference. Both describe the same appointment, but in two very different styles. One is written in a style appropriate to business and records only the facts. The other describes the meeting in a style appropriate for general readers interested in the feelings of the people involved.

Passage A

Yesterday at 10:00 A.M., Mark Spencer held a press conference. Eleanor Cartwright was present as well. Mr. Spencer talked about upcoming events at the Smithfield Museum of Art, where he is Director. Then he announced that Eleanor Cartwright had just been appointed Director of Development. This new position was created due to the planned building of a new wing, which will house the significant art collection that was donated to the Smithfield Museum last year. Mr. Spencer outlined Ms. Cartwright's qualifications and introduced her to the press. She discussed plans for the new wing, and she also took several questions from reporters before the press conference ended.

Passage B

Yesterday at 10:00 A.M., Mark Spencer, the popular Director of the Smithfield Museum of Art, held a press conference. The room was buzzing with reporters as Mr. Spencer took the podium. Standing to his right was a striking woman in a crimson suit. Mr. Spencer first discussed the soon-to-be-launched artist-in-residence program as well as the upcoming annual fundraising dinner, which has been the hottest ticket in town ever since Mr. Spencer came to the Smithfield.

The room was thick with curiosity as Mr. Spencer turned toward the mysterious woman and invited her to join him at the podium. Mr. Spencer then spoke in an excited and genuine tone, "I'm delighted to introduce to you the new Director of Development of the Smithfield Museum, Ms. Eleanor Cartwright." Mr. Spencer explained that this position was created due to the building of the new wing, for which construction is scheduled to start soon. The wing will house the impressive and significant art collection of Mr. and Mrs. Martin Buckner, which was donated to the museum last year. Mr. Spencer listed Ms. Cartwright's impressive credentials as the reporters hung on every word. Finally, Ms. Cartwright took the podium and wowed everyone with details about the new wing. She also took several questions. By the time she was done, everyone in attendance was charmed by her wit and sophistication, and they left the room convinced that the Smithfield Museum, once barely known, was truly becoming a major force in the art world.

Now, write down your observations about these two passages below. How are these two versions different? What did you notice about the sentence structure? About the degree of description and detail? About the degree of formality?

Your Observations:

Example: *I noticed that version B is almost twice as long as version A.*

Now, use your observations to answer the following questions:

11. Which version tells you more about Mark Spencer?
   a. passage A
   b. passage B

12. Which version tells you more about Eleanor Cartwright?
   a. passage A
   b. passage B

13. Which version is more objective?
   a. passage A
   b. passage B

14. Which version makes you feel excited about Eleanor Cartwright's appointment?
   a. passage A
   b. passage B

You noticed, of course, that passage B is much more descriptive than passage A—it tells you more about both Mark Spencer and Eleanor Cartwright. Passage A just provides the facts—specific details, but no description. Passage A is very objective. We do not learn anything about Mark Spencer other than his job title. For example, we don't know how people feel about him. In passage A, we also learn very little about Eleanor Cartwright other than her new job. We don't know what she looks like or how people in the room respond to her.

Passage B, however, tells us about Mark Spencer's reputation ("popular" and responsible for making the annual fundraising dinner "the hottest ticket in town"). Passage B also provides many details about Eleanor Cartwright ("striking woman in a crimson suit," "impressive credentials"). We also learn a good deal about the general tone of the room and how this announcement was received ("the room was buzzing,"

"reporters hung on her every word," "they left the room convinced that the Smithfield Museum, once barely known, was truly becoming a major force in the art world"). All these details help us feel something about the announcement and the people involved because the characters and the situation are presented visually; we can almost see what happens.

Summary

Style, as you can see, is an important aspect of reading comprehension. It can tell us about the writer's relationship to the reader; it can distance us with its objectivity or draw us in with its description and detail. As readers, we tend to react strongly to style, often without knowing why. But now you do know why, and you can use that knowledge to help you understand what you read.

TIP

- As you come across sentences or paragraphs written in different styles, see how they would sound if the style were altered. Change the level of formality, the degree of description and detail, or the sentence structure to create a new style.
- Do you have a favorite author? Take a second look at a particularly memorable work by this author, paying close attention to the style elements at work. If you are a Jane Austen fan, pick out features that make her novels enjoyable for you. Do you like her degree of formality, the way she uses detail to describe fancy parties, or the way she varies her sentence structure? After you've taken a close look at this work, try your own hand at it. Can you write a letter to a friend in the same style that Jane Austen would have? How about Ernest Hemingway or Stephen King?

14 ▶ HOW THEY SAY IT, PART TWO: TONE

Go three days without reading and your speech will become tasteless.

—Chinese proverb

LESSON SUMMARY
The way you perceive a person's tone of voice has a great deal to do with how you understand what that person is saying. The same is true of tone in writing; it's vital to pick up on clues to tone in order to understand a written piece fully. This lesson shows you how.

Say this word out loud: "Sure."

How did you say it? Did you say it with a smile, as in "Sure, anytime"? Or did you say it flatly, as if responding to a command? Or did you stretch the word out, "*Suuuurre*," as if you didn't believe what someone just said? Or did you ask it, as in, "Are you *sure* this is okay?"

Perhaps you didn't realize there were so many ways to say this one single word, *sure*. But there are. Why? The word itself isn't different; its denotation (dictionary meaning) isn't different; so how can the same word express so many different things?

The difference in the meaning of all these *sures* comes from the tone—how you say the word, and thus how your listeners will feel when they hear you say it.

When you speak and listen, you can hear the tone of your voice as well as the tone of the person to whom you are speaking. But how do you catch tone in writing? How do you know how the writer wants his or her words to sound? "Sure" by itself doesn't tell us whether you should whisper or shout it. You need to look at the context surrounding that word to find clues about the proper tone to use.

Think about how tone is created in speech. When you say "sure," the tone changes according to how loudly or softly you say the word and how slowly or quickly you say it. Tone is also conveyed (or supported) by the speaker's expressions and body language. In writing, of course, you do not have these visual resources, but you do have plenty of clues to help you determine tone. Those clues come from the elements of language and style that you've studied so far: point of view, diction, and style.

How Tone Influences Meaning

It may help you to think of a sentence as a collection of ingredients (words and phrases) that result in a dish (idea). These elements of language and style are like the spices that you need to give that sentence a certain flavor. Different spices will result in a different flavor (tone).

Look at the following two letters. Both convey essentially the same information, but they have two rather different tones.

Letter A
Dear Client:

Thank you for your letter. We will take your suggestion into consideration. We appreciate your concern.

Letter B
Dear Valued Customer:

Thank you for your recent letter regarding our refund policy and procedure. We are taking your suggestion quite seriously and truly appreciate your concern.

Which of these letters has a more positive tone? As you can see, letter B is more positive. Why? What do you notice about letter B that is different from letter A? List your observations below:

Example: *I noticed that letter A is addressed "Dear Client," while letter B is addressed "Dear Valued Customer."*

Perhaps you noticed that letter B uses key words like "*valued* customer" and "*truly* appreciate." Letter B also refers to the specific contents of the reader's letter, thus letting the reader know that his or her letter has been read. Furthermore, letter B tells the reader not just that the company "will take your suggestion into consideration"—which sounds a bit like an empty promise—but that the writers are taking the suggestion "quite seriously."

You may also notice that the sentences in letter B are longer than those in letter A, whose sentences are shorter and somewhat choppy. If you read those short sentences out loud, how do they sound? They're not very inviting, are they? They sound somewhat mechanical and empty of any feeling.

Use your observations to answer the following questions.

1. The tone of letter A is best classified as
a. sincere.
b. complimentary.
c. indifferent.

Choice **c**, indifferent, best describes the tone of letter A. There is no indication that the writers of letter A have actually read their client's letter, so there's no indication that they plan to take the client's suggestion seriously. They are indifferent to it. Also, the sentence structure indicates that the writers have not put much thought into writing this letter; as a result, the sentences sound abrupt and even unappreciative.

2. The tone of letter B is best classified as
a. cheerful.
b. sincere.
c. apologetic.

In contrast to letter A, the writers of letter B are sincere, choice **b**. They know exactly what their customer wrote about—there's the importance of specific details again! They've also taken the time to individualize the letter, and they've added words that show they value their customer and their customer's feedback.

Varieties of Tone

Just as there are endless varieties of tone when we speak, there are endless varieties of tone in writing.

Here's a short list of some of the more common words used to describe a writer's tone:

cheerful	sarcastic
complimentary	ironic
hopeful	wistful
sad	foreboding
gloomy	playful
apologetic	sincere
critical	insincere
insecure	authoritative
disrespectful	threatening
humorous	indifferent

If any of these terms are unfamiliar to you, please look them up in a dictionary now.

TIP

One way to identify an author's tone is to read several passages aloud. Listen carefully to the tone of your voice as you read, since tone is reinforced by the author's use of sentence structure and word choice: Does your voice sound as if you are upbeat and happy, or do you sound rushed, critical, or angry?

- What type of tone does a smoothly flowing, medium-length sentence with positive upbeat words convey?
- What type of tone does a short, choppy sentence filled with dark imagery convey?

Practice

Now look at several sentences and paragraphs to see if you can correctly identify their tone. As you read them, think of how the paragraphs sound. You may even want to read them out loud. With what kind of voice do you read? What's your tone? Use your instincts, as well as your observations, to choose the correct tone for each paragraph. Answers and explanations come immediately after the practice paragraphs.

3. Mr. Jones, since you obviously appear to know everything, would you like to come up here and teach this class for me?
   a. sarcastic
   b. critical
   c. disrespectful

4. Did you see what he just did? My goodness!
   a. insecure
   b. humorous
   c. surprised

5. Your essay? Oh, it was just fabulous. Really, I've never seen anything like it.
   a. insincere
   b. critical
   c. disrespectful

6. This is one of the best essays I've ever seen. It's clear, concise, and convincing.
   a. complimentary
   b. wistful
   c. hopeful

7. Bill had stayed up all night preparing for this presentation. He had everything ready: charts, graphs, lists, statistics. This was the biggest meeting of his career. He was ready. He smiled as the cab pulled up to 505 Park Avenue, and he gave the taxi driver an extra large tip. He entered the building confidently and pushed #11 on the elevator. Suddenly, as the doors of the elevator closed, he realized that he had left his briefcase in the cab.
   a. cheerful
   b. ironic
   c. critical

Answers

3. a. Since it is generally understood that students don't "know everything," it is clear that the teacher doesn't mean what she says in a literal sense. Teachers are there to instruct students because the students need to learn from their teacher. Therefore, the teacher is using sarcasm to point out that the student isn't listening to instruction because he or she feels they have nothing to learn from the teacher.

4. c. The exclamation mark that follows the question is a clue revealing that the observer is surprised. Exclamation points are often used to denote surprise.

5. a. Because of the opening question and because the next sentences are so vague, a reader can assume that the writer either hasn't read the essay or didn't like it. Also, *really* indicates that the writer is afraid the reader won't be convinced by the statement, so he tries to emphasize it. Furthermore, "I've never seen anything like it" isn't necessarily a compliment—it could really mean many different things, not all of them good.

6. a. Unlike question 5, this paragraph really is complimentary. The writer specifies three things that make the reader's essay exceptional: It's "clear, concise and convincing." The use of more specific adjectives makes this writer's praise seem sincere.

7. b. *Irony* is the mood created when things happen in a manner that is opposite of what was expected to happen. Here, Bill had prepared diligently for the big meeting and had everything ready. But contrary to his expectations of having a very successful presentation, he had no presentation at all because he left his materials in the cab. The irony is heightened by his confidence.

Summary

An ability to determine tone is an essential component of reading comprehension. Often, writers will let their tone convey their meaning, so you need to look carefully for clues in their language and style to determine how writers want their words to sound.

TIP

When you want to define an author's tone, think about the author's use of imagery. When you think about the imagery in Edgar Allan Poe's works, do you visualize stormy nights and menacing black ravens, or chirping robins and bright sunny days? If you answered yes to the former description, you are correct, because with very few exceptions, Poe's tone is mysterious and dark.

15 ▶ WORD POWER: PUTTING IT ALL TOGETHER

The limits of my language mean the limits of my world.
—LUDWIG WITTGENSTEIN, Austrian philosopher (1889–1951)

LESSON SUMMARY

This lesson pulls together what you've learned in Lessons 11–14, as well as in previous lessons. It shows you how to use point of view, diction, style, and tone to understand what a writer means.

You've learned a lot this week about language and how much it affects meaning. Before you add this information to the knowledge you already have about structure and the basics of reading comprehension, take a minute for a brief review of the last four lessons. It's always a good idea to stop and review material you've learned before you go on to new material.

Review: Language and Style

Point of view is the perspective from which the writer speaks. Sometimes, writers use the first-person point of view (*I, me, my, we, our, us*) to express their personal feelings and experiences directly to the reader. This point of view creates a sense of intimacy between the reader and the narrator because it expresses an extremely subjective perspective. When writers use the second-person point of view, they address the reader directly by using the pronoun *you*. This point of view is often used to give directions and to make the reader feel directly involved in the action described by the writer. The third-person point of view is the objective perspective of a "third person," someone who is not directly involved in the action or ideas expressed in the passage. This point of view establishes a distance between the reader and writer and uses the pronouns *he, his, him; she, hers, her; it, its*; and *they, them*, and *their*.

Diction refers to the specific words chosen by the author to express his or her ideas. Because words have both a *denotation* (exact or dictionary meaning) and a *connotation* (implied or suggested meaning), as well as an emotional register, the words an author chooses are very significant. Authors, like politicians, must choose their words carefully to express exactly the right idea with exactly the right impact.

Style is the manner in which writers express their ideas in writing. Style is composed of three main elements: sentence structure, degree of description and detail, and degree of formality. Some writers use a very formal style; others may write in a casual style. Certain styles are best for particular audiences or purposes. For example, a high degree of formality with specific details but without any unneccessary description would be appropriate for business, where time is money and writers should get to the point as quickly as possible.

Finally, *tone* is the mood or attitude conveyed by the writing. Tone is created by a combination of point of view, diction, and style. Tone is extremely important in determining meaning because as we noted, a word as simple as *sure* can have many different meanings depending upon the tone in which it is said. To determine the tone, you have to look for clues as to how the writer wants his or her words to sound.

Practice

In today's practice, you'll combine these aspects of language with everything else you've learned in this book about reading comprehension:

- finding the facts
- determining the main idea
- determining vocabulary meaning through context
- distinguishing facts and opinions
- chronological order
- cause and effect
- compare and contrast
- order of importance

Practice Passage 1

Begin with a paragraph someone might see in a local newspaper: a profile of a town figure. Read the paragraph carefully, marking it up as you go, and write your observations in the space provided.

Ms. Crawford has been a model citizen since she moved to Springfield in 1985. She started out as a small business owner and quickly grew her business until it was one of the major employers in the region. In 1991, her company was profiled in *Business Week* magazine. Her innovative business model includes a great deal of community work and fundraising, the rewards of which have brought deep and lasting benefits to Springfield and its citizens. Today, she is being honored with Springfield's Citizen of the Century Award to honor all her cutting-edge efforts on behalf of our community.

Your Observations:

Now answer the following questions:

1. Ms. Crawford's company was profiled in *Business Week*
   a. in 1985.
   b. in 1991.
   c. today.

2. Which sentence best sums up the main idea of the paragraph?
   a. Ms. Crawford is very smart.
   b. Ms. Crawford is a dedicated citizen.
   c. Springfield would be nowhere without Ms. Crawford.

3. "Ms. Crawford has been a model citizen since she moved to Springfield in 1985" is a
   a. fact.
   b. opinion.
   c. point of view.

4. Innovative means
   a. helpful.
   b. remarkable.
   c. inventive.

5. This paragraph is organized according to what structure?
   a. cause and effect
   b. compare and contrast
   c. chronological order

6. This paragraph uses what point of view?
   a. first-person point of view
   b. second-person point of view
   c. third-person point of view

Answers

1. a. The passage states, "In 1991, her company was profiled in *Business Week* magazine."

2. b. While it does seem that Ms. Crawford must be very smart since she has been so successful, that is not the main idea that governs the whole paragraph. Instead, the paragraph highlights her dedication to the town and local community since she moved there. Choice **c** can't be correct because although the paragraph indicates that Ms. Crawford is very valuable, it does not say that Springfield would be nowhere without her. This is an inference you might make but cannot support.

3. b. Although the sentence does contain fact (Ms. Crawford moved to Springfield in 1985), the sentence makes an assertion about those years since 1985: Ms. Crawford has been a model citizen all those years. This is an assertion, an opinion that needs evidence. The rest of the paragraph provides that evidence.

4. c. The best clue to determine the meaning of this word is found in the last sentence, which says that Ms. Crawford is being honored for "all her cutting-edge efforts on behalf of our community." Since her efforts on behalf of the community have been *cutting-edge*, we can assume that her business model, which includes a great deal of community work and fundraising and is described as *innovative,* must also be *cutting-edge.* Therefore, the definition of *innovative* must be similar to *cutting-edge,* so the likely choice is *inventive.*

5. c. The paragraph follows Ms. Crawford's contribution to the community from the time she moved to Springfield in 1985 to the present.

6. c. This paragraph uses the objective third-person point of view. There is no *I* or *we* (first person) or *you* (second person), and the only pronouns the paragraph uses are the third-person pronouns *she* and *her*.

How did you do? If you got all six answers correct, good work. This table shows you which lesson to study for each question you missed.

IF YOU MISSED:	THEN STUDY:
Question 1	Lesson 1
Question 2	Lesson 2
Question 3	Lesson 4
Question 4	Lesson 3
Question 5	Lesson 6
Question 6	Lesson 11

Practice Passage 2

Now try another paragraph. Don't forget to mark it up as you read and make observations. Pay special attention to language and style.

There will be dire consequences for residents if a shopping mall is built on the east side of town. First, the shopping mall will interfere with the tranquil and quiet atmosphere that we now enjoy. Second, the mall will attract a huge number of shoppers from a variety of surrounding areas, which will result in major traffic congestion for those of us who live here. But most importantly, to build the shopping mall, many of us will be asked to sell our homes and relocate, and this kind of displacement should be avoided at all costs.

7. The main idea of this passage is that the shopping mall would
   a. be great for the community.
   b. not change things much.
   c. be bad for the community.

8. *Displacement* is a good word choice because
   a. it is compatible with general reading level and the formal writing style of the article.
   b. the writer likes to impress readers by using big words.
   c. it is the only word that is suitable or appropriate.

9. This passage is organized
   a. in chronological order.
   b. by cause and effect.
   c. by order of importance.
   d. both **a** and **c**
   e. both **b** and **c**

10. This passage uses which point of view?
   a. first person
   b. second person
   c. third person

11. This passage is written from whose perspective?
   a. that of the residents
   b. that of an outside consultant
   c. that of the shopping mall developer

12. The choice of the word *dire* suggests that the consequences of the merger would be
   a. minimal.
   b. expected.
   c. disastrous.

13. Which words best describe the style of this passage?

    a. informal, conversational

    b. descriptive, story-like

    c. formal, businesslike

14. The tone of this passage is

    a. sad.

    b. foreboding.

    c. threatening.

Answers

7. c. The first sentence is the topic sentence, which establishes that the shopping mall will be bad for residents of the town. The remaining sentences support that idea.

8. a. The style of the article is businesslike and formal, and is targeted to a sophisticated reader who would be capable of understanding a word such as displacement. Therefore, displacement is compatible with the style of the article. Choices b and c are not correct. The words remove, move, or *replace* are less sophisticated, less formal word choices and therefore would not be preferred word choices for this article even though they communicate the intended concept. The writer is not attempting to impress the reader by choosing words based solely on their length, or to create an impression of superiority.

9. e. The writer warns the readers of the effects that a shopping mall will have on residents of the town and arranges those effects in order of importance, saving the most important effect for last.

10. a. The first-person point of view is reflected in the use of the pronouns *us* and *we*.

11. a. The writer says that the shopping mall will have "dire consequences" for the residents and then uses the pronouns *us* and *we*— which identifies the writer with the residents—when listing those dire consequences.

12. c. The effects the writer includes here are all very serious, especially the third effect— displacement. The writer has chosen the word *dire* to emphasize that seriousness.

13. c. The passage avoids any unnecessary description or details and uses formal rather than casual language.

14. b. Each sentence explains a negative effect that the shopping mall will have on the residents and the negativity of this passage is heightened by the word *dire* and the phrase *avoided at all costs*. Though the shopping mall itself might be described as threatening, (choice **c**), the writer is not *threatening* anybody.

How did you do? Once again, congratulations if you got them all correct. If not, this table tells you what to do.

IF YOU MISSED:	THEN STUDY:
Question 7	Lesson 2
Question 8	Lesson 3
Question 9	Lessons 7 and 9
Question 10	Lesson 11
Question 11	Lesson 11
Question 12	Lesson 12
Question 13	Lesson 13
Question 14	Lesson 14

TIP

Acquaint yourself with different styles of writing and diction by comparing and contrasting articles in magazines targeted towards different audiences. Some types of magazines that you might want to explore are

- literary and small press magazines such as *Poetry*.
- regional magazines such as *Time Out New York*.
- news magazines such as *Time*.
- travel magazines such as *Culture & Travel*.
- research journals such as *The New England Journal of Medicine*.
- scientific magazines such as *Popular Science*.
- entertainment magazines such as *Entertainment Weekly*.
- special interest magazines such as *Vogue* and *American Photo*.
- business magazines such as *Business Week*.

What differences and/or similarities do you detect in the style and diction of the authors of the featured articles? Do you also notice differences and similarities in the style and diction of the advertising copy in those magazines?

READING BETWEEN THE LINES

Now that you've studied the way authors use structure and language to organize and express their ideas, you're ready to tackle more difficult passages: those in which the writers don't provide clear topic sentences or do not clearly indicate their intentions. To understand this type of text, you have to "read between the lines." This means you really have to put your observation skills to use and scour the passage for clues to meaning. Like Sherlock Holmes, you will really have to notice what you see.

By the end of this section, you should be able to

- determine an implied main idea.
- determine an implied cause or effect.
- distinguish between logical and emotional appeals.
- determine the theme of a piece of literature.

You'll look at a variety of texts, including some literature, and then put it all together in a review lesson.

16 ▶ FINDING THE IMPLIED MAIN IDEA

Don't tell me the moon is shining; show me the glint of light on broken glass.

—Anton Chekhov, Russian writer (1860–1904)

LESSON SUMMARY
This lesson shows you how to determine the main idea of a passage in which the writer has not provided a topic sentence or made the topic clear from the start.

Oh, the power of suggestion. Advertisers know it well—and so do writers. They know that they can get an idea across to their readers without directly saying it. Instead of providing a topic sentence that expresses their main idea, many times, they simply omit that sentence and instead provide a series of clues through structure and language to get their ideas across.

Finding an implied main idea is much like finding a stated main idea. If you recall from Lesson 2, a main idea is defined as an assertion about the subject that controls or holds together all the ideas in the passage. Therefore, the main idea must be general enough to encompass all the ideas in the passage. Much like a net, it holds everything in the passage together. So far, all but one of the passages in this book have had a topic sentence that stated the main idea, so finding the main idea was something of a process of elimination: You could eliminate the sentences that weren't general enough to encompass the whole passage. But what do you do when there's no topic sentence?

You use your observations to make an inference—this time, an inference about the main idea or point of the passage.

How to Find an Implied Main Idea

Finding an implied main idea requires you to use your observations to make an inference that, like a topic sentence, encompasses the whole passage. It might take a little detective work, but now that you know how to find details and how to understand word choice, style, and tone, you can make observations that will enable you to find main ideas even when they're not explicitly stated.

Practice Passage 1

For the first example of finding an implied main idea, let's look at a statement from a parking garage manager in response to recent thefts:

> Radios have been stolen from four cars in our parking garage this month. Each time, the thieves have managed to get by the parking garage security with radios in hand, even though they do not have a parking garage identification card, which people must show as they enter and exit the garage. Yet each time, the security officers say they have seen nothing unusual.

Now, there is no topic sentence in this paragraph, but you should be able to determine the main idea of this statement from the facts provided and from the tone. What does the statement suggest?

1. Which of the following best summarizes the statement's main idea?
   a. There are too many thefts in the garage.
   b. There are not enough security guards.
   c. There is something wrong with the security in the parking garage.

Answer

The correct answer is choice **c**, "There is something wrong with the security in the parking garage." How can you tell that this is the main idea? For one thing, it's the only one of the three choices general enough to serve as a "net" for the paragraph; choice **a** is implied only in the first sentence; and choice **b** isn't mentioned at all. In addition, each sentence on its own suggests that security in the parking garage has not been working properly. Furthermore, the word *yet* indicates that there is a conflict between the events that have taken place and the duties of the security officers.

Practice Passage 2

Now examine the following statement that a neighbor wrote about Mr. Miller, who owned one of the cars that was vandalized in the parking garage:

> Well, Mr. Miller's a pretty carefree person. I've borrowed his car on several occasions, and a few times, I've found the doors unlocked when I arrived at the garage. He often forgets things, too, like exactly where he parked the car on a particular day or where he put his keys. One time, I found him wandering around the garage looking for his keys, which he thought he had dropped on the way to the car, and it turned out the car door was unlocked anyway. Sometimes, I wonder how he remembers his address, let alone to take care of his car.

2. What is Mr. Miller's neighbor suggesting?
   a. Mr. Miller forgets everything.
   b. Mr. Miller may have left his car door unlocked the day the radio was stolen.
   c. Mr. Miller is too carefree for his own good.

Answer

You can attack the question this way: Which of these three statements do the sentences in the neighbor's statement support? Try a process of elimination. Do all of the sentences support choice **a**? If not, cross **a** out. Do all of the sentences support choice **b**? Choice **c**?

The correct answer is **b**, "Mr. Miller may have left his car door unlocked the day the radio was stolen." How can you tell? Because this is the only idea that all of the sentences in the neighbor's statement support. You know that Mr. Miller often doesn't lock his car doors; you also know that he often forgets things. The combination makes it likely that Mr. Miller left his car door unlocked on the day his car radio was stolen.

TIP

Good writers *show* you instead of *telling* you by using symbolism, metaphor, and other literary devices that help illustrate meaning. When working to find the main idea in a text, it's important to use your knowledge, logical thinking skills, and your own ideas to infer what symbols and other clues signify. Before concluding what the main idea is, be sure you can support your theories based on information presented in the text.

Practice Passage 3

Now look at a paragraph in which the *language* the writer uses is what enables you to determine meaning. Here is a description of Coach Lerner, a college basketball coach, written by one of his players. Read the paragraph carefully and see if you can determine the implied main idea of the paragraph.

Coach Lerner, my basketball coach, is six feet ten inches tall with a voice that booms like a foghorn and the haircut of a drill sergeant. Every morning, he marches onto the basketball court at precisely 8:00 and dominates the gymnasium for the next three hours. He barks orders at us the entire time and expects that we will respond like troops on a battlefield. And if we fail to obey his commands, he makes us spend another 45 minutes under his rule.

Before you decide on the implied main idea, list your observations. What did you notice about the language in this paragraph? An example is provided to get you started.

Your Observations:

Example: *I noticed that Coach Lerner's voice is compared to a foghorn.*

3. Which of the following best expresses the implied message of the passage?
   a. Playing on Coach Lerner's team is difficult.
   b. Playing on Coach Lerner's team is like being under the command of an army general.
   c. Coach Lerner is a terrible basketball coach.

Answer

The correct answer is choice **b**, "Playing on Coach Lerner's team is like being under the command of an army general." There are many clues in the language of this paragraph that lead you to this inference. First, you probably noticed that Coach Lerner's voice "booms like a foghorn." This comparison (called a *simile*) suggests that Coach Lerner wants his voice to be heard and obeyed.

Second, the description of Coach Lerner's haircut is a critical part of the way the author establishes the tone of this paragraph. To say that he has "the haircut of a drill sergeant" (also a *simile*) makes us think of a military leader whose job it is to train soldiers. A writer wouldn't use this comparison unless he or she wanted to emphasize military-like discipline.

The author tells us that Coach Lerner "marches onto the basketball court," "barks orders," and expects his players to respond like "troops on a battlefield." The writer could have said that Coach Lerner "strides" onto the court, that he barks "instructions," and that he expects his players to act like "trained dogs." However, since the author is trying to paint a picture of Coach Lerner that will bring to mind a military leader, he uses words that convey military ideas. Thus, though choices **a** and **c** may be true—it *might* be difficult to play for Coach Lerner and he *might* be a terrible basketball coach—choice **b** is the only idea that all of the sentences in the paragraph support.

Of course, this person's description of Coach Lerner is very subjective, since it uses the first-person point of view. As an active reader, you should wonder whether everyone sees Coach Lerner this way or if this player is unable to be objective.

Practice Passage 4

Many people find reading literature a difficult task because in literature (fiction, drama, and poetry), the main idea is almost never expressed in a clear topic sentence. Instead, readers have to look for clues often hidden in the language of the text. For example, the following fictional paragraph describes a character. Read it carefully, make your observations, and then identify the main idea of the paragraph:

> Every morning when Clara arrives at the gym, she is greeted with a buzz of warm hellos. She starts her workout in the weight room, where her exercise regimen is always peppered with lively chats with those around her. She then moves on to the pool, where she stops and converses with other friends and acquaintances before diving in and swimming laps. As she swims, her sole focus is the calming sound of her body gliding through the water—a rare moment in her always very social days.

Your Observations:

Example: *I noticed that Clara talks with many people.*

4. The main idea of this paragraph is that
   a. Clara is shy.
   b. Clara knows everyone at the gym.
   c. Clara is very friendly.

Answer

Although it is possible that **b** "Clara knows everyone at the gym" (choice **b**), there is no evidence in this paragraph to support that inference. Thus, choice **b** cannot be the main idea. Choice **a**, "Clara is shy," cannot

be the correct answer either, since everything in the paragraph suggests that Clara is, in fact, quite outgoing.

Furthermore, the language of the paragraph creates a feeling of warmth and friendliness: Clara is greeted with "warm hellos" and she has "lively chats" and conversations with friends and acquaintances. She also has "very social days." All these words work together in the paragraph to paint a picture of someone who is very friendly and social. Thus, without directly saying so, the writer tells us that, "Clara is very friendly," choice **c**.

Summary

Many writers use implication to convey meaning rather than directly stating their ideas. This is especially true in literature, where readers generally prefer suggestion to direct statements. Finding the implied main idea requires a little detective work, but it is not as difficult as you may have thought, now that you know more about language and the way words can be used to suggest ideas.

TIP

- Listen carefully to people today. Are there times when they *imply* things without directly saying them? Are there times when *you* use suggestion to get your ideas across? How do you do this? Be aware of how you and others use indirect language and suggestion to convey meaning.

- Write a paragraph that does not have a topic sentence. You should have a clear idea of the main idea before you write your paragraph and make sure your sentences use language that will help your readers understand your main idea. For example, think of a topic sentence about the kind of person you are, but don't write it down. Then, write several sentences that support your topic sentence with language that leads your reader to the proper conclusion. You may want to show your paragraph to others to see if they can correctly infer your main idea.

LESSON

17

ASSUMING CAUSES AND PREDICTING EFFECTS

Cause and effect are two sides of one fact.
—RALPH WALDO EMERSON, American philosopher
(1803–1882)

LESSON SUMMARY
Today's lesson focuses on how to determine cause and effect when they are only implied, rather than explicitly stated.

Have you ever regretted just "telling it like it is"? Many times, you can't come right out and say what you'd like, but like writers, you can get your ideas across through *implication* or inference.

This lesson focuses on two specific types of implication: reading between the lines to *determine cause* and reading between the lines to *predict effects*.

In case you need a reminder: A *cause* is the person or thing that makes something happen or produces an effect. An *effect* is the change that occurs as a result of some action or cause. Cause tells us why something happened; effect tells us what happened after a cause (or series of causes).

Determining Implied Causes

In order to see how to determine causes that are implied rather than stated, look at the following brief fictional passage. Read the passage carefully and actively. After you make your observations, see if you can use the writer's clues to determine why the characters are fighting.

Anne sat with her feet up on the couch, drinking a soda. She heard footsteps by the front door. Brenda was right on time, as usual. Never a minute early or late—for her, everything was very exact.

Anne placed her feet on the floor, reached for the remote, and turned off the television. She knew Brenda would demand her complete attention. She knew Brenda would hang up her coat in the closet by the door (third hanger from the left) and then head to the kitchen for her daily inspection (exactly seven steps). She knew this because they had been roommates for six months. Taking a deep breath, she thought about what she would say to Brenda. She waited and watched from her spot on the couch.

A moment later, Brenda stepped into the kitchen and surveyed the scene. Anne watched her expression, watched her eyes focus on the sink, and watched her face harden when she saw the dishes piled high. Pointing to the dishes, Brenda said disappointedly, "I don't believe what I'm seeing. I thought we agreed to share the responsibilities. I thought it was your turn to clean the kitchen this week?"

"I haven't gotten to them yet," Anne replied. "I've been really busy. Relax. I've got all night." She walked into the kitchen and added her empty glass to the top of the pile.

Brenda fumed. "You know I'm having company tonight! Somehow I thought you would have done your share in the kitchen. If we want to remain roommates, things have to change."

The phone rang, and Anne darted to answer it.

Brenda said in the background, "Tell them to call back; we need to settle this now. I told you I'm having company soon."

Anne ignored Brenda's comment and continued to engage in conversation with a good friend of hers. "Did I ever tell you about the time when . . ."

Look carefully at the dialogue between these two characters. What do they say to each other? How is it said? What other clues from the author can you find in this passage to help you understand the cause of their conflict? List your observations below and then answer the questions that follow.

Your Observations:

Example: *I noticed that Anne was relaxing and watching TV when Brenda arrived.*

1. Why does Brenda get angry?
   a. because Anne is unfriendly
   b. because she had a bad day at work
   c. because Anne didn't do the dishes

2. Why didn't Anne do the dishes?
   a. She had just arrived home.
   b. She wanted to start a fight.
   c. She wants Brenda to get a new roommate.

3. What does Anne do that shows she doesn't intend to shoulder her share of the responsibilities?

   a. She turns off the television.

   b. She begins to wash the dishes in the sink.

   c. She talks on the phone with a friend.

Answers

1. c. Brenda's face "hardens" with anger when she sees the dishes in the sink. You can tell she expects the kitchen to be clean when she comes home. Anne waits for Brenda to begin her "daily inspection," and when she walks in, she looks around the kitchen as if she's inspecting it. Then she sees the dishes and her face hardens. She asks why the dishes are still in the sink. Further, she reminds Anne about the company she is expecting.

2. b. You can tell Anne is not worried about Brenda's reaction because she is watching television instead of cleaning the kitchen. She knows Brenda is going to check the kitchen and that Brenda is going to be mad about the dishes when she sees them. As Anne waits, she thinks about what she is going to say to Brenda.

3. c. Anne's actions speak loudly. She answers the phone and discontinues a conversation that is important if the two of them intend to remain roommates.

> ### TIP
>
> Remember, in some stories the effect can be witnessed before the cause, while in other stories the cause is presented before the reader witnesses its effects.
>
> - Effect followed by cause: A withering natural landscape that has been badly damaged by environmental toxins is vividly described before the cause of the devastation is explained.
> - Effect followed by cause: A shattered window is discovered before the details about the cause of the breakage are revealed.
> - Cause followed by effect: A professor discovers that her student has been cheating on exams and files a disciplinary complaint the next day.
> - Cause followed by effect: A person starts eating extra portions of fast food and has to purchase larger pants to accommodate an expanding waistline.

Finding Implied Effects

Just as writers can imply cause, they can also suggest effects. In the practice passage you just read, Anne clearly had a specific goal. She purposely decided not to do the dishes in an act of rebellion. Why? You know a little bit about Anne and Brenda from the passage. Use that knowledge to answer the following question. What do you think Anne was hoping to achieve? What effect do you think she was looking for?

1. Brenda would do the dishes herself for once.

2. Brenda would get herself a new roommate.

3. Brenda would stop being so neat and so regimented.

How can you tell that number 3 is the best answer? You have to look carefully at the passage. Anne says, "Relax. I've got all night." But Brenda has her own priorities. She says she is expecting company. Anne responds by ignoring her and turning to a phone conversation.

The passage doesn't directly say so, but from these clues, you can conclude that Anne's personality is more relaxed than Brenda's. That's why she didn't do the dishes and that's also why she gladly took a phone call.

But will she get the effect she hoped for? Take another look at the passage, paying close attention to the end. What do you think? Will Anne get her wish? Will Brenda change her ways? Why do you think so?

Most likely, Anne won't get her wish. How can you tell? The end of the passage offers a strong clue. Brenda clearly wants to resolve the situation, but she can't compete with the telephone and probably not with Anne's relaxed personality.

Determining Implied Effects

In order to learn how to determine implied effects, take another look at Mr. Miller (the man who had a radio stolen from his car) and the parking garage where he parks. Reread the statement of the parking garage manager as well as the one from Mr. Miller's neighbor and then use these statements to predict how the robbery will affect Mr. Miller and the parking garage.

Parking garage manager
Radios have been stolen from four cars in our parking garage this month. Each time, the thieves have managed to get by the parking garage security with radios in hand, even though they do not have a parking garage identification card, which people must show as they enter and exit the garage. Yet each time, the security officers say they have seen nothing unusual.

Mr. Miller's neighbor
Well, Mr. Miller's a pretty carefree person. I've borrowed his car on several occasions, and a few times, I've found the doors unlocked when I arrived at the garage. He often forgets things, too, like exactly where he parked the car on a particular day or where he put his keys. One time, I found him wandering around the garage looking for his keys, which he thought he had dropped on the way to the car, and it turned out the car door was unlocked anyway. Sometimes, I wonder how he remembers his address, let alone to take care of his car.

Based on these two paragraphs, which of the following effects would be logical results (effects) of the thefts? Circle the correct answers.

1. Security will be tighter in the parking garage from now on.

2. People walking in and out of the garage will be required to show their identification cards with no exceptions.

3. The security officers will be fired.

4. Mr. Miller will get his radio back.

5. Mr. Miller will be more careful about locking his car door.

6. Mr. Miller will get a new car.

7. Some people who currently park in the garage will find a new garage where they park their cars.

8. Mr. Miller will be more careful with his keys.

Answers

Effects 1, 2, 5, 7, and 8 are logical predicted outcomes.

Effect 3 is not likely because it is too extreme; the parking garage manager's statement does not suggest that he plans to fire security guards. Rather, it suggests that he plans to look into the security problem.

There is nothing in either statement to suggest that effect 4 (Mr. Miller will get his radio back) is correct.

Finally, there is no reason at all to think that Mr. Miller will get a new car because his radio was stolen. He'll likely get a new radio and perhaps he'll look for a new parking garage, but there's no evidence from the two statements to suggest that a new car is a likely possibility.

Summary

In reading, particularly in reading literature, as well as in real life, you often have to figure out what the causes of a particular event or situation might have been. The same is true of effects: Both in reading and in life, you spend a lot of time trying to predict the outcomes of real or predicted actions or events. If you "read between the lines" without going too far beyond what the passage (or real-life event) actually contains, you can usually do a pretty good job of predicting these causes and effects.

> **TIP**
>
> When you are trying to determine the cause of a particular event or action, remember that there are various factors that influence the cause, including
>
> - social
> - emotional
> - cultural
> - environmental
> - economic
> - psychological
> - physical
> - religious
> - familial

18 ▶ EMOTIONAL VERSUS LOGICAL APPEALS

Let us read with method, and propose to ourselves an end to which our studies may point. The use of reading is to aid us in thinking.

—EDWARD GIBBON, English historian (1737–1794)

LESSON SUMMARY

Writers often appeal to your emotions to try to persuade you of something. But unless they also provide logical evidence to back up their claims, you have no *reason* to accept their argument as valid. This lesson helps you see how to distinguish between appeals to your emotions and appeals to your sense of reason.

magine that you are about to do something when someone runs up to you and says, "You can't do that!"

"Why not?" you ask.

"Because! You just can't, that's all."

Now, "Because!" is not likely to convince you that you shouldn't do what you were about to do, is it? Why not? Well, "Because!" does not provide you with a *reason* for not doing what you wanted to do. It is not, therefore, a very convincing argument.

The Difference between Logical and Emotional Appeals

When writers want to convince people of something or influence them to think a certain way, they generally rely on two means of persuasion: appealing to the reader's sense of logic and appealing to the reader's emotions. It is important to be able to distinguish between these two types of appeal because when writers rely *only* on appeals to emotion, they neglect to provide any real *evidence* for why you should believe what they say. Writers who rely solely on emotional appeals usually hope to get their readers so angry, scared, or excited that they will forget to look for reason or sense in the argument.

Unfortunately, many readers aren't aware of this strategy, so they may accept arguments that are unfounded, manipulative, or both. Political leaders who use the emotional strategy in speaking to crowds are called *demagogues*. Calling a leader a demagogue is no compliment, since it means that he or she relies on prejudice and passion rather than clear thinking to persuade people of his or her position. Sound reasoning requires that you are able to look beyond emotional appeals to determine if there is any *logic* behind them.

Logical: according to reason; according to conclusions drawn from evidence or good common sense

Emotional: relating to emotions; arousing or exhibiting strong emotion

While it is true that an appeal to emotions can help *strengthen* an argument based in logic, an argument cannot be valid if it is based solely on emotional appeal.

Distinguishing between Logical and Emotional Appeals

The best way to see the difference between logical and emotional appeals is to look at some examples. Actively read the passages that follow, trying to discern whether the author is appealing primarily to your sense of reason or to your emotions.

Practice Passage 1

The City Council of Ste. Jeanne should reject mandatory recycling. First, everyone knows that recycling doesn't really accomplish very much and that people who support it are mostly interested in making themselves *feel* better about the environment. They see more and more road construction and fewer and fewer trees and buy into the notion that sending bottles and cans to a recycling plant rather than a landfill will reverse the trend. Unfortunately, that notion is no more than wishful thinking.

Second, the proponents of mandatory recycling are the same people who supported the city's disastrous decision to require an increase in the number of public bus routes. After the mayor spent hundreds of thousands of dollars for the new buses and for street signs, bus shelters, and schedules, we all quickly learned that there was little to no interest in using public transportation among the people for whom the new routes were intended. Mandatory recycling would add yet another chapter to the book of wasteful government programs.

Finally, I'd like every citizen to answer this question in the privacy of his or her own heart: Would the mandatory recycling law really influence behavior? Or would most people, in fact, go on doing what they are doing now? That is, wouldn't the recyclers keep on recycling and the people who throw their bottles and cans in the trash continue to do just that (only being a little bit more careful, burying the bottles inside "legal" trash such as pizza boxes and coffee filters)? Why should any of us be forced to be surreptitious about something so simple as throwing away a soft drink can? I urge both the council and the mayor to reject this misguided proposal.

Chances are that no matter how you *feel* about mandatory recycling programs, this passage provoked a reaction in you. Perhaps you found some of the writer's arguments convincing; perhaps they simply made you want to argue back. But take another look at the passage. Is there any appeal to your sense of logic here—reason, evidence, or common sense? Or is the author only appealing to your preexisting ideas and feelings about environmentalism and government programs?

What Reasons Does the Writer Offer?

To help you see whether the writer's appeals are based on logic or emotion, break down her argument. The writer offers three different reasons for opposing the mandatory recycling proposal. List them here.

1.

2.

3.

You probably noticed that each of the three paragraphs deals with a different reason that the writer opposes the mandatory recycling program. They are:

1. Recycling programs do not help the environment, and people who support the mandatory recycling program do so simply in order to make themselves feel better about a declining environment.

2. The people who support mandatory recycling also supported a failed program to increase city bus routes.

3. A mandatory recycling program would not actually cause people who do not presently recycle to begin recycling.

Are the Appeals Logical?

The next step is to see if these reasons are *logical*. Does the author come to these conclusions based on reason, evidence, or common sense? If you look carefully, you will see that the answer is *no*. Each of the writer's arguments is based purely on emotion without any logic to support it.

Begin with the first reason: *Recycling programs do not help the environment and people who support the mandatory recycling program do so simply in order to make themselves feel better about a declining environment.* Is there any logic behind this argument? Is this statement based on evidence, such as poll data showing a link between feeling bad about the environment and supporting the program, or environmental reports showing that recycling doesn't improve the environment to any appreciable degree?

Regardless of whether you agree or disagree with this author, you can probably see that this argument is based only in emotion rather than in logic. The argument crumbles when you break it down. The author tries to blunt any skepticism about her argument by saying that "everyone knows" that recycling doesn't accomplish very much and that people support it mostly for selfish reasons. She states this as if it were an established fact, but she fails to establish it with evidence. Even though many people may agree, no one can correctly claim that everyone knows this to be true—as presented, it is mere opinion. In fact, many people would argue in turn that recycling does a great deal to help clean up the environment. And if the writer cannot say for a fact that recycling doesn't work, how can she convincingly assert that people support it for selfish reasons?

Even without this flaw, the writer's argument is not logical because there is no evidence in this essay that the particular mandatory recycling program being discussed by the city council will not work. The author moves from stating her opposition to the program in the first sentence to a paragraph of unconvincing generalities about recycling programs in general.

The author's second argument is that *the people who support mandatory recycling also supported a failed program to increase city bus routes.* Is there any logic in this statement? No, not if we bear in mind that the point of the argument is the recycling program and not the bus route program. Readers who are sympathetic to the underlying message that many government programs are wasteful may get caught up in the emotion of their opinion and lose sight of the fact that the author is not even talking about the proposed mandatory recycling plan. The argument is designed to succeed by appealing to this underlying sympathetic response rather than by addressing the merits and demerits of the proposal being considered.

The third argument is that *a mandatory recycling program would not actually cause people who do not presently recycle to begin recycling.* Again, the author offers no evidence for this claim. Instead, she works on her readers' sense of shame about their own failure to comply with local ordinances or on their cynicism about whether their fellow citizens will comply with such rules. She doesn't offer evidence that people won't comply, or that the law enforcement authorities will be ineffective in forcing compliance, instead suggesting that the proposed program would be an undue burden, forcing good people to act "surreptitious," or stealthy, about everyday, innocent actions. Again, she avoids supporting her argument with logic, reason, or evidence.

TIP

Certain words are sometimes used to communicate or reinforce *bias*, a person's individual opinion or interpretation of something. Biased words often illustrate the writer's emotions, and can also trigger emotions in a reader. Biased words are not rooted in fact. Instead, they convey judgment and personal belief. Here are some words that demonstrate bias:

- best
- favorite
- horrible
- awful
- mailman (this word is gender-biased, as it pertains only to the male sex)
- strange
- smart
- stupid

Practice Passage 2

Now look at another argument for the same position. Notice how much more logical this essay is—regardless of whether you agree with the author—simply because the author gives explanations and evidence for his position rather than appealing solely to the readers' emotions.

The City Council of Ste. Jeanne should reject mandatory recycling. Although many good people support this idea, the proposal facing us is so deeply flawed that I believe their support is misplaced. The most glaring problem is that the mandatory recycling program proposed here would create at least as much pollution as it would eliminate. Our neighbors in Youngsville could testify to that: Greensleaves Recycling, the proposed contractor, got the recycling contract in Youngsville five years ago, and their machinery spewed so much toxic gas out of its smokestacks that the city government stopped all recycling, mandatory or optional, for a solid year.

One of the biggest concerns people have is that the bottles and cans they throw away today will either accumulate in unsightly, unsanitary landfills or go up in smoke from an incinerator. But the fact of the matter is that new waste treatment facilities in nearby counties soon will eliminate most of the need for landfills and incinerators. By compacting unsorted trash into blocks comparable in hardness to concrete, the new facilities make it available for use in building foundations, dikes, and road construction. This form of "recycling"—not part of the present proposal—doesn't require us to collect the garbage in any new way because it doesn't matter whether the content is coffee grounds or juice bottles.

An argument in favor of the recycling proposal for which I have some sympathy is that mandatory recycling will raise people's awareness of our beautiful and fragile environment. Reflecting on this, however, I recalled our wonderful educational programs, both in the schools and in the mass media. Voluntary recycling is at an all-time high

level of participation; both anglers and environmentalists are celebrating the recent reopening of the Ste. Jeanne Waterway to fishing; and downtown Ste. Jeanne won the "Greening of the State" award just last year. Taken together, these facts suggest to me a populace already deeply engaged with environmental issues and now looking hard for new, well-conceived proposals to do even more. The present proposal simply doesn't measure up to our city's high standards.

You probably noticed immediately that this passage also gives three reasons for not supporting the mandatory recycling program—so the authors don't differ over whether to reject the proposed program. The two passages don't have as much in common in their style of argument, though, and that is our focus here. Let's take a closer look at passage 2.

What Reasons Does the Writer Offer?

Break this argument down as you did the first one. Here are the reasons the author of passage 2 provides in arguing that the mandatory recycling program should be rejected. Underneath each reason, make a note about the *logic* behind the reason; say what reasoning, evidence, or common sense the author points to in support of the argument.

1. The proposed mandatory recycling program would cause as much pollution as it would eliminate.

2. New waste treatment facilities lessen the need for recycling programs.

3. The mandatory recycling program is not needed to raise people's awareness of the environment.

Are the Appeals Logical?

Regardless of whether you agree with the author, you can see that this is a much more effective argument because the writer uses logic and common sense in backing up what he has to say.

The first argument is supported in the following way:

- The proposed contractor caused a great deal of pollution from smokestacks in a nearby city five years earlier.
- The smokestack toxicity in the nearby city was so extensive that even voluntary recycling was halted for a year, meaning that even less recycling took place than before the mandatory recycling program began.

The second argument is supported by the following logic:

- New waste treatment facilities allow all waste to be reused without the need for sorting it into waste to be recycled and waste to be incinerated or put in a landfill, but the proposed plan does not involve these new facilities.

Finally, the third argument is supported this way:

- The populace of Ste. Jeanne is already highly conscious of the environment, and benefit from educational programs in the schools and the mass media.
- The high level of environmental consciousness of the people shows in (a) the high rate of voluntary recycling, (b) the celebrated reopening of the Ste. Jeanne Waterway to fishing, and (c) the city's downtown winning a state environmental award the previous year.

More Practice

Now that you've examined two brief essays—one that appeals to emotion and one that appeals to logic—see if you can correctly identify the approaches used by the writers of the following sentences. Look carefully for a sense of logic. If the writer is appealing to your emotions, is the author's argument also backed up by logic (common sense, reason, or evidence)? Write an E in the blank if it appeals *only* to your sense of emotion and an L if it appeals to logic.

_____ **1.** Texting while driving is dangerous and anyone who does this is stupid.

_____ **2.** Texting while driving is dangerous because when drivers concentrate on a cell phone in their hands, they're using only one hand to control their motor vehicle, which makes them much more likely to have an accident.

_____ **3.** Many states have banned cell phone use when driving because it is dangerous. These laws have been put into effect because of startling statistics that point to the elevated risk of car accidents due to cell phone use.

_____ **4.** Dogs should always be kept on a leash in public places. What if you were walking down the street minding your own business and a loose dog ran up and attacked you?

_____ **5.** Dogs should always be kept on a leash in public places. A leash can protect dogs from traffic, garbage, dangerous places, and getting lost. It can also protect people from being harmed by overzealous, angry, or agitated dogs.

Answers

Argument 1 is an appeal to emotion without any logic, and arguments 2, 3, and 5 use common sense, evidence, and reason. But argument 4 might not be so obvious, since it may seem like a reasonable argument. However, it does not address all the logical reasons that leashes are necessary, but instead points to one frightening possibility. Yes, we would all like to avoid being attacked by a dog, which is a scary and threatening possibility, and by using only this scenario in the argument, the writer is appealing directly to our emotions.

Summary

Looking for appeals to logic will make you a more critical reader and thinker. And once you learn to read between the lines in an argument (to look behind emotional appeals for some sort of logical support), you'll have more confidence as a reader and be a better judge of the arguments that you hear and read.

TIP

- Language is often more powerful than we realize. Think about a situation in which you were enticed to buy a new game, food, movie, article of clothing, perfume, or other product or service. Was there a particular word, phrase, or sales pitch that was particularly persuasive?
- Listen carefully to how people around you try to convince you (or others) when they want you to think or act a certain way. For example, if a friend wants you to try a new place for lunch, how does he or she try to convince you: with appeals to your sense of logic ("The food is great—and so are the prices!") or to your emotions ("What, are you afraid to try something new?")? If your boss asks you to work overtime, does he or she appeal to your sense of logic ("You'll make lots of extra money") or to your emotions ("I could really, really use your help")? See which arguments you find most convincing and why.
- Read an editorial from the Opinion-Editorial page of your local newspaper. Look at how the writer supports his or her argument. Is the editorial convincing? Why? What reasons or evidence does it use to support its position?

19 ▶ FINDING MEANING IN LITERATURE

Curiosity is one of the most permanent and certain characteristics of a vigorous intellect.

—SAMUEL JOHNSON, English author (1709–1784)

LESSON SUMMARY

Many people are intimidated by reading literature—stories, poems, and plays—especially if they have to answer questions about it, as in a test situation. But now that you know so much about finding an implied main idea, you can also find the *theme*, or main idea, of a work of literature. This lesson works with poetry to show you how to do it.

L iterature (novels, poems, stories, and plays) can be quite intimidating to many readers. In literature, meanings are often implied, and messages and themes are not conveniently housed in a topic sentence. However, no matter what you are reading, you can feel confident that the author has left behind clues that will help you to find the theme (*the main idea*). As an active reader, you are now well-equipped to read between the lines to find meaning in anything you read.

Throughout these pages, you have spent a great deal of time locating the main ideas in various pieces of writing. Finding the theme of a work of literature is similar to finding the main idea in an article, passage, or memo. Just as the main idea is more than the subject of a given article, passage, or memo, the theme of a work of literature is also more than just its subject: It is what the text says *about* that subject. Theme, in other words, is the overall message or idea that a work of literature conveys. For example, you can probably figure out from the title that the *subject* of John Donne's poem "Death Be Not Proud" is death. However, the *theme* is not merely "death," but what the poem says *about* death, which happens to be that death is a gift if one believes in God.

There isn't room in this short lesson to look at theme in a short story, novel, or play. So this lesson will introduce you to a few poems. But don't be frightened: Reading poetry is really just like reading anything else. You just have to read a little more carefully and rely a little more on your sense of observation. You find themes in poetry the same way you do in other kinds of writing: by looking for clues in what happens and in the words the writer uses to describe what happens.

How Action Conveys Theme

First, look at an example of how the action of a poem—what happens in it—leads you to understand the theme.

Practice Passage 1

Read the following poem by William Blake from his book *Songs of Experience,* published in 1794. Read it out loud, because poetry is meant to be *heard* as well as read. Then read it again with your pen in hand: Read actively, making your observations and comments in the margins. Then answer the questions that follow.

A Poison Tree

I was angry with my friend;
I told my wrath, my wrath did end.   *wrath = anger*
I was angry with my foe: *foe = enemy*
I told it not, my wrath did grow.

And I water'd it in fears,
Night & morning with my tears;
And I sunned it with smiles,
And with soft deceitful wiles.   *wiles = trickery, deceit*

And it grew both day and night,
Till it bore an apple bright;
And my foe beheld it shine,
And he knew that it was mine.

And into my garden stole

When the night had veil'd the pole: *veiled = concealed*
In the morning glad I see
My foe outstretch'd beneath the tree.

What Happened?

To understand the author's theme, you need to look carefully at what happened, and why. Look at each of the four stanzas (a stanza is a poetic "paragraph"; each stanza in this poem is four lines long) to track the action.

What happens in the first stanza?

1. The speaker was angry with
   a. a friend.
   b. a foe.
   c. a friend and a foe.

2. How did the speaker handle his anger toward his friend?
   a. He told his friend about it and it went away.
   b. He kept it to himself and it grew.
   c. He kept it to himself and it went away.

3. How did the speaker handle his anger toward his foe?
   a. He told his friend about it and it went away.
   b. He kept it to himself and it grew.
   c. He kept it to himself and it went away.

You probably figured out the answers without too much trouble: **1. c, 2. a, 3. b.**

Now look at the second stanza. The key to understanding this stanza is knowing what *it* refers to. Reread the first and second stanzas carefully in order to answer the next question.

4. *It* refers to
   a. tears.
   b. smiles.
   c. wrath.

Choice **c**—*wrath*—is the last thing mentioned in the first stanza, so it follows that *wrath* is what *it* refers to.

The second stanza tells us that the speaker "water'd" it (his wrath) with fears and "sunned" it with smiles and wiles. How can this be? Can you literally water and sun your anger? No, but the speaker is not being literal here. Instead, he is using figurative language. Like the similes we saw earlier about Coach Lerner, comparing his voice to a foghorn and his haircut to that of a drill sergeant, this stanza uses a *metaphor*—a comparison that doesn't use the words *like* or *as*—to compare the speaker's wrath to something that grows with water and sun. Now, given these clues (and the best clue of all, the title of the poem), to what exactly is the speaker comparing his wrath?

5. The speaker compares his wrath to
   a. a flower.
   b. a tree.
   c. the sun.

The answer is **b**, a tree. The title gives this away. Also, a tree is the only plant that could bear "an apple bright," as in the third stanza.

What else happens in the third stanza?

6. In the third stanza, the foe
   a. grows his own apple.
   b. shines the speaker's apple.
   c. sees the speaker's apple.

The answer is **c**, the foe sees the speaker's apple ("my foe beheld it shine").

Finally, what happens in the fourth stanza? This stanza is somewhat trickier than the others, because in this stanza, something happens that is not directly stated. You know that the foe sneaks into the speaker's garden ("And into my garden stole"), but what else happens?

The poem doesn't exactly tell you, but you can guess. The speaker had an apple; you know that this apple grew on a tree and that this tree is a metaphor for the speaker's anger. You also know that the poem is called "A Poison Tree." You read in the fourth stanza that, in the morning, the speaker finds his foe "outstretch'd beneath the tree." What can you conclude?

7. At the end of the fourth stanza, the foe
   a. is waiting to ambush the speaker and kill him with the apple.
   b. has been killed by the apple he stole because it was poisonous.
   c. is waiting to share the apple with the speaker.

Which answer do your clues add up to? The only one that can be correct is **b**. The speaker was angry; the tree (and so the apple) was poisonous. You know that the foe, seeing the apple, snuck into the speaker's garden. Apparently he ate the apple, because now he's "outstretch'd beneath the tree." You also know that the speaker is "glad" to see his foe outstretched this way—he's glad to see him dead.

What Does It Mean?

Okay, so that's what happened in the poem. But what does it all mean?

Look again at the action. What the speaker *did* was to tell his friend about his wrath. What the speaker *didn't* do was to tell his enemy about his wrath. The results of the speaker's action and his inaction are your clues to the meaning of the poem as a whole, its theme.

8. Which of the following best summarizes the theme of the poem?
   a. Don't steal; it can kill you.
   b. Choose your enemies carefully.
   c. If you don't talk about your anger, it can be deadly.

Before you go any further, think about your answer again. Like a main idea, a theme must be general enough to encompass the whole work, not just a piece of it. Does the answer you chose encompass the whole poem and not just part of it?

You should have selected choice **c**, for this is the idea that sums up the message or "lesson" of the poem. In the first two lines, the speaker's wrath for his friend vanished when he talked about it, but he did not talk about his wrath for his enemy. Instead, he let it grow until it was poisonous and deadly.

How Language Conveys Emotion

In addition to conveying a theme, poems also often use language to create a powerful image or emotion. After looking at how poets use language to convey an emotion or a picture, you'll be ready to put your understanding of the action and the language together to understand the meaning of a poem.

Practice Passage 2
Take a look at the following poem by British poet Alfred Lord Tennyson as an example of how language can convey a strong feeling by conveying an image or picture. Read "The Eagle" twice out loud—remember, poetry is meant to be heard, not just seen. Then mark it up and write your observations in the margin.

The Eagle

He clasps the crag with crooked hands;   *crag = steep*
Close to the sun in lonely lands,   *or rugged rock*
Ringed with the azure world, he stands.   *azure = sky blue*

The wrinkled sea beneath him crawls;
He watches from his mountain walls,
And like a thunderbolt he falls.

The Sound of Words
What did you notice about the language in this poem? Did you notice the rhyme in each stanza—*hands, lands, stands* and *crawls, walls, falls*? Did you notice the repetition of the "k" sound in *clasps, crag,* and *crooked*? This repetition of sounds (especially at the beginning of words) is called *alliteration*.

9. Which other line of this poem uses alliteration?
   a. line 2
   b. line 3
   c. line 6

The answer is line 2, which repeats the *l* sound in "*lonely lands*."

Picture Language
You may have noticed another poetic device at work in this poem. In line 1, the poet tells us that the eagle ("he") "clasps" the rock "with crooked hands." Do eagles have hands? No, they do not, but Tennyson gives the eagle human characteristics. When an animal is given human characteristics, or when an inanimate thing (like a rock, for example) is given animate characteristics (human or animal), it is called *personification*.

10. Which other line of this poem uses personification?
   a. line 2
   b. line 4
   c. line 6

The other example of personification is found in line 4, where the sea "crawls" like a baby or a turtle.

Here's a memory test:

11. Line 6, "And like a thunderbolt he falls," uses which of the following poetic devices?
   a. personification
   b. simile
   c. irony

This line uses, choice **b**, a simile that compares the eagle to a thunderbolt. What is the effect of this comparison?

12. The comparison of the eagle to a thunderbolt makes the reader think of the eagle as
   a. a weak, timid creature.
   b. an unpredictable creature.
   c. a powerful, fast creature.

Like all good similes, this comparison creates a vivid image that not only helps us actually picture the eagle's flight, but also tells us *something about* the eagle by comparing it to the incredible force of nature that is lightning. The eagle, this simile suggests, is as powerful, as fast, as dangerous—and as impossible to catch—as a thunderbolt. We should, in short, be as awed by the eagle as we are by lightning—and that feeling, more than an idea we might call a theme, is what this poem is all about.

TIP

Poets often use figurative language or descriptive words that are not commonly used in casual speech. For example, a poet might use an archaic form of English or write in an unfamiliar vernacular. If you are having trouble understanding a particular passage that contains unfamiliar words, or words that are arranged in unusual patterns, it can be helpful to rewrite the passage in words you use more commonly in your daily life. That way, you can easily find the meaning of the passage. (It's like cracking a code!)

Action + Language = Theme

In the final poem for today, by American poet Stephen Crane, see if you can determine the theme of the poem by looking at both the action of the poem and its language (diction, style, and tone). As before, begin by reading the poem carefully, first out loud and then with pen in hand.

Practice Passage 3

A Man Said to the Universe

A man said to the universe:
"Sir, I exist!"
"However," replied the universe,
"The fact has not created in me
A sense of obligation."

13. Which sentence best summarizes the theme of this poem?
   a. The universe is too big for humanity.
   b. The universe is indifferent to humanity.
   c. Humanity has an obligation to the universe.

The best choice is **b**, "The universe is indifferent to humanity." This idea is conveyed in part by the action of the poem: what the man says to the universe and the universe's reply. But the universe's indifference is also reflected in the language of the poem.

14. Which of the following best describes the tone of this poem?
   a. warm, caring
   b. hot, angry
   c. cold, formal

The words of this poem—especially *sir, fact,* and *sense of obligation*—are cold, formal words that reflect the way the universe feels about humans: indifferent. There is no sense of intimacy, no relationship, no warmth in these words. The poet's diction and style help to reveal the theme of the poem.

Summary

Reading poetry wasn't so bad after all, was it? If you are an active reader who is sensitive to the language used by the poet, you can use the clues the poet gives you to help you enjoy the pictures and emotions created through words and understand the poem's theme. And if you can do this for poems, you can certainly do it for stories, novels, and plays as well.

TIP

One way to become a skilled reader is to learn how to react to a text in an interactive manner. You are an active and participatory reader if you:

1. Read carefully and pay attention to important organizational and content clues, such as titles.
2. Grant yourself the freedom to question the author's theories and/or motivations.
3. Allow yourself to be impressed or moved by what you have read.
4. Spend the time it takes to fully absorb the text. Some texts can be read in a single sitting, while more challenging subjects or texts might require a lengthier, closer reading or multiple readings.

L E S S O N

DRAWING CONCLUSIONS: PUTTING IT ALL TOGETHER

Reading furnishes the mind only with materials of knowledge; it is thinking that makes what we read ours.

—JOHN LOCKE, English philosopher (1632–1704)

LESSON SUMMARY

This lesson wraps up your study of reading comprehension by reviewing everything you've learned so far.

Y ou're almost at the end of this book. If you've been doing a lesson every weekday, you've spent almost a month building your reading skills. Congratulations! This lesson uses a longer passage than the ones you've read so far to give you a chance to practice all the skills you've learned. Here's a quick review of what you've learned since the last review lesson:

- **Lesson 16: Finding an implied main idea.** You practiced looking for clues in structure, language, and style, as well as the facts of the passage, to determine the main idea.
- **Lesson 17: Understanding implied causes and effects.** You learned to "read between the lines" to determine causes and make predictions about effects.
- **Lesson 18: Emotional and logical appeals.** You learned that arguments that appeal to readers' emotions must be supported by logic as well in order to be convincing.
- **Lesson 19: Finding the theme in literature.** You used your detective skills to find the main idea implied by the structure, language, style, and action in a work of literature.

Practice

Today, you'll practice these skills in combination with skills covered earlier in this book:

- finding the facts
- determining the main idea
- determining the meaning of unfamiliar words
- distinguishing between fact and opinion
- chronological order
- order of importance
- cause and effect
- comparison and contrast
- point of view
- diction
- language and style
- tone

If this seems like a monumental task, don't worry: It isn't. You've already mastered some of these skills and should be very comfortable with the others. In fact, you will probably be surprised at how easy you find this exercise to be.

Practice Passage

Are you ready? Read the following essay. Remember, read actively and make observations in the space provided on the next page. Then answer the questions that follow. This will give you a chance to see how well your reading skills are coming along.

Although many companies offer tuition reimbursement, most companies reimburse employees only for classes that are relevant to their positions. This is a very limiting policy. A company that reimburses employees for all college credit courses—whether job related or not—offers a service not only to the employees, but to the entire company.

One good reason for giving employees unconditional tuition reimbursement is that it shows the company's dedication to its employees. In today's economy, where job security is a thing of the past and employees feel more and more expendable, it is important for a company to demonstrate to its employees that it cares. The best way to do this is with concrete investments in them.

In turn, this dedication to the betterment of company employees will create greater employee loyalty. A company that puts out funds to pay for the education of its employees will get its money back by having employees stay with the company longer. It will reduce employee turnover, because even employees who don't take advantage of the tuition reimbursement program will be more loyal to their company, just knowing that their company cares enough to pay for their education.

Most importantly, the company that has an unrestricted tuition reimbursement program will have higher quality employees. Although these companies do indeed run the risk of losing money on employees who go on to another job in a different company as soon as they get their degree, more often than not, the employee will stay with the company. And even if employees do leave after graduation, it generally takes several years to complete any degree program. Thus, even if the employee leaves upon graduating, throughout those years, the employer will have a more sophisticated, more intelligent, and therefore more valuable and productive employee. And, if the employee stays, that education will doubly benefit the company: Not only is the employee more educated, but now that employee can be promoted so the company doesn't have to fill a high-level vacancy from the outside. Open positions can be filled by people who already know the company well.

Though unconditional tuition reimbursement requires a significant investment on the employer's part, it is perhaps one of the wisest investments a company can make.

Your Observations

Record your observations about the passage in the space below.

Questions

1. According to the practice passage, the most important result of unrestricted tuition reimbursement is that
   a. employees are happier and work harder.
   b. companies with unrestricted tuition reimbursement have higher quality employees.
   c. it shows the company's dedication to its employees.

2. How, according to the passage, will unconditional tuition reimbursement reduce employee turnover?
   a. by making employees more loyal
   b. by paying employees more money
   c. by promoting education

3. The first sentence of the passage, "Although many companies offer tuition reimbursement, most companies reimburse employees only for classes that are relevant to their positions," is
   a. fact.
   b. opinion.
   c. neither.

4. The second sentence of the passage, "This is a very limiting policy," is
   a. fact.
   b. opinion.
   c. neither.

5. This passage is organized according to which of the following strategies? (Mark all that apply.)
   a. chronological order
   b. order of importance
   c. cause and effect

6. The point of view used in this passage is the
   a. first-person point of view.
   b. second-person point of view.
   c. third-person point of view.

7. The writer most likely chose this point of view because
   a. the writer is describing a personal experience.
   b. it enables readers to identify with the situation.
   c. its objectivity encourages the reader to take the writer's ideas seriously.

8. The writer most likely uses the word *wisest* in the last sentence, rather than words such as *profitable, practical,* or *beneficial,* because
   a. wisdom is associated with education, the subject of the essay.
   b. the writer is trying to appeal to people who are already highly educated.
   c. the writer believes tuition reimbursement is a good choice even though it does not benefit companies.

9. Which logical conclusion can be reached after reading the passage?
   a. Unrestricted tuition reimbursement is a big expense.
   b. Some companies like to educate their employees.
   c. Companies benefit greatly by offering unrestricted tuition reimbursement.

10. The passage suggests that, compared to employees of companies that offer unconditional tuition reimbursement, employees of companies that do not offer this benefit are
   a. less loyal.
   b. more likely to be promoted.
   c. not as smart.

11. Expendable (paragraph 2) most nearly means
   a. expensive.
   b. flexible.
   c. replaceable.

12. The writer appeals primarily to the reader's
   a. emotions.
   b. sense of logic.
   c. senses.

13. The main idea of the passage is that
   a. companies should reimburse employees for work-related courses.
   b. both companies and employees would benefit from unconditional tuition reimbursement.
   c. companies should require their employees to take college courses.

Answers

1. b. The first sentence in the last paragraph uses the transitional phrase "most importantly" to specify that the most important effect of unrestricted tuition reimbursement is "higher quality employees." While other positive effects had also been mentioned, they were not mentioned in conjunction with the phrase "most importantly."

2. a. The idea that employees will become more loyal is stated in the third paragraph: "A company that puts out funds to pay for the education of its employees will get its money back by having employees stay with the company longer. It will reduce employee turnover because even employees who don't take advantage of the tuition reimbursement program will be more loyal . . ."

3. a. The sentence is a fact; you could verify it by surveying companies to find out about their tuition reimbursement policies.

4. b. The sentence is an opinion; it shows how the author feels about the policy.

5. b, c. The author lists the ways companies would benefit by having unconditional tuition reimbursement in order of importance from least to most important. The author also shows the positive effects unconditional reimbursement would have on the company.

6. c. There is no *I* or *you* here; the writer doesn't refer directly to herself or to the reader. Instead, everything is spoken of in the third person.

7. c. The writer most likely uses the third-person point of view because it is objective, and her argument is more likely to be taken seriously. If she used the first person, readers might think she was an employee who wanted her employer to pay for her tuition, and she wouldn't be taken seriously.

8. a. By using a word associated with education, the writer stresses the importance of education for the company.

9. c. Although tuition reimbursement is a considerable expense for many companies, that was not the topic being addressed. Instead, the main idea of the passage and the focus throughout is on the benefits that companies receive by offering unrestricted tuition reimbursement. The article states that such programs may help to motivate employees, but never implies that the programs are the only way to accomplish this.

10. a. If employees of companies that offer unconditional tuition reimbursement are more loyal to their companies (see the second and third paragraphs), it follows that other employees will be less loyal because their company isn't showing enough dedication to their betterment.

11. c. Your best clue that *expendable* means *replaceable* is that the writer uses the word immediately after saying that job security is a thing of the past, so that workers don't feel they are important or valuable to a company that can fire them on a moment's notice.

12. b. There is common sense or reason behind each of the writer's arguments. Indeed, there are few, if any, emotional appeals in this passage.

13. b. This main idea is explicitly stated in the last sentence of the first paragraph (a good place to look for the main idea of a longer passage like this one) and repeated at the end of the passage.

How did you do? If you got all of the answers correct, congratulations! Good work. If you missed a few, you might want to take time to review the corresponding lessons.

IF YOU MISSED:	THEN STUDY:
Question 1	Lesson 1
Question 2	Lesson 1
Question 3	Lesson 4
Question 4	Lesson 4
Question 5	Lessons 6–10
Question 6	Lesson 11
Question 7	Lesson 11
Question 8	Lesson 12
Question 9	Lesson 14
Question 10	Lessons 16 and 17
Question 11	Lesson 3
Question 12	Lesson 18
Question 13	Lessons 2 and 16

Congratulations!

You've completed 20 lessons and have seen your reading skills increase. If you're preparing for a standardized test, you should check out Appendix A, which provides tips on how to prepare and what to do during the test. And don't forget Appendix B, which gives suggestions for how to continue to improve your reading skills, along with a list of suggested books organized by subject categories.

Now it's time to reward yourself for a job well done. Buy yourself a good book and enjoy!

TIP

Look up the word **syllogism** in the dictionary. Then, locate syllogism exercises in books or on the Internet to help your practice your deductive reasoning skills and improve your ability to draw logical conclusions while reading.

Posttest ▶

Now that you've spent a good deal of time improving your reading comprehension, take this posttest to see how much you've learned. If you took the pretest at the beginning of this book, you can compare what you knew when you started the book with what you know now.

When you complete this test, grade yourself, and then compare your score with your score on the pretest. If your score now is much greater than your pretest score, congratulations—you've profited noticeably from your hard work. If your score shows little improvement, perhaps you need to review certain chapters. Do you notice a pattern to the types of questions you got wrong? Whatever you score on this posttest, keep this book around for review and refer to it when you need tips on how to read more efficiently.

Use the answer sheet on the next page to fill in the correct answers. Or, if you prefer, simply circle the answers in this book. If the book doesn't belong to you, write the numbers 1–50 on a piece of paper and record your answers there. Take as much time as you need to do this short test. When you finish, check your answers against the answer key that follows. Each answer tells you which lesson of this book teaches you about the reading strategy in that question.

	a	b	c	d			a	b	c	d			a	b	c	d
1.	a	b	c	d		18.	a	b	c	d		35.	a	b	c	d
2.	a	b	c	d		19.	a	b	c	d		36.	a	b	c	d
3.	a	b	c	d		20.	a	b	c	d		37.	a	b	c	d
4.	a	b	c	d		21.	a	b	c	d		38.	a	b	c	d
5.	a	b	c	d		22.	a	b	c	d		39.	a	b	c	d
6.	a	b	c	d		23.	a	b	c	d		40.	a	b	c	d
7.	a	b	c	d		24.	a	b	c	d		41.	a	b	c	d
8.	a	b	c	d		25.	a	b	c	d		42.	a	b	c	d
9.	a	b	c	d		26.	a	b	c	d		43.	a	b	c	d
10.	a	b	c	d		27.	a	b	c	d		44.	a	b	c	d
11.	a	b	c	d		28.	a	b	c	d		45.	a	b	c	d
12.	a	b	c	d		29.	a	b	c	d		46.	a	b	c	d
13.	a	b	c	d		30.	a	b	c	d		47.	a	b	c	d
14.	a	b	c	d		31.	a	b	c	d		48.	a	b	c	d
15.	a	b	c	d		32.	a	b	c	d		49.	a	b	c	d
16.	a	b	c	d		33.	a	b	c	d		50.	a	b	c	d
17.	a	b	c	d		34.	a	b	c	d						

Posttest

The posttest consists of a series of reading passages with questions that follow to test your comprehension.

Grunge Music and American Popular Culture

The late 1980s found the landscape of popular music in America dominated by a distinctive style of rock and roll known as *glam rock* or *hair metal*—so called because of the over-styled hair, makeup, and wardrobe worn by the genre's ostentatious rockers. Bands like Poison, Whitesnake, and Mötley Crüe popularized glam rock with their power ballads and flashy style, but the product had worn thin by the early 1990s. Just as superficial as the 80s, glam rockers were shallow, short on substance, and musically inferior.

In 1991, a Seattle-based band called Nirvana shocked the corporate music industry with the release of its debut single, "Smells Like Teen Spirit," which quickly became a huge hit all over the world. Nirvana's distorted, guitar-laden sound and thought-provoking lyrics were the antithesis of glam rock, and the youth of America were quick to pledge their allegiance to the brand-new movement known as *grunge*.

Grunge actually got its start in the Pacific Northwest during the mid-1980s. Nirvana had simply mainstreamed a sound and culture that got its start years before with bands like Mudhoney, Soundgarden, and Green River. Grunge rockers derived their fashion sense from the youth culture of the Pacific Northwest: a melding of punk rock style and outdoors clothing like flannels, heavy boots, worn out jeans, and corduroys. At the height of the movement's popularity, when other Seattle bands like Pearl Jam and Alice in Chains were all the rage, the trappings of grunge were working their way to the height of American fashion. Like the music, the teenagers were fast to embrace the grunge fashion because it represented defiance against corporate America and shallow pop culture.

The popularity of grunge music was ephemeral; by the mid- to late-1990s, its influence upon American culture had all but disappeared, and most of its recognizable bands were nowhere to be seen on the charts. The heavy sound and themes of grunge were replaced on the radio waves by boy bands like the Backstreet Boys, and the bubblegum pop of Britney Spears and Christina Aguilera.

There are many reasons why the Seattle sound faded out of the mainstream as quickly as it rocketed to prominence, but the most glaring reason lies at the defiant, anti-establishment heart of the grunge movement itself. It is very hard to buck the trend when you are the one setting it, and many of the grunge bands were never comfortable with the fame that was thrust upon them. Ultimately, the simple fact that many grunge bands were so against mainstream rock stardom eventually took the movement back to where it started: underground. The fickle American mainstream public, as quick as they were to hop on to the grunge bandwagon, were just as quick to hop off and move on to something else.

1. The best word to describe grunge music is
   a. flashy.
   b. rebellious.
   c. fickle.
   d. antithetical.

2. Teenagers embraced grunge fashion because
   a. they were tired of Glam Rock fashion.
   b. it defied corporate America and the shallowness of pop culture.
   c. grunge rockers told them to embrace it.
   d. it outraged their parents.

3. By stating that "glam rockers were shallow, short on substance, and musically inferior," this author is
   a. using a time-honored form of reporting that dignifies his or her position.
   b. resorting to a subjective, emotional assertion that is not an effective way to build an argument.
   c. making an objective, logical assertion based on facts.
   d. merely quoting what others say about glam rock and detaching herself or himself from the opinion.

4. This writer is trying to document
   a. the popularity of glam rock.
   b. Nirvana's role in popularizing grunge music.
   c. the rise and fall of grunge music.
   d. the reasons young people responded so enthusiastically to grunge music.

5. According to this passage, what is the difference between glam rock and grunge?
   a. Glam rock is flashier and superficial, while grunge is thought-provoking and anti-establishment.
   b. Glam rock appeals to teenagers, while grunge appeals to adults.
   c. Glam rock faded quickly, while grunge is still prominent.
   d. Glam rock was more commercially successful than grunge.

6. The tone of the sentence, "The fickle American mainstream public, as quick as they were to hop on to the grunge bandwagon, were just as quick to hop off and move on to something else" can be best described as
   a. authoritative.
   b. gloomy.
   c. cynical.
   d. ironic.

7. Which of the following bands is not associated with grunge?
   a. Nirvana
   b. Mudhoney
   c. Pearl Jam
   d. Poison

Food Trucks on Parade
(excerpt from a feature article in a local newspaper)

When you're hungry and pressed for time, there's nothing like a food truck to fit the bill (and fill your stomach). Made popular by features on the Food Network and a constant presence at events like street fairs and concerts, local food trucks offer a great variety of snacks, meals, and desserts for people on the go. To celebrate this growing community, the Bloomville Town Council is sponsoring its first Mobile Food Fest this Sunday in Bentley Park.

If you think today's food trucks are anything like the traditional hot dog cart, think again. When you visit Bentley Park this weekend, you're likely to find these "open-air restaurants" serving *banh mi* (Vietnamese sandwiches), Texas-style BBQ ribs, vegan tacos, lobster rolls, and falafel sandwiches alongside the more traditional burgers, hot dogs, and soft-serve ice cream cones.

Event organizers hope to make this an annual festival, starting with more than 20 local vendors in its inaugural year. One of these will be Max Bartlett, owner of The Sandwich Guy truck (which serves—you guessed it—sandwiches). Bartlett is a veteran of Bloomville's "food truck circuit" at local events, and is looking forward to serving his signature grilled cheese to the Bentley Park crowd: "These events are always so much fun—you get to mingle and try all sorts of different foods, practically in your backyard."

According to town clerk Audrey Marshall, the numbers of food truck operators in Bloomville are growing. "We've seen a 35% increase in permit applications this year," she commented. "And we expect that number to grow next year as well. It's a great boon to our small-business community."

The festival runs from noon until 8:00 pm on Sunday. For more details, please visit the festival's website.

8. What is the main idea of this article?
   a. Bloomville Town Hall's policy on food truck permits
   b. the Mobile Food Fest
   c. different types of food served by trucks
   d. food you can eat on the go

9. This tone of this article can best be described as
   a. informative.
   b. biased.
   c. sarcastic.
   d. excited.

10. From the context of the article, you can infer that the word *boon* likely means which of the following?
   a. drain
   b. food
   c. drawback
   d. benefit

11. Which of the following conclusions can you draw from this article?
   a. There are 62 food trucks in Bloomville.
   b. Audrey Marshall will be attending the festival.
   c. Food trucks are growing in popularity in Bloomville.
   d. There will not be hot dogs served at the festival.

12. According to the article, *banh mi* is a type of
   a. Vietnamese rice dish.
   b. falafel sandwich.
   c. gourmet grilled cheese sandwich.
   d. Vietnamese sandwich.

13. Max Bartlett's statement that "these events are always so much fun" is
   a. a fact.
   b. an opinion.
   c. an emotional appeal.
   d. a logical appeal.

14. From the context of the article, you can infer that the word *inaugural* most likely means which of the following?
   a. first
   b. future
   c. popular
   d. past

15. The tone of the sentence, "One of these will be Max Bartlett, owner of The Sandwich Guy truck (which serves—you guessed it—sandwiches)" can best be described as
   a. mean.
   b. playful.
   c. vengeful.
   d. sad.

"Mrs. Rachel Lynde is Surprised"
(an excerpt from *Anne of Green Gables* by Lucy Maud Montgomery)

Mrs. Rachel Lynde lived just where the Avonlea main road dipped down into a little hollow, fringed with alders and ladies' eardrops and traversed by a brook that had its source away back in the woods of the old Cuthbert place; it was reputed to be an intricate, headlong brook in its earlier course through those woods, with dark secrets of pool and cascade; but by the time it reached Lynde's Hollow it was a quiet, well-conducted little stream, for not even a brook could run past Mrs. Rachel Lynde's door without due regard for decency and decorum; it probably was conscious that Mrs. Rachel was sitting at her window, keeping a sharp eye on everything that passed, from brooks and children up, and that if she noticed anything odd or out of place she would never rest until she had ferreted out the whys and wherefores thereof.

There are plenty of people in Avonlea and out of it, who can attend closely to their neighbor's business by dint of neglecting their own; but Mrs. Rachel Lynde was one of those capable creatures who can manage their own concerns and those of other folks into the bargain. She was a notable housewife; her work was always done and well done; she "ran" the Sewing Circle, helped run the Sunday-school, and was the strongest prop of the Church Aid Society and Foreign Missions Auxiliary. Yet with all this Mrs. Rachel found abundant time to sit for hours at her kitchen window, knitting "cotton warp" quilts—she had knitted sixteen of them, as Avonlea housekeepers were wont to tell in awed voices—and keeping a sharp eye on the main road that crossed the hollow and wound up the steep red hill beyond. Since Avonlea occupied a little triangular peninsula jutting out into the Gulf of St. Lawrence with water on two sides of it, anybody who went out of it or into it had to pass over that hill road and so run the unseen gauntlet of Mrs. Rachel's all-seeing eye.

She was sitting there one afternoon in early June. The sun was coming in at the window warm and bright; the orchard on the slope below the house was in a bridal flush of pinky- white bloom, hummed over by a myriad of bees. Thomas Lynde—a meek little man whom Avonlea people called "Rachel Lynde's husband"—was sowing his late turnip seed on the hill field beyond the barn; and Matthew Cuthbert ought to have been sowing his on the big red brook field away over by Green Gables. Mrs. Rachel knew that he ought because she had heard him tell Peter Morrison the evening before in William J. Blair's store over at Carmody that he meant to sow his turnip seed the next afternoon. Peter had asked him, of course, for Matthew Cuthbert had never been known to volunteer information about anything in his whole life.

And yet here was Matthew Cuthbert, at half-past three on the afternoon of a busy day, placidly driving over the hollow and up the hill; moreover, he wore a white collar and his best suit of clothes, which was plain proof that he was going out of Avonlea; and he had the buggy and the sorrel mare, which *betokened* that he was going a considerable distance. Now, where was Matthew Cuthbert going and why was he going there?

16. From the context of the passage, you can infer that the word *betokened* most likely means which of the following?
   a. lied
   b. implied
   c. confirmed
   d. required

17. Which of the following conclusions can you make from this passage?
   a. Matthew Cuthbert is being purposely secretive about his errand.
   b. Mrs. Rachel Lynde is very observant.
   c. Mrs. Rachel Lynde lives in a yellow house.
   d. Avonlea is famous for its many brooks.

18. The passage expresses which point of view?
  a. first-person
  b. second-person
  c. third-person
  d. narrative

19. If this passage were written from Mrs. Rachel Lynde's direct point of view, what would the switch to the first-person perspective achieve?
  a. The reader would be distanced from Mrs. Rachel's thoughts and feelings.
  b. The reader would learn more about Matthew Cuthbert's motives for leaving.
  c. The reader would be able to hear Mrs. Rachel's own thoughts in her own voice.
  d. The reader would know more about Thomas Lynde.

20. The author lists Mrs. Rachel's accomplishments as a member of the Avonlea community to demonstrate which of the following?
  a. the contrast between Mrs. Rachel and other people who typically devote all of their time to gossip
  b. the similarity between Mrs. Rachel and other residents of Avonlea
  c. the variety of activities available in Avonlea
  d. an informative tone

21. What is the main idea of this excerpt?
  a. Matthew Cuthbert is on an unknown errand, and Mrs. Rachel Lynde desperately wants to know why.
  b. Avonlea farmers should be home planting turnips on June afternoons.
  c. Mrs. Rachel Lynde knows everything about everyone in Avonlea.
  d. Matthew Cuthbert is shy.

22. From the context of the passage, you can infer which of the following?
  a. Matthew Cuthbert is going to the store to pick up turnip seeds.
  b. Matthew Cuthbert's errand is a formal one.
  c. Mrs. Rachel Lynde can control the flow of streams.
  d. Cotton warp quilts are very popular in Avonlea.

Security Information for Air Travelers
(excerpt from a pamphlet)

To accommodate security checks and your airline's pre-boarding policies, please plan to arrive at the airport at least one hour in advance of your flight's departure. Once you've checked in at your airline's terminal, please be sure you have your boarding pass and a photo ID in hand as you make your way to security.

Once you arrive at the security checkpoint, expect to remove your shoes and jacket, as well as any belts, jewelry, or other accessories containing metal—you will be able to put your items in a separate container to be scanned by security personnel, along with any carry-on luggage and/or electronics. You will be required to pass through a metal detector, and may be selected for further screening at the discretion of security personnel. Liquids in containers larger than three fluid ounces will not be allowed past the entrance of the Security area; please make sure that you have planned accordingly, or the completion of your screening may be delayed.

Please note that once you've passed through the security checks successfully, you will not be allowed to return to the main airline terminals or baggage check areas, so please make sure that all check-in procedures have been completed before you reach the security checkpoint. Non-passengers will not be allowed beyond the security area.

23. What type of reader would benefit the most from reading this article?
a. an experienced business traveler
b. a child
c. an inexperienced air traveler
d. a pilot

24. According to this article, when you arrive at the airport, when should you plan to say good-bye to the person dropping you off?
a. at the airplane's gate, after you've passed through the security checkpoint
b. before you pass through the security checkpoint
c. on the sidewalk outside of the airport
d. on the plane

25. What is the tone of this article?
a. sarcastic
b. business-like
c. angry
d. frivolous

26. Based on the information contained in the article, which of the following should you wear to make your security screening easiest?
a. slip-on shoes, a backpack containing bottles of water, and an easily removable jacket
b. slip-on shoes, an easily removable jacket, and a shoulder bag containing small, clearly labeled bottles
c. a backpack containing complicated electronics equipment and an easily removable jacket
d. slip-on shoes and any metal jewelry and accessories you didn't want to check with your luggage

Bear Story

Campers Gene and Marie Marsden took pride in being good citizens when in the wild. While driving the 300 miles from their home in Colorado to the Green River Lakes area of the Wind River Mountains in Wyoming, they instructed their children in the protocol they'd learned in the bear safety pamphlet put out by the Bridger-Teton Forest Service. The number-one rule was "Don't feed the bears!"—whether intentionally or not. Warning the kids not to go anywhere near a bear, the Marsdens had no problem with the intentional part, but the unintentional part was not as easy to avoid as they thought.

Mr. and Mrs. Marsden did their best to keep a tidy camp. While the bear manual had said to hang all food at least ten feet off the ground and four feet out from the trunk of a tree, they did what all the other people in the nearby public campground were doing and locked their food in their little utility trailer at night. Afraid that the scent of the bait might attract a bear, they even locked up Marie's fishing pole. It was always dark when they went to bed, but they perused the campsite with flashlights, making sure nothing was left out. Taking the recommended precaution of sleeping a hundred yards from where they cooked their food, they kept the car near their tents, unhitched from the trailer, which they left up at the other camp. Before going to bed each night, all of the Marsdens took off the clothes they had worn during the day while eating, replacing them with pajamas that they used only for sleeping. They were also careful to lock the dirty laundry in the trailer. As the pamphlet advised, they took no snacks into their tents.

Gene says he now regrets not having taken their dog into the tent at night, but they liked having him on guard. Small animals would often come sniffing around, and the dog would chase them back into the thickets, then return to the hollow he'd dug for himself in front of the children's tent. But on the night of the encounter, Spike would not stop barking, and Marie Marsden knew he must be sounding the alarm on something more dangerous and dauntless than a raccoon or squirrel. When she unzipped the tent and shined her flashlight in the direction of the cooking area, she saw Spike attempting to hold a young grizzly bear at bay.

They all managed to pile into the car, and with the kids sitting atop stuffed sacks full of clothes and gear, they drove quickly down the trail, calling out the window to Spike and abandoning the cargo trailer to whatever fate the bear might have in store for it. Uncertain whether the bear was following, one of the children opened a door and loaded Spike up on the run. They drove to a pay phone 20 miles away and called a Fish and Game Department ranger, who identified the bear by the white ruff the Marsdens had seen around his neck. The authorities informed the Marsdens that the bear was a young, recently weaned male that they'd been keeping an eye on.

The next morning, the Marsdens heard helicopters circling over the mountain above them and wondered if it might have something to do with the bear. After spending the night in the public campground, they drove back to their site. Wandering the area in search of clues, Marie came to a halt below the tallest spruce. She slapped her head and shouted, "Oh no!"

"What is it?" Gene asked.

Marie pointed at the ground where Spike's dog food bowl lay upside down.

A week after their return home, the Marsdens read the headline in their local paper. "Bear Euthanized in Wind Rivers." According to the article, the Fish and Game Department had shot the young bear because, having been rewarded for invading a human campsite, it would likely do so again.

The Marsdens knew they had been lucky in the encounter, yet much to their shame and sadness, they also knew that the bear had not.

27. Which of the following statements is false?
   a. The Marsdens like to camp.
   b. The Marsdens' dog chases squirrels and barks too much.
   c. The Marsdsens are a considerate and compassionate married couple.
   d. The Marsdens' dog cornered a young grizzly.

28. Who does the author imply is mostly to blame in the bear's death?
   a. the Marsdens, because they were not careful enough
   b. the bear, because he invaded a human camp
   c. the Fish and Game authorities, because of poor communication with campers
   d. the Forest Service, for putting out incomplete information

29. In paragraph 2, it can be determined from the context that the word perused means
   a. neglected.
   b. cleaned.
   c. studied.
   d. hid.

30. In paragraph 3, it can be determined from the context that the word dauntless means
   a. stupid.
   b. fearless.
   c. clumsy.
   d. spineless.

31. This story is arranged
   a. like a news story, with the most important event told first.
   b. in reverse chronological order, with the last event first.
   c. in standard chronological order, with events told in the order they occurred.
   d. in mixed, random order.

32. What was the "reward" referred to in the next to last paragraph?
   a. the bear seeing the Marsdens run from him
   b. the bear receiving no punishment for disturbing humans
   c. the bear being able to stand off Spike
   d. the bear getting the dog food

33. The tone and style of this piece make it appropriate for which of the following types of publications?
   a. a scientific report on human-bear interaction
   b. a pamphlet on bear safety such as the one the Marsdens read
   c. a statistical study on bear fatalities in the Western mountains
   d. a human interest article in the Sunday magazine of a newspaper

New Device Hits Stores
(excerpt from a news article)

Due to extremely high demand, customers hoping to buy the new MyBook tablet by TechGiant could be facing long lines and possible sellouts in its first weekend of release.

Introduced in November at the annual Gadgetry of the Future conference after months of speculation by technology bloggers and industry insiders, the MyBook is expected to break previous sales records going into the crucial holiday sales period. With market-leading network capabilities and improved video technology, the device is anticipated to outpace competitors like Stark Electronics's Tablette, and BGE's ReadMe.

According to TechGiant CEO Frank Jackson's public statement on the MyBook, the device "will revolutionize how we read, connect, and interact." However, critics have taken aim at the device's lackluster video capabilities and large size as potential flaws that could have sales *repercussions*.

Still, at the Digital World flagship store in midtown New York, customers dismissed the concerns. "This is going to be *the* gift this holiday season," said shopper Celia Nunez. "I'm hoping to buy them for several of my relatives, so I'm just hoping there are some left when I get through this line!"

34. What is the main idea of this article?
- **a.** There will be a consumer backlash against the MyBook device.
- **b.** Despite mixed reviews, the MyBook is selling well.
- **c.** The MyBook will revolutionize the electronics industry.
- **d.** Holiday sales are up overall this year.

35. From the context of the article, you can infer which of the following?
- **a.** The MyBook has strong word-of-mouth marketing behind its sales.
- **b.** Celia Nunez knows more about the MyBook's features than technology bloggers do.
- **c.** TechGiant stock will rise in the next month.
- **d.** Bloggers and industry insiders love the MyBook.

36. In the context of the article, the word *repercussions* most likely means
- **a.** profits.
- **b.** upward trend.
- **c.** assets.
- **d.** backlash.

37. The quotations featured in the article are examples of what?
- **a.** facts
- **b.** opinions
- **c.** consumer feedback
- **d.** fiction

Maine's Glacial Past

The coast of the State of Maine is one of the most irregular in the world. A straight line running from the southernmost coastal city to the northernmost coastal city would measure about 225 miles. If you followed the coastline between these points, you would travel more than ten times as far. This irregularity is the result of what is called a drowned coastline. The term comes from the glacial activity of the Ice Age. At that time, the whole area that is now Maine was part of a mountain range that towered above the sea. As the glacier descended, however, it expended enormous force on those mountains, and they sank into the sea.

As the mountains sank, ocean water charged over the lowest parts of the remaining land, forming a series of twisting inlets and lagoons of contorted grottos and nooks. The highest parts of the former mountain range, nearest the shore, remained as islands. Mt. Desert Island was one of the most famous of all the islands left behind by the glacier. Marine fossils found here were 225 feet above sea level indicating the level of the shoreline prior to the glacier.

The 2,500-mile-long rocky and jagged coastline of Maine keeps watch over nearly 2,000 islands. Many of these islands are tiny and uninhabited, but many are home to thriving communities. Mt. Desert Island is one of the largest, most beautiful of the Maine coast islands. Measuring 16 miles by 12 miles, Mt. Desert was very nearly formed as two distinct islands. It is split almost in half by Somes Sound, a very deep and very narrow stretch of water seven miles long.

For years, Mt. Desert Island, particularly its major settlement, Bar Harbor, afforded summer homes for the wealthy. Recently, though, Bar Harbor has become a burgeoning arts community as well. But the best part of the island is the unspoiled forest land known as Acadia National Park. Since the island sits on the boundary line between the temperate and subarctic zones, the island supports the flora and fauna of both zones as well as beach, inland, and alpine plants. It also lies in a major bird migration lane and is a resting spot for many birds.

The establishment of Acadia National Park in 1916 means that this natural monument will be preserved and that it will be available to all people, not just the wealthy. Visitors to Acadia may receive nature instruction from the park naturalists as well as enjoy camping, hiking, cycling, and boating. Or they may choose to spend time at the archeological museum learning about the Stone Age inhabitants of the island.

The best view on Mt. Desert Island is from the top of Cadillac Mountain. This mountain rises 1,532 feet, making it the highest mountain on the Atlantic seaboard. From the summit, you can gaze back toward the mainland or out over the Atlantic Ocean and contemplate the beauty created by a retreating glacier.

38. Which of the following statements best expresses the main idea of paragraph 4 of the selection?
   a. The wealthy residents of Mt. Desert Island selfishly kept it to themselves.
   b. Acadia National Park is one of the smallest of the national parks.
   c. On Mt. Desert Island, there is great tension between the year-round residents and the summer tourists.
   d. Due to its location and environment, Mt. Desert Island supports an incredibly diverse animal and plant life.

39. According to the selection, the large number of small islands along the coast of Maine are the result of
   a. glaciers forcing a mountain range into the sea.
   b. Maine's location between the temperate and subarctic zones.
   c. the irregularity of the Maine coast.
   d. the need for summer communities for wealthy tourists and artists.

40. The content of paragraph 5 indicates that the writer believes that
   a. the continued existence of national parks is threatened by budget cuts.
   b. the best way to preserve the environment on Mt. Desert Island is to limit the number of visitors.
   c. national parks allow large numbers of people to visit and learn about interesting wilderness areas.
   d. Mt. Desert Island is the most interesting tourist attraction in Maine.

41. According to the selection, the coast of Maine is
   a. 2,500 miles long.
   b. 3,500 miles long.
   c. 225 miles long.
   d. 235 miles long.

42. What is the meaning of the underlined phrase flora and fauna in paragraph 4 of this passage?
   a. insects and plants
   b. plants and animals
   c. deer and coyote
   d. birds and beaches

Immune Functions

The immune system is equal in complexity to the combined <u>intricacies</u> of the brain and nervous system. The success of the immune system in defending the body relies on a dynamic regulatory communications network consisting of millions and millions of cells. Organized into sets and subsets, these cells pass information back and forth like clouds of bees swarming around a hive. The result is a sensitive system of checks and balances that produces an immune response that is prompt, appropriate, effective, and self-limiting.

At the heart of the immune system is the ability to distinguish between self and nonself. When immune defenders encounter cells or organisms carrying foreign or nonself molecules, the immune troops move quickly to eliminate the intruders. Virtually every body cell carries distinctive molecules that identify it as self. The body's immune defenses do not normally attack tissues that carry a self-marker. Rather, immune cells and other body cells coexist peaceably in a state known as self-tolerance. When a normally functioning immune system attacks a nonself molecule, the system has the ability to "remember" the specifics of the foreign body. Upon subsequent encounters with the same species of molecules, the immune system reacts accordingly. With the possible exception of antibodies passed during lactation, this so-called immune system memory is not inherited. Despite the occurrence of a virus in your family, your immune system must "learn" from experience with the many millions of distinctive nonself molecules in the sea of microbes in which we live. Learning entails producing the appropriate molecules and cells to match up with and counteract each nonself invader.

Any substance capable of triggering an immune response is called an antigen. Antigens are not to be confused with allergens, which are most often harmless substances (such as ragweed pollen or cat hair) that provoke the immune system to set off the inappropriate and harmful response known as allergy. An antigen can be a virus, a bacterium, a fungus, a parasite, or even a portion or product of one of these organisms. Tissues or cells from another individual (except an identical twin, whose cells carry identical self-markers) also act as antigens; because the immune system recognizes transplanted tissues as foreign, it rejects them. The body will even reject nourishing proteins unless they are first broken down by the digestive system into their primary, nonantigenic building blocks. An antigen announces its foreignness by means of intricate and characteristic shapes called epitopes, which protrude from its surface. Most antigens, even the simplest microbes, carry several different kinds of epitopes on their surface; some may even carry several hundred. Some epitopes will be more effective than others at stimulating an immune response. Only in abnormal situations does the immune system wrongly identify self as nonself and execute a misdirected immune attack. The result can be a so-called autoimmune disease such as rheumatoid arthritis or systemic lupus erythematosis. The painful side effects of these diseases are caused by a person's immune system actually attacking itself.

43. What is the analogy used to describe the communications network among the cells in the immune system?
  a. the immune system's memory
  b. immune troops eliminating intruders
  c. bees swarming around a hive
  d. a sea of microbes

44. The immune cells and other cells in the body coexist peaceably in a state known as
  a. equilibrium.
  b. self-tolerance.
  c. harmony.
  d. tolerance.

45. What is the specific term for the substance capable of triggering an inappropriate or harmful immune response to a harmless substance such as ragweed pollen?
   a. antigen
   b. microbe
   c. allergen
   d. autoimmune disease

46. How do the cells in the immune system recognize an antigen as "foreign" or "nonself?"
   a. through an allergic response
   b. through blood type
   c. through fine hairs protruding from the antigen surface
   d. through characteristic shapes on the antigen surface

47. After you have had the chicken pox, your immune system will be able to do all of the following EXCEPT
   a. prevent your offspring from infection by the chicken pox virus.
   b. distinguish between your body cells and that of the chicken pox virus.
   c. "remember" previous experiences with the chicken pox virus.
   d. match up and counteract nonself molecules in the form of the chicken pox virus.

48. Which of the following best expresses the main idea of this passage?
   a. An antigen is any substance that triggers an immune response.
   b. The basic function of the immune system is to distinguish between self and nonself.
   c. One of the immune system's primary functions is the allergic response.
   d. The human body presents an opportune habitat for microbes.

49. Why would tissue transplanted from father to daughter have a greater risk of being detected as foreign than a tissue transplanted between identical twins?
   a. The age of the twins' tissue would be the same and therefore less likely to be rejected.
   b. The identical twin's tissue would carry the same self-markers and would therefore be less likely to be rejected.
   c. The difference in the sex of the father and daughter would cause the tissue to be rejected by the daughter's immune system.
   d. The twins' immune systems would "remember" the same encounters with childhood illnesses.

50. Antigens differ from allergens because
   a. allergens are usually harmless substances, while antigens can be harmful viruses, fungus or parasites.
   b. antigens trigger an immune system response and allergens do not.
   c. people sensitive to allergens experience visible physical symptoms while people with antigens do not suffer from obvious responses or symptoms.
   d. There is no difference between an antigen and an allergen.

Answer Key

1.	b.	Lesson 1	26.	b.	Lesson 20
2.	b.	Lesson 1	27.	b.	Lesson 20
3.	b.	Lesson 18	28.	a.	Lesson 16
4.	c.	Lesson 2	29.	c.	Lesson 3
5.	a.	Lesson 8	30.	b.	Lesson 3
6.	c.	Lesson 14	31.	c.	Lesson 6
7.	d.	Lesson 1	32.	d.	Lesson 16
8.	b.	Lesson 2	33.	d.	Lesson 13
9.	a.	Lesson 5	34.	b.	Lesson 1
10.	d.	Lesson 14	35.	a.	Lesson 16
11.	c.	Lesson 20	36.	d.	Lesson 3
12.	d.	Lesson 1	37.	b.	Lesson 4
13.	b.	Lesson 4	38.	d.	Lesson 2
14.	a.	Lesson 3	39.	a.	Lesson 9
15.	b.	Lesson 14	40.	c.	Lesson 4
16.	b.	Lesson 3	41.	a.	Lesson 1
17.	b.	Lesson 20	42.	b.	Lesson 3
18.	c.	Lesson 11	43.	c.	Lesson 8
19.	c.	Lesson 11	44.	b.	Lesson 1
20.	a.	Lesson 8	45.	c.	Lesson 3
21.	a.	Lesson 2	46.	d.	Lesson 9
22.	b.	Lesson 20	47.	a.	Lesson 6
23.	c.	Lesson 1	48.	b.	Lesson 2
24.	b.	Lesson 1	49.	b.	Lesson 9
25.	b.	Lesson 14	50.	a.	Lesson 8

Answer Explanations

1. Choice **a** is incorrect. The word *grunge* is presented as the opposite of *glam* and *flashy* in the second paragraph.

   Choice **b** is correct. The article continually contrasts grunge music with the more "corporate," mainstream pop music popular in the 1980s and later, illustrating the rebelliousness of bands like Nirvana, with their "distorted" sound.

   Choice **c** is incorrect. Although the article eventually discusses the end of the grunge movement, the primary descriptions of the music do not support the idea that grunge was inconsistent, or *fickle*.

   Choice **d** is incorrect. *Antithetical* means "opposite," and although grunge bands are portrayed as being the opposite of glam rockers and pop icons, it is not the defining characteristic, per the article.

2. Choice **a** is incorrect. The article never mentions how young people felt about glam rock fashion.

Choice **b** is correct. At the end of the third paragraph, the writer directly states that teenagers embraced grunge fashion because it was against corporate America and the slick pop culture.

Choice **c** is incorrect. The second paragraph states that grunge fashion was derived from the Pacific Northwest's youth culture, not from the musicians themselves.

Choice **d** is incorrect. There is no indication of how parents felt about grunge fashion, so this statement is not supported.

3. Choice **a** is incorrect. "Reporting" means that the writer is offering objective facts. Instead, this statement is an opinion.

Choice **b** is correct. This statement is the writer's subjective opinion. Words like *shallow* and *inferior* can carry a judgmental tone based on the writer's own feelings and emotions, and that is how the words are used here.

Choice **c** is incorrect. This pronouncement is not backed up by actual verifiable facts—just the writer's opinion.

Choice **d** is incorrect. There are no words or phrases that suggest that the statement is quoted from someone else, or that the author does not hold this opinion.

4. Choice **a** is incorrect. The writer uses glam rock as a comparison point, and portrays it as a negative, outdated influence that was replaced by grunge.

Choice **b** is incorrect. Nirvana is mentioned as one of the founding bands of the grunge movement, but it is not the primary focus of the overall piece.

Choice **c** is correct. The article is arranged chronologically, starting with the 1980s music that was replaced by grunge (the "rise"), and ending with the late 1990s music that eventually replaced grunge (the "fall"), with supporting details in the middle to support the overall narrative.

Choice **d** is incorrect. While the writer does mention some of the reasons that teenagers responded enthusiastically to grunge, those are part of the bigger narrative about grunge itself.

5. Choice **a** is correct. The writer uses the first and second paragraphs to establish glam rock's flashy superficiality and compare it unfavorably to grunge's grittiness and honesty.

Choice **b** is incorrect. In the second paragraph, the writer directly mentions that "the youth of America" were caught up in the grunge movement. There is no indication that adults were drawn to grunge.

Choice **c** is incorrect. The article discusses the end of the grunge movement, so it is clear that grunge music is no longer prominent.

Choice **d** is incorrect. There are no supporting details that discuss how commercially successful glam rock *or* grunge was. Both types of music are shown to be popular, although at different times.

6. Choice **a** is incorrect. While the tone is firm, *authoritative* is not the most prominent tone. Always be sure to read all answer choices to make sure that there is not a better option.

Choice **b** is incorrect. The tone is not particularly sad. The decisiveness suggests that there's a different emotion underneath the words.

Choice **c** is correct. The tone is *cynical* because the writer assumes the worst of people's intentions (that they have only a superficial attachment to grunge). The bitterness comes out in the writer's strong tone.

Choice **d** is incorrect. There is nothing to suggest that the writer might not mean what he or she is saying, so there is no apparent irony in the statement.

7. Choice **a** is incorrect. Nirvana is highlighted as one of the most important grunge bands, in the second paragraph.

   Choice **b** is incorrect. Mudhoney is mentioned in the second paragraph as one of the earliest grunge bands.

   Choice **c** is incorrect. Pearl Jam is mentioned in the second paragraph as well, as an example of a popular Seattle band.

   Choice **d** is correct. Poison is listed in the first paragraph as a glam rock band from the 1980s.

8. Choice **a** is incorrect. Although a town official is interviewed about the number of food truck permits, this is a secondary detail.

   Choice **b** is correct. The article's primary topic is the festival that will take place on Sunday, with supporting details that offer background on food trucks and the community.

   Choice **c** is incorrect. The types of foods served by trucks are offered as a supporting detail to let the reader know what will be available at the festival.

   Choice **d** is incorrect. Again, even though food is listed, the primary goal of the article is not to make specific food recommendations.

9. Choice **a** is correct. The article is an announcement, designed to inform the reader about what will be taking place, when it will take place, and where it will take place. The writer offers details to support that information.

   Choice **b** is incorrect. There is no language that suggests that the author is strongly biased in his or her reporting of the festival. Although the tone is light at times, there are no personal opinions included in the piece.

   Choice **c** is incorrect. The writer appears to be sincere; he or she does not mock the festival or any of the people interviewed for the article.

   Choice **d** is incorrect. The article is positive overall, but there are no strong statements or words that indicate excitement.

10. Choice **a** is incorrect. *Drain* is the opposite of what Audrey Marshall seems to be saying, as she talks about the increased numbers of vendors and future growth.

   Choice **b** is incorrect. *Food* would probably be an appropriate word for this article, but it is not the correct choice here. The concept of feeding the small business community is close, but there's a better option among the answer choices.

   Choice **c** is incorrect. A *drawback* is a negative aspect, and Audrey Marshall is talking about growth and progress, making this choice incorrect.

   Choice **d** is correct. *Boon* means a benefit, which makes sense with the rest of Audrey Marshall's statement about the growth of the community.

11. Choice **a** is incorrect. Aside from the statistic about food truck permits, there are no numbers given in the article, so there is not nearly enough information to draw this conclusion.

   Choice **b** is incorrect. There is no evidence that Audrey Marshall will attend the festival. If you look at her quote, she is not even commenting on the festival itself—just the number of food truck permits in Bloomville.

   Choice **c** is correct. If the number of food truck vendors is growing (and expected to grow further), it is reasonable to infer that there's a growing demand in town as well.

Choice **d** is incorrect. In the second paragraph, the writer lists hot dogs among the more "traditional" foods that are likely to appear at the festival, so there is no reason to believe (based on the rest of the article) that hot dogs will not be served.

12. Choice **a** is incorrect. No rice dishes are mentioned among the list of potential foods at the festival.

Choice **b** and choice **c** are incorrect for the same reasons that choice **d** is correct: a parenthetical description in the second paragraph describes *banh mi* as being a type of Vietnamese sandwich.

13. Choice **a** is incorrect. The reader cannot know for certain that events like these are always fun, so it is not a fact.

Choice **b** is correct. Max Bartlett believes that the events are fun, so that makes his statement an opinion.

Choice **c** is incorrect. The quote doesn't ask the reader to accept Max's premise (that the events are fun), or try to sway the reader to a particular point of view. It's just a statement offered as a supporting detail in the article.

Choice **d** is incorrect. Similarly, this is not a logical appeal because Max is not asking the reader to do or believe anything, nor does he use facts or logic to try to sway the reader.

14. Choice **a** is correct. There's no way to know what the number of vendors will be for future festivals, which means that the figure applies to this year's festival. Remember, the first paragraph established that this year's Mobile Food Fest would be the first.

Choice **b** is incorrect. Again, the article can't predict the future, so it is unlikely that *inaugural* refers to future festivals.

Choice **c** is incorrect. Just as the article can't predict the number of vendors at future events, it also can't predict the success of this year's as it hasn't happened yet. This should eliminate *popular* as an option.

Choice **d** is incorrect. There is no past Mobile Food Fest, as this is the first year it's being held. Therefore, *inaugural* can't be inferred to mean "past."

15. Choice **a** is incorrect. The sentence is more light than critical of Max or his sandwiches.

Choice **b** is correct. The writer is having a bit of fun with the name of Max's truck, and injecting some jokiness into the feature piece.

Choice **c** is incorrect. There is nothing in the article that suggests the writer is out for vengeance against Max (or his truck), or that the writer has any personal opinion that could lead to a vengeful tone.

Choice **d** is incorrect. There is also nothing to suggest that the writer is sad about Max's truck having a very literal name.

16. Choice **a** is incorrect. While Mrs. Rachel is highly curious about where Matthew Cuthbert is going, there are no words or tones in the passage to suggest that Matthew is being deceptive about where he's going. You can eliminate *lied*.

Choice **b** is correct. Mrs. Rachel is using evidence to piece together where Matthew might be going. *Implied* connects her certainty that he's leaving Avonlea to the idea that the sorrel mare and buggy mean he's going even further than she previously thought, painting a more coherent picture of where Matthew might be headed.

Choice **c** is incorrect. Despite her logic, Mrs. Rachel still doesn't know where Matthew is going. Therefore, *confirmed* is not the right word to describe her speculative evidence.

Choice **d** is incorrect. Even though the sorrel mare and buggy make it appear Matthew is going a considerable distance, it's not required that Matthew use them only to go far.

17. Choice **a** is incorrect. Mrs. Rachel may know nearly everything about her neighbors, and she may find it mysterious that she doesn't know what's going on with Matthew Cuthbert, but there's no evidence in the passage to suggest that he is hiding his destination on purpose.

Choice **b** is correct. The passage is very clear that Mrs. Rachel's "all-seeing eye" catches most everything around her. Of the choices, this is the only statement that is supported by the passage.

Choice **c** is incorrect. While the reader discovers that the Lynde house is located in Avonlea next to a brook, there is no detail to suggest what color the house is.

Choice **d** is incorrect. The narrator mentions only the one brook. The reader would need to know more about other brooks in town to make this inference.

18. Choice **a** is incorrect. The perspective is Mrs. Rachel's overall, but she is not presented as an "I."

Choice **b** is incorrect. The passage does not involve the reader as "you," meaning it can't be second-person.

Choice **c** is correct. The narrator is unseen and unacknowledged, but is able to convey all necessary information to the reader. The use of "she" in the first paragraph is the first indicator that this is a third-person text. You should always read carefully throughout the text to make sure that no "I"s or "you"s come up later in the writing, switching the perspective.

Choice **d** is incorrect. This passage is indeed a narrative story; however, *narrative* is not a specific point of view.

19. Choice **a** is incorrect. Moving inside Mrs. Rachel Lynde's perspective would give even more insight into her thoughts and feelings, not less.

Choice **b** is incorrect. Inside Mrs. Rachel Lynde's head or outside of it, she still doesn't know for sure where Matthew Cuthbert is going.

Choice **c** is correct. Even though the lens is kept closely on Mrs. Rachel for much of the passage, switching her to an "I" perspective would let the reader "hear" Mrs. Rachel's own voice, rather than the narrator's interpretation of it.

Choice **d** is incorrect. As a narrator, Mrs. Rachel *might* reveal more information about her husband, but there is no guarantee that such a thing would happen.

20. Choice **a** is correct. The narrator, trying to establish Mrs. Rachel as a strong and vivid character, wants to make sure the reader knows that Mrs. Rachel doesn't spend all of her time waiting by the window and speculating about the motives of her neighbors. This contrast between her and those "who can attend closely to their neighbor's business by dint of neglecting their own" serves to emphasize the mystery of Matthew's errand.

Choice **b** is incorrect. The passage depicts Mrs. Rachel as more productive than most of her fellow Avonlea citizens. Also, there is no information about what other people do with their time, so there's no way to know exactly how similar she is to her neighbors.

Choice **c** is incorrect. Again, we see only Mrs. Rachel's list of activities, no one else's, so it is impossible to know whether these activities represent Avonlea as a whole.

Choice **d** is incorrect. The list is informative in that it tells us more about Mrs. Rachel's character, but this is only one paragraph in the entire passage, and does not represent the overall tone.

21. Choice **a** is correct. The main idea isn't apparent until fairly late in the passage (the fourth paragraph). The first several paragraphs are meant to establish scene and character, leading up to the revelation of Matthew's odd departure.

Choice **b** is incorrect. The third paragraph states that Matthew is supposed to be home planting turnips, like Thomas Lynde is doing, but a closer read shows that this is only the case because he was overheard telling others that he *would* be home planting turnips. There is no evidence anywhere in the piece that this planting is required or expected of Avonlea's farmers.

Choice **c** is incorrect. While a lot of the passage is devoted to explaining how Mrs. Rachel knows everything that goes on around her, this is primarily used as a contrast to the one thing she *doesn't* know. That Mrs. Rachel is usually in the know about everything in Avonlea becomes a secondary topic after the reader is introduced to the Matthew mystery.

Choice **d** is incorrect. Matthew's shyness (his never "volunteer[ing] information about anything") is a supporting detail, not a main idea.

22. Choice **a** is incorrect. The narrator (and Mrs. Rachel) both note that Matthew *looks* like he's on a less ordinary errand, so it is unlikely that he's going to the store for an ordinary reason.

Choice **b** is correct. His outfit, his choice of buggy and horse, and the odd timing all suggest that Matthew is going somewhere more formal than one might expect in the middle of an afternoon.

Choice **c** is incorrect. The narrator playfully suggests that even running water behaves itself in Mrs. Rachel's yard, but there's no evidence that this is actually the case.

Choice **d** is incorrect. While her cotton warp quilts are shown to be impressive, there is not enough information to determine whether the quilts themselves are popular around Avonlea.

23. Choice **a** is incorrect. An experienced business traveler likely encounters security checks fairly often, and so wouldn't require instructions like these anymore.

Choice **b** is incorrect. A child would most likely be traveling with an adult, and probably would not be reading these instructions on his or her own. Also, the tone and diction are very straightforward and business-like—not child-friendly.

Choice **c** is correct. This article is meant for someone unfamiliar with the security check process, and who needs pointers and reminders.

Choice **d** is incorrect. Pilots are likely to have a different set of check-in procedures and policies than the customers who are flying. Also, pilots are likely to be more experienced with airport procedures.

24. Choice **a** is incorrect. The third paragraph of the article explicitly forbids guests from going through the security check area if they are not passengers.

Choice **b** is correct. From the article, you can infer that non-passengers are allowed to accompany passengers up to the security area, just not beyond that point.

Choice **c** is incorrect. While non-passengers are forbidden from crossing the security checkpoint, there are no stated rules that say they are required to stay outside the airport.

Choice **d** is incorrect. If non-passengers are not allowed past Security, they are certainly not going to be allowed in the final point of the journey through the airport: the airplane itself.

25. Choice **a** is incorrect. The article is meant to be informative on a serious topic, so there is little room for sarcasm, and no language to indicate that the writer is being *sarcastic*.

Choice **b** is correct. The article is designed to convey important security information efficiently, so the tone is kept *business-like* and professional.

Choice **c** is incorrect. There is no personal perspective in the article, and nothing to be *angry* about, so the tone is not emotional.

Choice **d** is incorrect. Again, the article features serious information and serious consequences for violating the policies—both of which are the opposite of *frivolous*.

26. Choice **a** is incorrect. The second paragraph states that containers of liquid larger than three ounces are not allowed, so the backpack containing water bottles would be problematic.

Choice **b** is correct. The shoes and jacket can be taken off easily to meet the security requirements, and the clearly labeled, regulation-size bottles show compliance with the liquid policy outlined in the second paragraph.

Choice **c** is incorrect. The second paragraph states that electronics are among the items to be screened separately; so carrying them with you could slow down your security check experience.

Choice **d** is incorrect. Jewelry could set off the metal detector, per the second paragraph, and this could disrupt the security check.

27. Choice **a** is incorrect. The first paragraph describes the Marsdens as eager to be good campers.

Choice **b** is correct. Spike chases squirrels, but the story makes it clear that his excessive barking tipped off the Marsdens that something was out of the ordinary. If Spike normally barked too much, this would likely not be the case.

Choice **c** is incorrect. The first paragraph tells the reader that the Marsdens are considerate about their camping behavior, and their regret at the bear's death suggests that they are compassionate as well.

Choice **d** is incorrect. Spike the dog did, in fact, corner the grizzly, as illustrated in the third paragraph.

28. Choice **a** is correct. The first paragraph sets up the idea that the Marsdens would not be able to avoid attracting bears. The last paragraph mentions their "shame" at the bear's death, indicating guilt.

Choice **b** is incorrect. The writer suggests that the bear was attracted to the campsite by the food left out by the Marsdens, and that he'd been "rewarded" for raiding the campsite, This, in turn, suggests that he was lured there, and not at fault.

Choice **c** is incorrect. The last paragraph (the first mention of the Fish and Game Department) suggests that the department was merely doing its job based on what had already happened with the Marsdens and the bear.

Choice **d** is incorrect. The first paragraph states that the "number-one rule" was not to feed the bears. The writer implies that this is a priority for the Forest Service. As the next sentence talks about the Marsdens not being able to follow that rule, it passes the responsibility along to the family.

29. Choice **a** is incorrect. The Marsdens were careful about their campsite, so *neglect* is unikely.

Choice **b** is incorrect. They had already cleaned their campsite, so it is unlikely that they would clean it again.

Choice **c** is correct. The writer offers the image of the Marsdens carefully combing the campsite with flashlights, looking closely to see if they had forgotten anything. Therefore, *studied* is the most likely meaning.

Choice **d** is incorrect. Their use of the flashlight suggests that they're not trying to hide, but rather trying to see.

30. Choice **a** is incorrect. There is no supporting information to indicate that the author believes raccoons or squirrels are stupid.

Choice **b** is correct. The Marsdens assume that whatever Spike has cornered, it has to be a creature that is not afraid of the barking. Therefore, *fearless* is the right choice.

Choice **c** is incorrect. The Marsdens also assume that the creature is dangerous—the word *clumsy* is not generally associated with threatening behavior.

Choice **d** is incorrect. As with *fearless*, *spineless* can be eliminated by the simple fact that the animal is not scared away by Spike's barking.

31. Choice **a** is incorrect. The most important event is the Marsdens' encounter with the bear, which doesn't take place until the third paragraph.

Choice **b** is incorrect. If the story were in reverse chronological order, the story would begin with the bear's death and work backwards.

Choice **c** is correct. The story starts with the beginning of the Marsdens' camping trip, and follows it through to the bear's death, keeping the events in the order in which they happened.

Choice **d** is incorrect. The story is told in order, from one event to the next. The writer uses time-related phrases (*the next morning, a week after they returned home*) to help the reader place the events chronologically.

32. Choice **a** is incorrect. The writer never gives the reader the bear's perspective, so we don't know whether the bear saw the Marsdens run.

Choice **b** is incorrect. The bear was ultimately shot, so the reader knows that he was punished in some way for his encounter with the Marsdens.

Choice **c** is incorrect. The bear's stand-off with Spike is used to announce the bear's presence to the reader; it is not presented as an accomplishment or a positive experience for the bear.

Choice **d** is correct. Near the end of the story, the writer indicates that the bear had gotten to Spike's dog food—the only food accessible to him. In the second-to-last paragraph, the writer suggests that the bear's nature would push him to go back for more. Food is the only incentive that exists for the bear.

33. Choice **a** is incorrect. There are no statistics or facts that would make this piece an appropriate scientific report. The focus is on the story, not the science behind it.

Choice **b** is incorrect. The story is too focused on the narrative to be useful to someone reading a bear-safety pamphlet. If the piece had more direct tips on how to keep bears away, it might be more suitable as part of a safety pamphlet.

Choice **c** is incorrect. As with choice **a**, there's not enough specific information or factual evidence to make this story a report or study. There is also no information on bears other than the one encountered by the Marsdens, so there is no way to draw conclusions about other bear fatalities.

Choice **d** is correct. Because the story is a chronological narrative with background information about the Marsdens, it would be most suitable as a general human interest story about one family's encounter with a bear.

34. Choice **a** is incorrect. While some critics speculate that there could be a backlash, there is no evidence yet that this is going to occur.

Choice **b** is correct. The story's first paragraph describes the lines and the potential sellouts, which contrasts with the mixed reviews in the third paragraph.

Choice **c** is incorrect. That the MyBook will "revolutionize" anything is not a fact, but a single quote from the company's CEO. This is presented as a supporting detail, not a main idea.

Choice **d** is incorrect. Sales information for anything but the MyBook is incomplete, so while the article speculates that holiday sales will be strong, this is a small part of the information conveyed.

35. Choice **a** is correct. Despite critics going public with their concerns, people like Celia Nunez are waiting in line because they had heard that the MyBook would be the most popular holiday gift this year.

Choice **b** is incorrect. All we know of Celia is her quote related to shopping. Her MyBook expertise is not discussed in enough detail to determine whether she knows more than the critics.

Choice **c** is incorrect. From the first paragraph, you know that the MyBook is already selling well, but there is no mention in the article of how these sales will affect TechGiant's stock.

Choice **d** is incorrect. Because the bloggers and insiders could easily be part of the group labeled "critics" in the third paragraph, there is not enough information to determine whether or not they love the MyBook.

36. Choice **a** is incorrect. Context words like *lackluster* and *flaws* are negative, while *profit* is generally seen as a positive word.

Choices **b** and **c** are incorrect. Similarly, it is unlikely that flaws and mediocre features would automatically lead to an *upward trend*, or positive *assets*.

Choice **d** is correct. *Backlash*, or hostile response, fits in with the negative tone established by the context of the rest of the sentence.

37. Choice **a** is incorrect. The quotes are personal statements, not things that are known to be true.

Choice **b** is correct. Again, these are personal statements. Even when they're authoritative, as with the TechGiant CEO's, they still represent ideas that the speakers *believe* to be true.

Choice **c** is incorrect. Only one of the quotes is from a consumer, and she isn't commenting on the product itself so much as her reasons for wanting to buy one.

Choice **d** is incorrect. This is a news article, presenting factual information and reasonable support—not fiction.

38. Choice **a** is incorrect. The fourth paragraph doesn't pass judgment on the wealthy residents—it explains the possible reasons why Mt. Desert Island has become a popular destination.

Choice **b** is incorrect. The paragraph contains no information on the park's size.

Choice **c** is incorrect. The paragraph focuses on the aspects of the island that attract people, not on the social issues among its residents.

Choice **d** is correct. The paragraph focuses on the diversity of its inhabitants (including the humans) to emphasize the appeal of Acadia National Park.

39. Choice **a** is correct. The second paragraph of the excerpt describes the glacier process that shaped the Maine coastline.

Choice **b** is incorrect. In the fourth paragraph, the temperate and subarctic zones are responsible for diverse flora and fauna, not for the islands.

Choice **c** is incorrect. The large number of small islands on the coast is due to glaciers, not irregularity.

Choice **d** is incorrect. The residents of coastal Maine are not discussed in terms of their needs, and so have nothing to do with the coastal islands.

40. Choice **a** is incorrect. There is no mention of budgets or budget cuts in the fifth paragraph.

Choice **b** is incorrect. The paragraph states that Acadia will be "available to all people," which is the opposite of limiting visitors.

Choice **c** is correct. The writer believes that Acadia should be open to everyone for activities of their choosing, per the paragraph.

Choice **d** is incorrect. The paragraph says nothing about other tourist attractions, which would be necessary to draw this conclusion.

41. Choices **a**, **b**, and **d** are incorrect. The first paragraph clearly states that the coast of Maine is 225 miles long.

Choice **c** is correct.

42. Choice **a** is incorrect. Insects are never mentioned anywhere in the passage.

Choice **b** is correct. The same paragraph describes the *plants and animals* found in Acadia, which means you can infer that those are the meanings of flora and fauna.

Choice **c** is incorrect. *Deer and coyote* are never mentioned anywhere in the passage.

Choice **d** is incorrect. *Birds and beaches* are mentioned in addition to flora and fauna in the same sentence, meaning they can't be the same as the underlined words.

43. Choices **a**, **b**, and **d** are incorrect. The first paragraph compares the immune system cell communication to bees swarming around a hive.

    Choice **c** is correct.

44. Choice **a** is incorrect. *Equilibrium* does mean a kind of balance, but according to the passage, it is not the correct choice.

    Choice **b** is correct. The second paragraph explicitly says that *self-tolerance* is the state in which immune cells coexist with other types of cells.

    Choice **c** is incorrect. *Harmony*, like equilibrium, would ordinarily work; however, the passage is very specific about which term it uses for this phenomenon.

    Choice **d** is incorrect. The prefix *self-* is the key to eliminating this one. The more specific you can be in verifying what a text actually said, the likelier you are to choose the best answer.

45. Choice **a** is incorrect. The third paragraph specifically says that *antigens* are not to be confused with allergens, so this choice is a trap. Read carefully!

    Choice **b** is incorrect. In the second paragraph, *microbes* are described as "the sea…in which we live," which is different from the definition in the question.

    Choice **c** is correct. The third paragraph states that *allergens* are the substances which trigger a harmful immune response.

    Choice **d** is incorrect. An *autoimmune disease* is described as "an immune system actually attacking itself," which is not the definition in the question.

46. Choice **a** is incorrect. An *allergic response* is defined as an "inappropriate and harmful response," which would likely come *after* the immune cells recognize an antigen as foreign.

    Choice **b** is incorrect. The passage never mentions *blood types*, so this is not the answer.

    Choice **c** is incorrect. The third paragraph states that antigens carry "epitopes," which are not described as hairs.

    Choice **d** is correct. The characteristic shapes, or epitopes, are defined in the third paragraph.

47. Choice **a** is correct. The second paragraph states that immune system memory is not inherited, and therefore can't be passed to offspring.

    Choice **b** is incorrect. The second paragraph also describes how the immune system will recognize "nonself" particles (in this case, the chicken pox virus), and react accordingly.

    Choice **c** is incorrect. The passage tells the reader that immune system memory will remember the specifics of the foreign body, if the foreign body ever returns.

    Choice **d** is incorrect. The last sentence of the second paragraph explains that the immune system will match up and counteract nonself particles, so this choice is not the correct answer.

48. Choice **a** is incorrect. That antigens are substances that trigger immune responses is a standalone fact, not the main idea supported by other facts and information.

    Choice **b** is correct. The second and third paragraphs are devoted to fleshing out that main topic, and describing how the immune system actually distinguishes between self and nonself particles.

    Choice **c** is incorrect. Allergic responses are specific (they are only one type of immune system response), which makes this choice too narrow to be a main idea.

    Choice **d** is incorrect. This statement is vague, and is not supported by information within the passage, so it is not the main idea.

49. Choice **a** is incorrect. Age is not listed as a factor in immune responses.

Choice **b** is correct. The second paragraph explicitly states that identical twins carry the same self-markers, so this is correct.

Choice **c** is incorrect. As with age, sex is not mentioned as a factor in immune responses. But because the father and daughter are not identical, they will have different self-markers, and therefore different immune responses.

Choice **d** is incorrect. Just because the twins are identical does not mean they will encounter the exact same illnesses. The passage states that their identical internal makeup is the driving force behind the match—not external factors like airborne diseases.

50. Choice **a** is correct. The first sentences of the third paragraph define and compare the two, confirming that allergens are harmless substances and antigens can be harmful substances.

Choice **b** is incorrect. The passage says specifically that allergens *can* trigger immune responses, despite being otherwise harmless substances.

Choice **c** is incorrect. The passage does not contain any information on symptoms, so there is no support to determine whether this statement is accurate.

Choice **d** is incorrect. The third paragraph states that while antigens can be harmful, while allergens are generally harmless. This is an explicit difference between the two, so this choice is incorrect.

APPENDIX

A ▶ STUDYING FOR SUCCESS

How successful you are at studying has less to do with how much time you put into it than with how you do it. That's because some ways of studying are much more effective than others, and some environments are much more conducive to studying than others. Another reason is that not everyone retains information in the same way. On the following pages, you will discover how to adapt your studying strategies to the ways you learn best. You will probably pick up some new techniques for studying, and will also gain insight on how to prepare for standardized tests.

Learning Styles

Think for a minute about what you know about how you learn. For example, if you need directions to a new restaurant, would you

- ask to see a map showing how to get there?
- ask someone to tell you how to get there?
- copy someone's written directions?

Most people learn in a variety of ways: seeing, touching, hearing, and experiencing the world around them. Many people find, however, that they are more likely to absorb information better from one learning source than from others. The source that works best for you is called your dominant learning method.

There are three basic learning methods: visual, auditory, and kinesthetic (also known as tactile).

- Visual learners understand and retain information best when they can see the map, the picture, the text, the word, or the math example.
- Auditory learners learn best when they can hear the directions, the poem, the math theorem, or the spelling of a word.
- Kinesthetic learners need to do—they must write the directions, draw the diagram, or copy down the phone number.

Visual Learners

If you are a visual learner, you learn best by seeing. Pay special attention to illustrations and graphic material when you study. If you color code your notes with colorful inks or highlighters, you may find that you absorb information better. Visual learners can learn to map or diagram information later in this appendix.

Auditory Learners

If you are an auditory learner, you learn best by listening. Read material aloud to yourself, or talk about what you are learning with a study partner or a study group. Hearing the information will help you to remember it. Some people like to tape-record notes and play them back on the tape player. If you commute to work or school by car or listen to a personal tape player, you can gain extra preparation time by playing the notes to yourself on tape.

Kinesthetic Learners

If you are a kinesthetic learner, you learn best by doing. Interact a lot with your print material by underlining and making margin notes in your textbooks and handouts. Rewrite your notes onto index cards. Recopying material helps you remember it.

How to Study Most Effectively

If studying efficiently is second nature to you, you're very lucky. Most people have to work at it. Try some of these helpful study methods to make studying easier and more effective for you.

Make an Outline

After collecting all the materials you need to review or prepare for the test, the first step for studying any subject is to reduce a large body of information into smaller, more manageable units. One approach to studying this way is to make an outline of text information, handout material, and class notes.

The important information in print material is often surrounded by lots of extra words and ideas. If you can highlight just the important information, or at least the information you need to know for your test, you can help yourself narrow your focus so that you can study more effectively. There are several ways to make an outline of print material. They include annotating, outlining, and mapping. The point of all three of these strategies is that they allow you to pull out just the important information that you need to prepare for the test.

Annotating

Annotations help you pull out main ideas from the surrounding text to make them more visible and accessible to you. Annotation means that you underline or highlight important information that appears in print material. It also involves responding to the material by engaging yourself with the writer by making margin notes. Margin notes are phrases or sentences in the margins of print material that summarize the content of those passages. Your margin notes leave footprints for you to follow as you review the text.

Here is an example of a passage that has been annotated and underlined.

Loction, Location, Location

Find a quiet spot, use a good reading light, and turn the radio off.

Find Quiet Places

For many adult test takers, it's difficult to find a quiet spot in their busy lives. Many adults don't even have a bedroom corner that isn't shared with someone else. Your quiet spot may be in a different place at different times of the day.

Different quiet places at different times

For example, it could be the kitchen table early in the morning before breakfast, your workplace area when everyone else is at lunch, or a corner of the sofa late at night. If you know you'll have to move around when you study, make sure your study material is portable.

Portable study material

Keep your notes, practice tests, pencils, and other supplies together in a folder or bag. Then you can easily carry your study material with you and study in whatever quiet spot presents itself.

If quiet study areas are nonexistent in your home or work environment, you may need to find a space elsewhere. The public library is the most obvious choice. Some test takers find it helpful to assign themselves study hours at the library in the same way that they schedule dentist appointments, class hours, household tasks, or other necessary uses of daily or weekly time. Studying away from home or work also minimizes the distractions of other people and other demands when you are preparing for a test.

Library!

Lights

Libraries also provide good reading lights. For some people, this may seem like a trivial matter, but the eyestrain that can come from working for long periods in poor light can be very tiring—which you can't afford when you're studying hard.

Need good light

At home, the bedside lamp, the semidarkness of a room dominated by the television, or the bright sunlight of the back porch will be of little help to tired eyes.

Outlining

You are probably familiar with the basic format of the traditional outline:

I. Main idea 1
    A. Major detail
    B. Major detail
        1. Minor detail
        2. Minor detail
II. Main idea 2
    A. Major detail
    B. Major detail

You may have used an outline in school to help you organize a writing assignment or take notes. When you outline print material, you're looking for the basic ideas that make up the framework of the text. When you are taking out the important information for a test, then you are looking for the basic ideas that the author wants to convey to you.

Mapping

Mapping is a more visual kind of outline. Instead of making a linear outline of the main ideas of a text, when you map, you make a diagram of the main points in the text that you want to remember. The following diagrams show the same information in a map form.

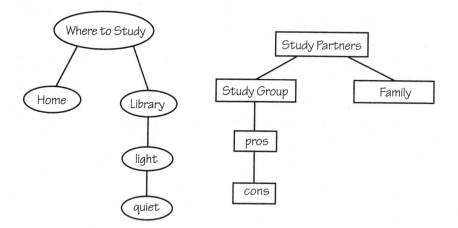

Make Study Notes

The next step after you have pulled out all the key ideas is to make notes from which you will study. You will use these notes for the intensive and ongoing study you'll do over the period of time before the test. They're the specific items that you targeted as important to know for the test. Your notes should help you understand the information you need to know and, in many cases, commit it to memory. You should be sure to include

- the main ideas you underlined or highlighted in the text.
- the main ideas and important details you outlined or mapped from the text.
- specific terms, words, dates, formulas, names, facts, or procedures that you need to memorize.

How Do You Make Study Notes?

Some people like to write study notes in the back pages of their notebooks or on paper folded lengthwise so that it can be tucked between the pages of a text or review book. This format is good to use for notes that can be written as questions and answers, cause and effect, or definition and examples. You can also make notes on index cards.

Using Index Cards

It can be very helpful to write your study notes—especially those that contain material to be memorized—on index cards. Vocabulary words are significantly easier to learn using index cards.

Advantages of making notes on index cards are:

- The information on each card is visually separated from other information. Therefore, it's easier to concentrate on just that one item, separate from the surrounding text. You remember the look of a vocabulary word or a math equation more clearly when it is set off by itself.
- Cards are small and portable. They can be carried in a purse or a pocket and pulled out at any time during the day for review.
- Study cards can help you with the necessary task of memorizing. If you write the key word or topic you are trying to learn on one side, and the information you must know on the other side, you have an easy way to quiz yourself on the material. This method is especially good for kinesthetic learners, who learn by doing.

Making Memorizing Easier

There are many ways to take the drudgery out of memorizing information.

Take Small Bites of Time

Most people memorize information best when they study in small periods over a long period of time.

Memorizing facts from index cards that can be carried with you and pulled out for a few ten-minute sessions each day will yield better results than sitting down with a textbook for an hour straight. Index card notes can be pulled out in odd moments: while you are sitting in the car waiting to pick up your friend, during the 15 minutes you spend on the bus in the morning, while you wait to be picked up from school or work, and so on.

You'll find that these short but regular practices will greatly aid your recall of lots of information. They're a great way to add more study time to your schedule.

Break It Up

When you have a list to memorize, break the list into groups of seven or any other odd number. People seem to remember best when they divide long lists into shorter ones—and, for some reason, shorter ones that have an odd number of items in them. So instead of trying to memorize ten vocabulary or spelling words, split your list into smaller lists of seven and three, or five and five, to help you remember them.

Create Visual Aids

Give yourself visual assistance in memorizing. If there's a tricky combination of letters in a word you need to spell, for example, circle or underline it in red or highlight it in the text. Your eye will recall what the word looks like. With some information, you can even draw a map or picture to help you remember.

Do It Out Loud

Give yourself auditory assistance in memorizing. Many people learn best if they hear the information. Sit by yourself in a quiet room and say aloud what you need to learn. Or give your notes to someone else and let that person ask you or quiz you on the material.

Use Mnemonics

Mnemonics, or memory tricks, are things that help you remember what you need to know.

The most common type of mnemonic is the acronym. One acronym you may already know is **HOMES**, for the names of the Great Lakes (Huron, Ontario, Michigan, Erie, and Superior). **ROY G. BIV** reminds people of the colors in the spectrum (**r**ed, **o**range, **y**ellow, **g**reen, **b**lue, **i**ndigo, and **v**iolet).

You can make a mnemonic out of anything. In a psychology course, for example, you might memorize the stages in death and dying by the nonsense word **DABDA** (**d**enial, **a**nger, **b**argaining, **d**epression, and acceptance.) Another kind of mnemonic is a silly sentence made out of words that each begin with the letter or letters that start each item in a series. You may remember "**P**lease **E**xcuse **M**y **D**ear **A**unt **S**ally" as a device for remembering the order of operations in math (Parentheses, Exponents, Multiply, Divide, Add, and Subtract).

Sleep on It

When you study right before sleep and don't allow any interference—such as conversation, radio, television, or music—to come between study and sleep, you remember material better. This is especially true if you

Take Small Bites of Time

Most people memorize information best when they study in <u>small periods over a long period of time</u>.

Memorizing facts from index cards that can be carried with you and pulled out for a few ten-minute sessions each day will yield better results than sitting down with a textbook for an hour straight. You'll find that these short but regular practices will greatly aid your recall of lots of information. They're a great way to add more study time to your schedule.

Break It Up

When you have a list to memorize, <u>break the list into groups of seven or any other odd number</u>. People seem to remember best when they divide long lists into shorter ones—and, for some reason, shorter ones that have an odd number of items in them. So instead of trying to memorize ten vocabulary or spelling words, split your list into smaller lists of seven and three, or five and five, to help you remember them.

Create Visual Aids

<u>Give yourself visual assistance in memorizing</u>. If there's a tricky combination of letters in a word you need to spell, for example, circle or underline it in red or highlight it in the text. Your eye will recall what the word looks like.

Do It Out Loud

<u>Give yourself auditory assistance in memorizing</u>. Many people learn best if they hear the information. Sit by yourself in a quiet room and say aloud what you need to learn. Or give your notes to someone else and let that person quiz you on the material.

Use Mnemonics

<u>Mnemonics</u>, or memory tricks, are things that help you remember what you need to know.

The most common type of mnemonic is the <u>acronym</u>. One acronym you may already know is **HOMES**, for the names of the Great Lakes (**H**uron, **O**ntario, **M**ichigan, **E**rie, and **S**uperior). **ROY G. BIV** reminds people of the colors in the spectrum (**r**ed, **o**range, **y**ellow, **g**reen, **b**lue, **i**ndigo, and **v**iolet).

review first thing after waking as well. A rested and relaxed brain seems to hang on to information better than a tired and stressed-out brain.

On the following pages, try out some of the learning strategies you discovered in this lesson. Then check your answers.

The following is a passage from this text to underline and annotate. Make margin summaries of the key points in each paragraph. Then make a mnemonic based on your margin notes.

Note Cards

Make note cards with definitions for each kind of learning modality:

- visual
- auditory
- kinesthetic

Mapping

Here is an outline of the learning strategies covered in this chapter. Using the same information, make a map or diagram of the same material.

   I. How to study most effectively
     A. Annotating
     B. Outlining
     C. Mapping
  II. How to make study notes
     A. Notebook pages
     B. Index cards
        1. Reasons for using index cards
 III. Memory methods

Completed Sample Annotation

Take Small Bites of Time

Distributed practice

Most people memorize information best when they study in <u>small periods over a long period of time</u>.

Memorizing facts from portable index cards that can be carried with you and pulled out for a few ten-minute sessions each day will yield better results than sitting down with a textbook for an hour straight. You'll find that these short but regular practices will greatly aid your recall of lots of information. They're a great way to add more study time to your schedule.

Break It Up

Divide lists

When you have a list to memorize, <u>break the list into groups of seven or any other odd number</u>. People seem to remember best when they divide long lists into shorter ones—and, for some reason, shorter ones that have an odd number of items in them. So instead of trying to memorize ten vocabulary or spelling words, split your list into smaller lists of seven and three, or five and five, to help you remember them.

Create Visual Aids

Visual Aids

Give yourself visual assistance in memorizing. If there's a tricky combination of letters in a word you need to spell, for example, circle or underline it in red or highlight it in the text. Your eye will recall what the word looks like.

Do It Out Loud

Auditory

Give yourself auditory assistance in memorizing. Many people learn best if they hear the information. Sit by yourself in a quiet room and say aloud what you need to learn. Or, give your notes to someone else and let that person ask you questions and quiz you on the material.

Use Mnemonics

Acronym

<u>Mnemonics</u>, or memory tricks, are things that help you remember what you need to know.

The most common type of mnemonic is the <u>acronym</u>. One acronym you may already know is **HOMES**, for the names of the Great Lakes (**H**uron, **O**ntario, **M**ichigan, **E**rie, and **S**uperior). **ROY G. BIV** reminds people of the colors in the spectrum (**r**ed, **o**range, **y**ellow, **g**reen, **b**lue, **i**ndigo, and **v**iolet).

Sample Mnemonics
DDVAA

Note Cards
Here are samples of how your note cards might look:

FRONT OF CARD

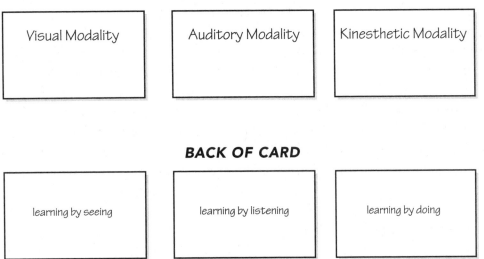

Visual Modality	Auditory Modality	Kinesthetic Modality

BACK OF CARD

learning by seeing	learning by listening	learning by doing

Mapping
Here is an example of how your map or diagram might look:

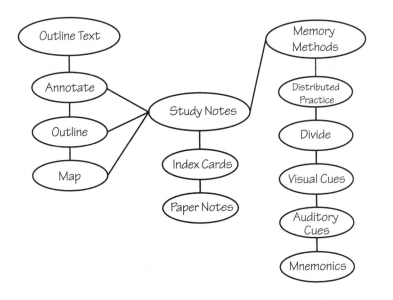

Studying for a Standarized Test

Most of us get nervous about tests, especially standardized tests, where our scores can have a significant impact on our future. Nervousness is natural—and it can even be an advantage if you know how to channel it into positive energy.

The following pages provide suggestions for overcoming test anxiety, both in the days and weeks before the test and during the test itself.

Two to Three Months before the Test

The number one best way to combat test anxiety is to **be prepared.** That means two things: Know what to expect on the test, and review the material and skills on which you will be tested.

Review the Material and Skills You'll Be Tested On

The fact that you are reading this book means that you've already taken this step. Now, are there other steps you can take? Are there other subject areas you need to review? Can you make more improvement in this or other areas? If you are really nervous or if it has been a long time since you reviewed these subjects and skills, you may want to buy a second study guide, sign up for a class in your neighborhood, or work with a tutor.

The more you know about what to expect on test day and the more comfortable you are with the material and skills to be tested, the less anxious you will be and the better you will do on the test itself.

The Days before the Test
Review, Don't Cram

If you have been preparing and reviewing in the weeks before the exam, there's no need to cram a few days beforehand. Cramming is likely to confuse you and make you nervous. Instead, schedule a relaxed review of all you have learned.

Physical Activity

Get some exercise in the days preceding the test. You'll send some extra oxygen to your brain and allow your thinking performance to peak on the day you take the test. Moderation is the key here. Don't exercise so much that you feel exhausted, but a little physical activity will invigorate your body and brain. Walking is a terrific, low-impact, energy-building form of exercise.

Balanced Diet

Like your body, your brain needs proper nutrients to function well. Eat plenty of fruits and vegetables in the days before the test. Foods high in lecithin, such as fish and beans, are especially good choices. Lecithin is a protein your brain needs for peak performance. You may even consider a visit to your local pharmacy to buy a bottle of lecithin tablets several weeks before your test.

Rest

Get plenty of sleep the nights before the test. Don't overdo it, though, or you'll make yourself as groggy as if you were overtired. Go to bed at a reasonable time, early enough to get the hours of rest you need to function **effectively.** You'll feel relaxed and rested if you've gotten plenty of sleep in the days before you take the test.

Trial Run

At some point before the test, make a trial run to the testing center to see how long it takes to get there. Rushing raises your emotional energy and lowers your intellectual capacity, so you want to allow plenty of time on test day to get to the testing center. Arriving ten or 15 minutes early gives you time to relax and get situated.

Motivation

Plan some sort of celebration—with family or friends, or just by yourself—for after the test. Make sure it's something you'll really look forward to and enjoy. If you have something planned for after the test, you may find it easier to prepare and keep moving during the test.

Test Day

It's finally here, the day of the big test. Set your alarm early enough to allow plenty of time to get to the testing center. Eat a good breakfast. Avoid anything that's really high in sugar, such as donuts. A sugar high turns into a sugar low after an hour or so. Cereal and toast, or anything with complex carbohydrates is a good choice. Eat only moderate amounts. You don't want to take a test feeling stuffed! Your body will channel its energy to your digestive system instead of your brain.

Pack a high-energy snack to take with you. You may have a break sometime during the test when you can grab a quick snack. Bananas are great. They have a moderate amount of sugar and plenty of brain nutrients, such as potassium. Most proctors won't allow you to eat a snack while you're testing, but a peppermint shouldn't pose a problem. Peppermints are like smelling salts for your brain. If you lose your concentration or suffer from a momentary mental block, a peppermint can get you back on track. Don't forget the earlier advice about relaxing and taking a few deep breaths.

Leave early enough so you have plenty of time to get to the test center. Allow a few minutes for unexpected traffic. When you arrive, locate the restroom and use it. Few things interfere with concentration as much as a full bladder. Then find your seat and make sure it's comfortable. If it isn't, tell the proctor and ask to move to something more suitable.

Now relax and think positively! Before you know it, the test will be over, and you'll walk away knowing you've done as well as you can.

Combating Test Anxiety

Okay—you know what the test will be on. You've reviewed the subjects and practiced the skills on which you will be tested. So why do you still have that sinking feeling in your stomach? Why are your palms sweaty and your hands shaking?

Even the brightest, most well-prepared test takers sometimes suffer bouts of test anxiety. But don't worry; you can overcome it. Here are some specific strategies to help you.

Take the Test One Question at a Time

Focus all your attention on the one question you're answering. Avoid thoughts about questions you've already read or concerns about what's coming next. Concentrate your thinking where it will do the most good—on the question you're answering now.

Develop a Positive Attitude

Keep reminding yourself that you're prepared. In fact, if you've read this book, you're probably better prepared than most other test takers. Remember, it's only a test, and you will do your **best**. That's all anyone can ask of you. If that nagging voice inside your head starts sending negative messages, combat them with positive ones of your own. Tell yourself:

- "I'm doing just fine."
- "I've prepared for this test."
- "I know exactly what to do."
- "I know I can get the score I'm shooting for."

You get the idea. Remember to drown out negative messages with positive ones of your own.

If You Lose Your Concentration

Don't worry about it! It's normal. During a long test, it happens to everyone. When your mind is stressed or overexerted, it takes a break whether you want it to or not. It's easy to get your concentration back if you simply acknowledge the fact that you've lost it and take a quick break. You brain needs very little time (seconds, really) to rest.

Put your pencil down and close your eyes. Take a deep breath, hold it for a moment, and let it out slowly. Listen to the sound of your breathing as you repeat this two more times. The few seconds this takes is really all the time your brain needs to relax and refocus. This exercise also helps you control your heart rate, so you can keep anxiety at bay.

Try this technique several times before the test when you feel stressed. The more you practice, the better it will work for you on test day.

If You Freeze

Don't worry about a question that stumps you even though you're sure you know the answer. Mark it and go on to the next question. You can come back to the "stumper" later. Try to put it out of your mind completely until you come back to it. Just let your subconscious mind chew on the question while your conscious mind focuses on the other items (one at a time—of course). Chances are, the memory block will be gone by the time you return to the question.

If you freeze before you ever begin the test, here's what to do:

1. Do some deep breathing to help yourself relax and focus.
2. Remind yourself that you're prepared.
3. Take some time to look over the test.
4. Read a few of the questions.
5. Decide which ones are the easiest and start there.

Before long, you'll be "in the groove."

Time Strategies

One of the most important—and nerve-wracking—elements of a standardized test is time. You'll only be allowed a certain number of minutes for each section, so it is very important that you use your time wisely.

Pace Yourself

The most important time strategy is **pacing yourself**. Before you begin, take just a few seconds to survey the test, noting the number of questions and the sections that look easier than the rest. Then, make a rough time schedule based on the amount of time available to you. Mark the halfway point on your test and make a note beside that mark of the time when the testing period is half over.

Keep Moving

Once you begin the test, **keep moving**. If you work slowly in an attempt to make fewer mistakes, your mind will become bored and begin to wander. You'll end up making far more mistakes if you're not concentrating. Worse, if you take too long to answer questions that stump you, you may end up running out of time before you finish.

So don't stop for difficult questions. Skip them and move on. You can come back to them later if you have time. A question that takes you five seconds to answer counts as much as one that takes you several minutes, so pick up the easy points first. Besides, answering the easier questions first helps build your confidence and gets you in the testing groove. Who knows? As you go through the test, you may even stumble across some relevant information to help you answer those tough questions.

Don't Rush

Keep moving, but **don't rush**. Think of your mind as a seesaw. On one side is your emotional energy; on the other side, your intellectual energy. When your emotional energy is high, your intellectual capacity is low. Remember how difficult it is to reason with someone when you're angry? On the other hand, when your intellectual energy is high, your emotional energy is low. Rushing raises your emotional energy and reduces your intellectual capacity. Remember the last time you were late for work? All that rushing around probably caused you to forget important things—like your lunch. Move quickly to keep your mind from wandering, but don't rush and get yourself flustered.

Check Yourself

Check yourself at the halfway mark. If you're a little ahead, you know you're on track and may even have a little time left to check your work. If you're a little behind, you have several choices. You can pick up the pace a little, but do this *only* if you can do it comfortably. Remember—**don't rush!** You can also skip around in the remaining portion of the test to pick up as many easy points as possible.

Avoiding Errors

When you take the test, you want to make as few errors as possible in the questions you answer. Here are a few tactics to keep in mind.

Control Yourself

Remember that comparison between your mind and a seesaw? Keeping your emotional energy low and your intellectual energy high is the best way to avoid mistakes. If you feel stressed or worried, stop for a few seconds. Acknowledge the feeling ("Hmmm! I'm feeling a little pressure here!"), take a few deep breaths, and send yourself a few positive messages. This relieves your emotional anxiety and boosts your intellectual capacity.

Directions

In many standardized testing situations, a proctor reads the instructions aloud. Make certain you understand what is expected. If you don't, **ask**. Listen carefully for instructions about how to answer the questions and make certain you know how much time you have to complete the task. Write the time on your test if you don't already know how long you have to take the test. If you miss this vital information, **ask for it**. You need it to do well on your test.

Answers

This may seem like a silly warning, but it is important. Place your answers in the right blanks or the corresponding ovals on the answer sheet. Right answers in the wrong place earn no points—depending on the test, you may even lose points for incorrect answers. It's a good idea to check every five to ten questions to make sure you're in the right spot. That way, you won't need much time to correct your answer sheet if you have made an error.

Choosing the Right Answers by Process of Elimination

Make sure you understand what the question is asking. If you're not sure of what's being asked, you'll never know whether you've chosen the right answer.

So determine what the question is asking. If the answer isn't readily apparent, look for clues in the answer choices. Notice the similarities and differences in the answer choices. Sometimes, this helps to put the question in a new perspective, making it easier to answer. If you're still not sure of the answer, use the process of elimination. First, eliminate any answer choices that are obviously wrong. Then, reason your way through the remaining choices. You may be able to use relevant information from other parts of the test. If you can't eliminate any of the answer choices, you might be better off to skip the question and come back to it later. If you can't eliminate any answer choices to improve your odds when you return, make a guess and move on.

If You're Penalized for Wrong Answers

You **must know** whether there's a penalty for wrong answers before you begin the test. If you don't, ask the proctor before the test begins. Whether you make a guess depends on the penalty. Some standardized tests are scored in such a way that every wrong answer reduces your score by one-fourth or one-half of a point. Whatever the penalty, if you can eliminate enough choices to make the odds of answering the question correctly better than the penalty for getting it wrong, make a guess.

Let's imagine you are taking a test in which each answer has four choices and you are penalized one-fourth of a point for each wrong answer. If you have no clue and cannot eliminate any of the answer choices, you're better off leaving the question blank because the odds of answering correctly are one in four. This makes the penalty and the odds equal. However, if you can eliminate one of the choices, the odds are now in your favor. You have a one in three chance of answering the question correctly. Fortunately, few tests are scored using such elaborate means, but if your test is one of them, know the penalties and calculate your odds before you take a guess on a question.

If You Finish Early

Use any time you have left at the end of the test or test section to check your work. First, make certain you've put the answers in the right places. As you're doing this, make sure you've answered each question only once. Most standardized tests are scored in such a way that questions with more than one answer are marked wrong. If you've erased an answer, make sure you've done a good job. Check for stray marks on your answer sheet that could distort your score.

After you've checked for these obvious errors, take a second look at the more difficult questions.

You've probably heard the folk wisdom about never changing an answer. It's not always good advice. If you have a good reason for thinking a response is wrong, change it.

After the Test

Once you've finished, *congratulate yourself.* You've worked hard to prepare; now it's time to enjoy yourself and relax. Remember that celebration you planned before the test? Go to it!

B ▶ ADDITIONAL RESOURCES

Reading is like exercise: If you don't keep doing it, you'll get out of shape. Like muscles that grow stronger and bigger with each repetition, your reading skills grow stronger and stronger with everything you read. But if you stop working out, your reading comprehension muscles will deteriorate, and you may find yourself struggling with material you could have easily understood several months ago.

So don't stop now! You've really just begun. Reading comprehension is a skill to build throughout your whole lifetime.

Tips for Continuing to Improve Your Reading

The following are some ways you can continue to strengthen your reading comprehension skills:

- **Read!** Read anything—books, newspapers, magazines, novels, poems. The more you read, the better. Set yourself a reading goal: maybe one book a month, two books while you're on vacation, or a half hour of reading every night before bed. There's a list of suggested books at the end of this section; try some.
- **Discover new authors.** Check out the best-seller list and try the books on that list. If it's a best-seller, it's probably a book that appeals to a wide variety of readers, and chances are, you'll like it.
- **Spend time in bookstores and libraries.** There are bound to be books and authors out there that appeal to some of your interests. Don't be afraid to ask a salesperson or librarian to help you: Describe your interests and your preferences in style, and he or she can help you find books you'll enjoy reading.
- **Join a reading group.** Most cities and towns have a club that meets every two weeks or each month to discuss a selected book. In these groups, you'll be able to discuss your ideas and questions with a group of friends and associates in an informal setting. If your area doesn't have a reading group, start your own. You and your friends can take turns choosing which book you'll read and discuss.
- **Review this book periodically to refresh yourself about the basics.** Try some of the skill building exercises at the end of each lesson on a regular basis.

Suggested Reading List

On the following pages is a list of great reads. These suggestions are just the tip of the iceberg! It is broken down into different subjects, so try reading some of the books in the categories that interest you.

Autobiography

A Moveable Feast by Ernest Hemingway
I Know Why the Caged Bird Sings by Maya Angelou
My Life by Bill Clinton
Narrative of the Life of Frederick Douglass, an American Slave by Frederick Douglass
Night by Elie Wiesel
The Story of My Life by Helen Keller
Africa In My Blood: An Autobiography in Letters by Jane Goodall and Dale Peterson
Dreams from My Father by Barack Obama

Coming of Age

The Catcher in the Rye by J. D. Salinger
Great Expectations by Charles Dickens
Little Women by Louisa May Alcott
Peace Like a River by Leif Engler
Random Family: Love, Drugs, Trouble, and Coming of Age in the Bronx by Adrian Nicole LeBlanc

Historical/Social Issues

The Journal of Crazy Horse: A Lakota History by Joseph M. Marshall III
Pride and Prejudice by Jane Austen
Raisin in the Sun by Lorraine Hansberry
The Jungle by Upton Sinclair
The Grapes of Wrath by John Steinbeck
The Color of Water by James McBride

Inspirational/Spiritual

Awake My Soul: Spirituality for Busy People by Timothy K. Jones
A New Earth: Awake To Your Life's Purpose by Eckhart Tolle
Simple Path by Mother Theresa
The Five People You Meet in Heaven by Mitch Albom
The Prayer of Jabez: Breaking Through to the Blessed Life by Bruce Wilkinson
Live in a Better Way: Reflections on Truth, Love, and Happiness by His Holiness the Dalai Lama

Mystery/Thriller

2nd Chance by James Patterson
American Psycho by Bret Easton Ellis
On the Street Where You Live by Mary Higgins Clark
State of Fear by Michael Crichton
Murder on the Orient Express by Agatha Christie
The Girl with the Dragon Tattoo by Stieg Larsson

Poetry

Collected Poems of Langston Hughes by Langston Hughes
The Collected Poems of Emily Dickinson by Emily Dickinson
The Sonnets by William Shakespeare
The Vintage Book of Contemporary American Poetry by J.D. McClatchy
The Collected Poems of William Carlos Williams Vol. 1: 1909–1939 by William Carlos Williams

Science Fiction/Fantasy

Brave New World by Aldous Huxley
Frankenstein by Mary Shelley
Harry Potter (series) by J.K. Rowling
The Lord of the Rings (trilogy) by J.R.R. Tolkien
The Alchemist by Paulo Coelho

Short Stories

Drinking Coffee Elsewhere by Z.Z. Packer
Everything's Eventual: 14 Dark Tales by Stephen King
The Complete Tales and Poems of Edgar Allan Poe by Edgar Allan Poe
Collected Short Stories of F. Scott Fitzgerald by F. Scott Fitzgerald
Interpreter of Maladies by Jhumpa Lahiri
Birds of America by Lorrie Moore

Science/Health

Bioterrorism and Public Health by John G. Bartlett
Black Death: AIDS in Africa by Susan Hunter
Blood Evidence by Henry C. Lee
Cognitive Neuroscience: The Biology of the Mind by Michael S. Gazzaniga
An Inconvenient Truth: The Planetary Emergency of Global Warming and What We Can Do about It by Al Gore

War

Black Hawk Down: A Story of Modern War by Mark Bowden
Born on the Fourth of July by Ron Kovic
The Greatest Generation by Tom Brokaw
Unbroken by Laura Hillenbrand

Glossary

active reading   the first essential step to comprehension, active reading forces you to *see* what you're reading, and to look closely at what's in the text. Active reading involves the questions "Who? What? When? Where? Why? How?" Active readers mark up passages by identifying unfamiliar vocabulary, underlining key words and ideas, and recording their reactions and questions in the margins.

cause   a person or thing that makes something happen or produces an effect

cause and effect   ideas are arranged so readers can see which events, or series of events, *caused* something to take place, or what *effect* an event or series of events had

chronological order   ideas are arranged in the order in which they occurred (or in the order in which they should occur)

compare and contrast   ideas are arranged so parallel aspects of item A and item B are compared and contrasted either in block style (AAAABBBB) or point-by-point style (ABABABAB)

comparison   showing how two or more things are similar

connotation   the implied or suggested meaning

context   the surrounding text in which a word is used. A close look at an unfamiliar word's context can often help you find its meaning without using a dictionary.

contrast   showing how two or more things are different, or not alike

contributing cause   one factor that contributes to the cause of something. A contributing cause helps make something happen, but can't make that thing happen by itself.

degree of formality   the extent to which a piece of writing is formal or casual. For example, a writer may use slang as if speaking to a friend, or jargon (specific technical language) as if speaking to colleagues.

denotation   the exact or dictionary meaning

diction   the particular words chosen and used by the author to express his or her ideas. Diction includes denotation, connotation, and the emotional register chosen by the writer.

effect   a change produced by an action or cause

emotional appeal   an argument that appeals to the reader's or listener's emotions, arousing or exhibiting strong emotion. Emotional appeals may strengthen an argument, but the argument cannot be valid based solely on this type of appeal.

fact   something we know *for certain* to exist, to be true, or to have happened. A fact is evidence that supports a truth.

first person point of view   a highly individualized, personal point of view in which the writer or narrator speaks about his or her own feelings and experiences directly to the reader using three pronouns: *I, me, mine; we, our, us.*

hierarchy   a group of things arranged by rank or order of importance

language and style   words used by the writer and the types of sentences in which he or she uses them. Different aspects of language and style include point of view, diction, style, and tone.

logical appeal   an argument that appeals to the reader's or listener's sense of reason. This type of argument is based on conclusions drawn from facts, evidence, or good common sense.

main idea   an assertion about the subject; the general idea that controls or holds together the paragraph or passage

making observations   looking carefully at the text and noticing specific things about how it is written; making inferences

opinion   something *believed* to exist, to be true, or to have happened. An opinion is the opposite of a fact, as it is not evidence of something—an opinion is something a person believes.

order of importance   ideas are arranged in order of increasing importance (least important idea to most important idea) or in order of decreasing importance (most important idea to least important idea). This organizational pattern arranges things by hierarchy, not chronology.

point of view   the person or perspective through which the writer channels his or her information and ideas. Point of view determines who is speaking to the reader.

reasonable opinion   an opinion that is based on a fact. A reasonable opinion is one that is supported by facts or other evidence.

second-person point of view   another personal point of view in which the writer speaks directly to the reader, addressing the reader as *you.*

style a distinctive way of writing or speaking, or doing something; the manner in which something is done. Style is composed of three main elements: sentence structure, degree of description and detail, and degree of formality.

sufficient cause a cause that is strong and effective enough to make something happen on its own

third-person point of view an impersonal, objective point of view in which the perspective is that of an outsider (a "third person") who is not directly involved in the action. There is no direct reference to either the reader (second person) or the writer (first person). The writer chooses from these pronouns: *he, him, his; she, her, hers; it, its;* and *they, them, theirs.*

tone the mood or attitude conveyed by words or speech. Tone is created by a combination of point of view, diction, and style.

topic sentence a sentence that clearly expresses the main idea of a paragraph or passage

transitional words and phrases words and phrases that signal a shift from one idea to the next, such as *first, then,* and *when.* Transitional words keep events linked together in chronological order.

ADDITIONAL ONLINE PRACTICE ▶

hether you need help building basic skills or preparing for an exam, visit the LearningExpress Practice Center! Using the code below, you'll be able to access additional reading comprehension practice. This online practice will also provide you with:

- **Immediate scoring**
- **Detailed answer explanations**
- **Personalized recommendations for further practice and study**

Log in to the LearningExpress Practice Center by using the URL: **www.learnatest/practice**

This is your access code: **8998**

Follow the steps online to redeem your access code. After you've used your access code to register with the site, you will be prompted to create a username and password. For easy reference, record them here:

Access Code: _____   Password: _____

With your username and password, you can log in and access your additional practice material. If you have any questions or problems, please contact LearningExpress customer service at 1-800-295-9556 ext. 2, or e-mail us at **customerservice@learningexpressllc.com**.